MW00561063

Wisdom
FROM ABOVE

365 DEVOTIONS FROM THE BOOK OF PROVERBS

BRIAN SIMMONS
WITH SARA PERRY

BroadStreet
PUBLISHING

BroadStreet Publishing® Group, LLC
Savage, Minnesota, USA
BroadStreetPublishing.com

Wisdom from Above: 365 Devotions from the Book of Proverbs

Written by Brian Simmons with Sara Perry.

9781424563708 (faux leather)
9781424563715 (ebook)

Stock or custom editions of BroadStreet Publishing titles may be purchased
in bulk for educational, business, ministry, fundraising, or sales promotional
use. For information, please email orders@broadstreetpublishing.com.

Cover and interior by Garborg Design Works | garborgdesign.com

Printed in China

23 24 25 26 27 5 4 3 2 1

Wisdom is a gift
from a generous God,
and every word he speaks
is full of revelation
and becomes a fountain
of understanding within you.

PROVERBS 2:6

JANUARY

WORDS TO LIVE BY

Here are kingdom revelations, words to live by, and words
of wisdom given to empower you to reign in life.

PROVERBS 1:1

The book of Proverbs is full of wonderful revelations of
the kingdom of God. There is food for the hungry soul,
direction for the longing heart, and healing oil for the
hurting. The wisdom of Christ leads us to the abundance of
his life within us. Where he dwells, there he moves. Where
he moves, there he transforms. We are living vessels, filled
with the life-changing power of the Spirit of God.

As our minds are drenched in the living water of
God's wisdom, we are filled with all we need to thrive in
this life, no matter what circumstances may come our
way. As we submit to the waterfall of loving instruction
throughout Proverbs, we will find that clarity comes as we
walk in obedience to God's wonderful Word.

**Wonderful Lord, I submit my heart to you, and I
humble myself before you today. Fill me with the
wonders of your Word and satisfy my heart as I follow
you in obedience. I want to live in your victory here and
now. Thank you.**

ADVICE FOR LIFE

Those who cling to these words will receive discipline to
demonstrate wisdom in every relationship and to choose
what is right and just and fair.

PROVERBS 1:3

Do you sometimes find it difficult to put your ideas into
practice? Have you ever heard great advice but failed to
follow through on it? Every day is an opportunity to grasp
the present grace of God that empowers those who look
to him. When we set our hearts, as well as our minds, on
the wisdom of the Lord, his Spirit gives us the strength we
need to implement discipline in our lives and to choose
his loving ways over our own preferences.

As we invite the Prince of Peace to lead us in
life, he counsels us with this innate wisdom and gives
us discernment to choose what is right, fair, and just.
Whatever we are lacking is found in abundance in his
kingdom. As we lean into his Spirit, we find that he
imparts the treasures of his generous mercy into our very
hearts and lives.

**Wise One, I take your Word seriously, and I look to you
as my teacher. Guide me into your truth and transform
my heart, mind, and soul with your incomparable
wisdom. Thank you.**

DESIGNED WITH A DESTINY

These proverbs will give you great skill to teach the immature and make them wise, to give youth the understanding of their design and destiny.

PROVERBS 1:4

We were each designed with intention and creativity. The Creator of the Universe is the one who shaped us with flesh and bone, and he molds us still into his loving image as we look to him. He gave us our quirks and our talents, our unique imprints, and our most pronounced features. Why would we disparage what God so thoughtfully created?

If we want to grow in our ability to teach others, then we first need to adopt an avid learner's posture. God is the Master, and we are his apprentices. We will never be greater than our teacher, so let's remember to remain humble and receptive to his wisdom throughout our lives. All that we need is found in him, and we don't have to look anywhere else!

Father, thank you for creating not only me in your image but also every person. Give me your merciful and compassionate perspective as I engage with others, and lead me into deeper and more grounded love as I fellowship with your Spirit. I know that there is purpose in every life.

BRILLIANT STRATEGIES

For the wise, these proverbs will make you even wiser,
and for those with discernment, you will be able to
acquire brilliant strategies for leadership.

PROVERBS 1:5

Wherever you find yourself today in spiritual, emotional,
or physical health, that is your starting point. You can
grow, define, and improve from the place where you
begin at this moment—the place of your progress. Don't
spend time feeling guilty over lost time or opportunities;
you only have this moment to choose what you will do
and how you will live. Let the loving arms of God wrap
around you, encourage your heart in hope, and guide you
into his goodness.

God has brilliant strategies to share with you
if you listen. His ways are far better than the ways of
humankind. His problem-solving skills are unmatched.
Lay down your worries about how you will get from point
A to point B (whatever those may be) and ask the Lord
for his right-now word for you. You have only to take
the step that is directly in front of you, do what is at your
fingertips to do, and follow his direction.

**Savior, thank you for your wonderful wisdom that
simplifies the complex. Speak to my life today, giving
me insight into strategies that will help me lead with
wisdom and discernment.**

THE POWER OF DEVOTION

We cross the threshold of true knowledge
when we live in obedient devotion to God.

PROVERBS 1:7

Obedient devotion to God is much more than the idea of fearing him. As we submit, worship him with awe, and revere who God is, we align our hearts and lives with his nature. We trust his faithfulness to follow through on his promises, we cling to his loyal love, and we wait for his power to do what we cannot do on our own.

True knowledge is not something that happens with our minds. We are whole beings, which is so much more than what we think. We are body, spirit, and soul. As we approach the Lord and his leadership with every part of who we are holistically, we break through the barriers of simply admiring God to living for him. His grace becomes our strength. His mercy becomes our passion. His compassion both melts and moves us. What a way to live!

Dearest Lord, there is no one like you. The ways that I have known to survive fall short of what it means to live wholeheartedly in and for you. I want to thrive, to come alive in the power of your wisdom as your presence makes me whole.

ADORNED WITH ADVICE

Pay close attention, my child, to your father's wise words and never forget your mother's instructions. For their insight will bring you success, adorning you with grace-filled thoughts and giving you reins to guide your decisions.

PROVERBS 1:8–9

As we seek to live wholeheartedly for the Lord, we should not throw away the wisdom of those who have raised us. The wisdom of God is found in each generation. While our understanding falls short in some ways, we can learn important lessons through experience. Instead of starting fresh, we should allow the insight of others to weigh in on our choices and guide us in decision-making.

The fruit of wisdom can be found anywhere. We simply need to know how to spot its characteristics. Don't let the faults of others overshadow what they get right. Every person is a mixture of mistakes and successes, so let's give grace where it is required and respect where it is due.

Father, I know that you are the only perfect parent. Help me to sift the things that don't guide me to you and to embrace the good that will help me in life as I consider the advice, wisdom, and living example of those around me. Thank you for your guidance.

CELEBRATION
OF WISDOM

Wisdom's praises are sung in the streets
and celebrated far and wide.

PROVERBS 1:20

Wisdom leads to much more than success in life. It is a steady and firm foundation in every season—through the dark valleys of life as well as the mountaintops. It is a guiding light through storms and a clear beacon in the dark of night. When wisdom is heeded, we find peace, love, and joy along with light, life, and healing.

Let's celebrate how wisdom has set us free. Jesus Christ is wisdom personified. If we struggle to find where true wisdom shines through, we have to look no further than the work of Christ in our lives. His mercy-kindness is full of the clarity of God's heart. May we see the many miracles of God's faithful character reaching through the details of our lives, awakening our hearts in awe of the one who pursues us endlessly with love.

Jesus, your life, ministry, death, and resurrection all speak of the wonders of God's wisdom. It is so unlike the wisdom of this world. The fruit of your loyal and loving nature lasts longer than anything in existence. As you reach out to me, I grab hold of your goodness and celebrate your wonders in my life.

WONDERFULLY PRESENT

Wisdom's song is not always heard in the halls of higher learning. But in the hustle and bustle of everyday life its lyrics can always be heard above the din of the crowd.

PROVERBS 1:21

No matter where we are in life or where we find ourselves in this world, we can find wisdom. Just as the Spirit of God is everywhere, more vast and accessible than we can imagine, so is the wisdom of God. We don't have to enter a church or dedicated holy space in order to encounter the King of kings. He is as present in the back alleys as he is in the church pews. Let's never forget how very near he is.

We do not need to go to seminary to learn the wisdom of God. We do not need to obtain higher degrees in order to grow in understanding. The loving hand of God guides us wherever we are—in whatever sphere or occupation. We can listen for wisdom's voice ringing out as we go about our days and look for God's mark wherever we go. If we listen, we will hear. If we look, we will perceive. God is faithful to reveal himself to those who are searching for him.

Spirit, open my ears to hear what you are saying. Amen.

WISDOM'S INVITATION

"Come back to your senses and be restored to reality.
Don't even think about refusing my rebuke! Don't you
know that I'm ready to pour out my spirit of wisdom
upon you and bring to you the revelation of my words
that will make your heart wise?"

PROVERBS 1:23

When we stop resisting the facts, we can yield to what
God is saying. When our hearts resist listening to
wisdom—even when it comes from places and people
we would normally reject—we let pride keep us from
growing in understanding. If we will humble ourselves
before the Lord and listen for where his voice is and what
it is saying, cynicism, judgment, and dismissiveness have
no place.

Let's look to the Lord and acknowledge that he
knows far better than we ever could. He loves more fully,
heals more completely, restores more readily, and forgives
like no one else. If left unchecked, overconfidence and
self-importance can keep us from growing in wisdom.
Wisdom calls us to trust God, submit to his mercy, and
offer it to others. Is this the wisdom that we follow?

**Holy Spirit, I humble myself before you. Correct me,
redirect me, and open my heart to understand your
ways. I trust you.**

PLENTIFUL PEACE

"The one who always listens to me
will live undisturbed in a heavenly peace."

PROVERBS 1:33

How readily do we listen to the leading of the Lord?
When we hear what he says but disregard his instruction,
we may find ourselves wandering from the path of his
peace. This peace doesn't come from undisturbed lives;
every one of us will experience loss in this world. We
will experience setbacks, and we will sometimes fail. But
our peace is not contingent upon our circumstances. It is
reliant on Christ within us.

May we, with humble and open hearts, submit
ourselves to the leadership of Christ in every way. We
read his words, and the Spirit moves within us and
speaks, but we practice true wisdom when we live it
out. If we exercise the things that we say we believe to
be true, then we are true listeners. The peace of God
is undisturbed in the one who has nothing to fear and
nothing to regret. Even so, each time we fail, marvelous
mercy can restore us.

**Prince of Peace, you are the one who settles my soul
when I can feel the talons of fear gripping my heart.
You are my steady foundation and my sure salvation. I
trust you, and I follow you, all because I belong to you.**

COURAGE AND CONFIDENCE

"Free from fear, confident and courageous, that one will rest unafraid and sheltered from the storms of life."

PROVERBS 1:33

Even when storms rage, we can rest unafraid. Jesus lived this out. When he and the disciples were traveling by boat, they went through a terrifying storm. We know it was a terrible storm because the disciples thought they were going to die, and they marveled (perhaps feeling a bit annoyed) that Jesus was in the bottom of the boat sleeping through it all. When Jesus awoke to his disciples begging him to save them from death, his response was a rebuke. "Why are you gripped with fear?" he asked. "Where is your faith?" (Matthew 8:26).

Directly after this, Jesus quieted the wind and waves with a simple statement. The courage and confidence that Jesus had in the midst of a violent storm is available to us today, no matter what we face. He is our peace, and he will shelter us and keep us. Let's put our full faith and trust in the one who calms the storm.

Jesus, I don't want to be overcome with fear or distracted by the things that threaten to take me out. Instead, I want to trust so fully in you that I can peacefully rest in the midst of even the harshest storm. Be my peace today.

HIDDEN WITHIN

My child, will you treasure my wisdom? Then, and only then, will you acquire it. And only if you accept my advice and hide it within will you succeed.

PROVERBS 2:1

We cannot resist the teachings of Christ or the wisdom of his Word and expect to become successful in his kingdom. Though we may apply the wisdom of this world and find a modicum of success by its standard, that does nothing to reflect on our impact in or for the kingdom of Christ.

When we hide God's Word in our hearts, it becomes part of our worldview, informing how we live, move, and act. When we truly treasure something, then we do whatever we can to promote it, align with it, and find it. The mercy-kindness of God cannot be exaggerated. His justice is far superior to any we find in this world's systems. Let's allow his Word to go deep, meditating on the values of his kingdom and soaking in his nature. Our goal should be to live out a partnership with Christ, yielded to and moved by his love above all things.

All-Knowing One, I value your wisdom more than the wisdom of any other. Lead me, and I will follow. I want your ways to be such a part of my own heart that I become a reflection of your nature. Mold me in your image.

Pass It Along

Train your heart to listen when I speak and open your
spirit wide to expand your discernment—then pass it on
to your sons and daughters.

PROVERBS 2:2

The love of God is larger than we can imagine, and his
mercy reaches further than we would ever dare go. There
is no place in this universe where we could escape from
his Spirit. There is no place we could possibly hide from
him. Why, then, would we try to keep our understanding
of him within the parameters of our own limited
experience?

   We don't have to grasp what God is doing in order
to trust him. We don't have to fear those who are different
from us or who worship differently either. God is a
faithful leader to all who look to him, and he answers all
who call on his name. Let's take the opportunity of today
to open our spirits wide to expand our discernment,
training our hearts to listen when God speaks. When he
does, let's share it with those we love.

**Loving Lord, I don't want to keep your goodness to
myself. I don't want to live so privately that my loved
ones don't know the conversations you and I have. Help
me to be intentional about sharing my breakthroughs
and revelation with those around me.**

TREASURE HUNT

Keep seeking it like a man would seek for sterling silver,
searching in hidden places for cherished treasure.

PROVERBS 2:4

God does not discourage us from asking questions. In
fact, he encourages it! Verse 3 of this chapter says, "Yes,
cry out for comprehension and intercede for insight."
Jesus said in Matthew 7:7, "Ask, and the gift is yours. Seek,
and you'll discover. Knock, and the door will be opened
for you." We shouldn't be timid about the questions we
ask or shy about our pursuit of God. He is not offended by
what he already knows of us.

We develop intimacy with God when we are
vulnerable with him. Do we trust his love to actually meet
and satisfy us? Do we truly believe that his mercy covers
all the weaknesses and doubts within us? There's no need
to hold back a single thing for fear of being found out.
Instead, we can bring him all that we are and trust him to
hold us together. We are free to go after him with all that
we have. His wisdom is a valuable treasure waiting to be
discovered.

**King of Glory, I will not let fear keep me from pressing
further into your heart today. Overwhelm my senses
with the tangible power of your presence and reveal
what I could never understand outside of you.**

ALIVE IN HIS PRESENCE

Wisdom is a gift from a generous God, and every word
he speaks is full of revelation and becomes a fountain of
understanding within you.

PROVERBS 2:6

What a generous God we have! Every word he speaks is
full of revelation, bringing light to the shadows and clarity
to our confusion. He unveils his glory, and we catch
a glimpse of his unmatched goodness. Sometimes we
cannot even put the deep understanding we experience
in his presence into words. That's okay! The power of
his presence can blind the proud, as we know happened
with Paul, and make blind eyes see, as we know Jesus did.
There is so much possibility.

The fruit of an encounter with wisdom is finding
ourselves alive, refreshed, at peace, full of joy and wonder,
and comforted. The pure love of God is like a never-ending
fountain that revives the weary heart, satisfies the thirsty
soul, and makes wise the simple. Let's refrain from getting
distracted by unnecessary arguments with others today. A
place of life-giving mercy is available to us even now.

**Generous God, you are always full of more to give
than we could ever receive. Thank you! I want to be
filled by your Spirit and refreshed by your love today.
Overwhelm me with the kindness of your presence
once again.**

PROTECTED BY THE MOST HIGH

He becomes your personal bodyguard ? *DON'T LIKE THIS TERM* "THE ANGEL OF THE LORD ON *as you follow his ways, protecting and guarding you* CAMPS AROUND THESE WHO FEAR HIM" *as you choose what is right.*

PROVERBS 2:7–8

We never need to be overcome by fear with God as our loving Shepherd and strong defense. Though we will encounter many circumstances where fear is a factor, we can courageously face whatever comes, knowing that God is faithful and will not leave us. When he beckons us, let's answer his call. When he propels us with the passion of his heart, let's partner with him over our worries. In fact, we can give every worry we have to him because he cares for us. First Peter 5:7 instructs that we leave all our worries and stress with God and not take them with us.

We can lay down at his feet everything that overwhelms us. He tenderly cares for us like a loving Shepherd and good Father. He will not let our fear sweep us away. He is better, bigger, and far more powerful than whatever we face.

Good Shepherd, watch over me as I come and go. Be with me, guide me, and protect me. Give me the grace to choose the right thing and the path of peace.

WON OVER

When wisdom wins your heart and revelation breaks in,
true pleasure enters your soul.

PROVERBS 2:10

There are many small pleasures we can find in this life.
None, however, comes close to the true satisfaction of the
light of revelation that breaks through when Christ wins
our hearts. His mercy completely covers us, cleansing us
from all unrighteousness—from anything and everything
that ever stood between us and God.

How could we not be overcome with delight when
we know the value of our salvation? Our souls come alive
in the glory-light of his powerful mercy-kindness. His
loyal love washes over our souls and revives our fading
hope. There is always more revelation in his wisdom.
There is always more to discover in his presence. What
great reasons to press in to know him more today, inviting
him to move in power, breaking every mold we have put
him in. He is far greater than we have yet known. He is far
sweeter than we have yet tasted. He is far better than we
could imagine. Let's dive deep into his presence.

**King of Glory, break through the fog of my mind
and burn off the confusion of yesterday. Bring light,
revelation, and peace to my heart as I look to you. I am
undone in your loving arms.**

WORTH ITS
WEIGHT IN GOLD

If you <u>choose</u> to follow good counsel, divine design will
watch over you and understanding will protect you from
making poor choices.

PROVERBS 2:11

<u>The counsel we keep is more important than we may
realize.</u> Whom do we go to for advice when we are unsure
of how to move forward? Whose advice do we trust and
why? <u>While wisdom can be found in many places, we
should not overlook the importance of including voices
that know us well.</u> It is also important to consider the
lifestyles and fruit of the lives of those who counsel us.
Good advice can stand on its own, but there is power
in witnessing and supporting those around us through
shared encouragement and guidance.

What do we do when God is calling us into
something new and those around us are hesitant or
unsupportive? We can heed the wisdom of the Lord and
take others' perspectives into account. Proverbs 15:22
says, "<u>If you first seek out multiple counselors, you'll
watch your plans succeed.</u>" <u>We can cast our net wide,
taking in the perspectives of others, but only we can make
our choice.</u>

Great God, thank you that there is so much grace in you.
I don't fear failure because even if I mess up, you are
with me. You redeem, restore, and repair. I trust you.

GROUNDING WISDOM

Only wisdom can save you from the
flattery of the promiscuous woman—
she's such a smooth-talking seductress!

PROVERBS 2:16

Not only is this a warning against adultery, but it is also speaking to any areas where we might be tempted to compromise—physically, emotionally, or spiritually. With the promise of fleeting pleasure, we may be tempted and drawn in, but wisdom begs us to be more prudent than that. Many ideologies floating around sound promising but are nothing more than thinly veiled bids at control.

May we thoroughly trust in the mercy of Christ to keep us, guard us, and deliver us from the temptation to compromise. When others advise that we angrily retaliate against those who have hurt us, Christ instructs us to turn the other cheek. While some make excuses for their ready judgment against people they disagree with, Jesus calls us to break bread with them. Let's follow the loving lead of the Lord, for he can always be trusted.

Christ, have mercy on me and all the ways that I have compromised. Thank you for your abundance of grace. I submit to your laid-down love and give up the fight for rights you never guaranteed. I choose your way. I choose your wisdom.

FOLLOW THE FRUIT

Follow those who follow wisdom
and stay on the right path.

PROVERBS 2:20

When it comes to wisdom, we should be aware of the path we find ourselves on. Are we walking in the ways of this world, or are we following the path of laid-down love that Christ first walked? There are no perfect people to follow, but there is a path consistently walked by those who follow Jesus' wisdom in their lives. When they mess up, they seek forgiveness and work to make amends. They live out the belief that restoration is partnering with God's heart of redemption. They are merciful and compassionate to all kinds of people. They are kind to others, and they don't make power plays.

Following the way of Christ is worth it. It is not easy, but no one promised that the wise way would be. To live a life of integrity and mercy is not what most people choose, though that's no reason for us to give it up. Christ sees every movement of our hearts, and he will reward what we do in secret, including the many sacrifices we make along the way.

Loving Lord, I want to walk in your ways and follow your truth. I don't want to have only the appearance of being good. I want to live connected to your values of mercy, repentance, restoration, and justice.

DIVINE DESTINY

*All my godly lovers will enjoy life to the fullest
and will inherit their destinies.*

PROVERBS 2:21

It is at once possible to follow the Lord and to enjoy life to the fullest. Are you convinced of that truth? We have got to get over the fear of missing out as Christians. The pure delight we find in the freedom of Christ is far better than the bondage to cycles of shame, fear, and sin.

If there is any area of your life where you feel as if you are missing out on something, ask the Lord for his perspective. Ask him to show you where he is in that area, what he is doing on your behalf, and the opportunity that you have in him. The value system of the kingdom of Christ is far superior to the value systems of this world—and that includes religious systems. We can encounter liberty in his love, endless fields of opportunity in his kingdom, and far more satisfying fruit in his fellowship than we have yet understood. We won't miss out on anything he has for us.

Merciful One, thank you for the freedom I've found in you. Flood me with joy as I delight in your presence even now.

SOULS OF HONOR

The treacherous ones who love darkness will lose not only all they could have had, but even their own souls!

PROVERBS 2:22

What our hearts seek, they will find. What we desire, we will go after. It is important, then, that we look at the driving forces behind our motivations. We cannot account for anyone else's choices, but we certainly can take agency of our own. The Lord can transform even the coldest heart in the life-giving light of his love. Will we surrender our hearts to the Lord, allowing his mercy to renew our desires in the purity of his purposes?

May we be found not only as lovers of the light but also as people of honor. Let's dare to follow the path of Jesus that pushes us outside of our self-protected lives into the broader scope of his compassion. Jesus said, "Those who let go of their lives for my sake and surrender it all to me will discover true life" (Matthew 10:39). What a beautiful invitation this is to stop clinging so tightly to our own control and instead to start submitting to the one who makes the rays of sunlight dance upon the horizon each morning.

Loving Creator, I don't want to cling so tightly to my life that I miss the opportunity to be free in your mercy. I want to know you more than I want to control my comfort.

TRUE SATISFACTION

My child, if you truly want a long and satisfying life, never forget the things that I've taught you. Follow closely every truth that I've given you. Then you will have a full, rewarding life.

PROVERBS 3:1–2

We can find a wealth of satisfaction in the wisdom of God. He who knew no sin laid down his life for us. We find freedom in his embrace of love though it does not make sense, according to our logic, why he would sacrifice himself for us. He reconciled us not so that we would become slaves but sons and daughters. We share in his inheritance, in the bounty of his kingdom, because he wanted it this way.

When we find where we truly belong, in the restorative mercy of God's heart that does not withhold affection whenever we come to him, our souls know the satisfaction of true acceptance. We do well to follow his wisdom, to incorporate his truth, and to nurture the fellowship of his Spirit throughout our lives. No matter is too small that he cannot give us insight. No concern is too great that he cannot help us. Let's look to him and find ourselves loved to life over and over again in his glorious presence.

Lord, thank you for your wisdom that guides me through the hills and valleys of this life. I look to you.

SHAPED BY LOYAL LOVE

Hold on to loyal love and don't let go, and be faithful to all that you've been taught. Let your life be shaped by integrity, with truth written upon your heart.

PROVERBS 3:3

When the trials of life shake us, we can take the courage offered to us through this verse and "hold on to loyal love and [not] let go." The forever-faithful love of God will never let go of us, but we can lean in and hold on with all our strength. We should strive to root and ground ourselves in the mercy-presence of God every chance we get, turning our attention to the nearness and faithfulness of our God.

As we choose to live with integrity, letting our lives match up with the values of our hearts, shaped by Christ's kingdom, every movement of mercy reflects the power of God at work within us. If we keep holding on to the wonderful nature of God, following in his footsteps, we will not stray to the right or to the left. Let's keep first things first and fix our eyes on the one who never leaves or forsakes us. As we behold him, we will become more like him.

Loyal God, no one is more trustworthy than you. I hold on to you with all my soul, strength, and attention. Transform me in your life-changing mercy.

FAVORABLE INTEGRITY

That's how you will find favor and understanding
with both God and men—you will gain the reputation
of living life well.

PROVERBS 3:4

How can we find favor with both God and others?
By living true to our word, living according to the
kingdom values of Jesus Christ, and clothing ourselves
in compassion. This does not mean everyone will like
us, but integrity has more to do with us than with others'
expectations. When there is no lie to get caught up in and
nothing to expose, we are living truly and humbly before
God as well as before others.

When your life matches your values and your
actions represent your words, others can count on you
to follow through on what you say. Let your focus be not
on how much honor or attention you get from others but
on what you do with your time and how you respond to
those in your life. Do what is yours to do—the simple
tasks as well as the great ones—and concern yourself with
those things. Simply put your hand to your own plow
and follow through on your part. Then you will know the
satisfaction and favor of living well before God and men.

**Father, help me to keep from being distracted by things
that don't matter and aren't mine to worry about.**

TRUSTWORTHY AND RELIABLE

Trust in the Lord completely, and do not rely on your own opinions. With all your heart rely on him to guide you, and he will lead you in every decision you make.

PROVERBS 3:5

God is the best leader, the most intuitive healer, the kindest listener, and the most generous provider. Whatever we are looking for is found completely and wholly in him. Whatever your reservations or questions today, bring them to the Lord. He can handle them. Don't be swayed by your fear and don't be convinced to stay small by the logic of others.

God is more than able to lead you. He is full of abundant grace to empower you for each new day and each new obstacle that you face. Rely on him to guide you, for he will not let you down. He is reliable and true. He is faithful and strong. He does not forget a single word he has spoken, and he does not neglect his promises. Trust in him completely, for he cares for you.

Faithful Father, I choose to trust you more than I do any other. You never go back on your word, and you do not leave those who rely on you. I'm leaning on you today, and I trust you to guide me in every decision I make.

Intimate Fellowship

Become intimate with him in whatever you do,
and he will lead you wherever you go.

Proverbs 3:6

When we know people deeply, we can almost predict what they will do, what choices they will make, and how they will respond in certain circumstances. It is the same with the Lord. The more we get to know him, the more familiar his ways become to us. The more familiar he is, the more confident we become in his responses as well.

Pursuing the Lord with all we have allows us to cultivate close fellowship with him. His presence is with us even now. He gives revelation and deeper understanding to broaden our perspective of his Word in line with his character. We know him well when we can begin to anticipate his mercy-kindness before we even hear his voice or feel him move. Any movement of our hearts toward the Lord is a seed of hope, trust, and reliance. He is far better than we can imagine, so let's not hold back even a moment from knowing him more today.

Precious Lord, as I go throughout my day, I invite you to interrupt my thoughts with your truth. Wrap around me with the tangible grace of your presence and fill me with your love. I love you!

LIFELONG LEARNING

Don't think for a moment that you know it all,
for wisdom comes when you adore him with undivided
devotion and avoid everything that's wrong.

PROVERBS 3:7

Wisdom is laced with humility, always willing to listen to correction and ready to hear instruction. Pride is not a rite of maturity; it is the attitude of fools. As long as we live, there is more to discover, more wonder to uncover, and more transformation to take place. If we think we have made it, we will resist opportunities to change instead of embracing them.

When we give our attention to the Lord, worshiping him with our undivided devotion, every opportunity for forgiveness and restoration is a chance to become more like him. We cannot venture to be perfect in life; we are all just trying our very best with whatever we have been given. If we do not have to be experts, we can simply be learners—ever evolving and growing in mercy, grace, joy, peace, patience, and self-control. May we embrace the invitation to continue to cultivate the fruit of the Spirit as long as we live.

Wise God, I devote my heart to you and to learning your ways. I humble myself before you and ask for your compassion to guard my heart and mind in every interaction I have today.

FREE-FLOWING GENEROSITY

Glorify God with all your wealth, honoring him with your firstfruits, with every increase that comes to you. Then every dimension of your life will overflow with blessings from an uncontainable source of inner joy!

PROVERBS 3:9–10

God is a generous Father. He freely offers us the bounty of his kingdom, and we get to pour out our generosity right back to him. When we offer God the firstfruits of our labor, we honor the knowledge that what we have received originated with him. Why would we withhold anything from him when he so freely offers us the abundance of his life-giving love?

The Scriptures teach us to be intentional about the practice of generosity—not only with the Lord but also with others. We have been given much, so let's not forget to sow those resources into the communities where we dwell. Generosity is a trait of a merciful and magnanimous God. We become beacons of his goodness as we practice giving God glory through the way we delegate our time and income.

Generous God, thank you for all that I have and for the gracious way in which you provide for me. I choose to honor you not only with my words but also with my wealth. All that I have is yours.

KIND CORRECTION

The Father's discipline comes only from his passionate
love and pleasure for you. Even when it seems like his
correction is harsh, it's still better than any father on earth
gives to his child.

PROVERBS 3:12

The Lord is kind to his children. He does not ridicule or
shame us. He is a good Father, and he is kind even in his
correction. There is infinite and inherent wisdom in God's
discipline. He does not humiliate us or berate us; he calls
us up instead of beating us down. He reminds us who he
is and who he has created us to be, lovingly aligns us, and
rights our false mindsets in his truth.

If you have not known kindness in correction,
may today be the day you trust the Lord to lead you into
his merciful truth a bit deeper. Dare to be known and
to stop hiding. The Lord disciplines those he loves, but
he does not abuse them. He is full of compassion, and
his gentleness leads us to restoration. As we continue to
humble ourselves before him, God transforms us with his
loyal love. He is so very approachable.

**Trustworthy One, I will not hide from your correction
today. Speak to me, Lord, for I am listening. I long to
know your kindness even as you set me straight.**

DRAWN INTO HEALING

The ways of wisdom are sweet, always drawing you
into the place of wholeness. Seeking for her brings the
discovery of untold blessings, for she is the healing tree of
life to those who taste her fruits.

PROVERBS 3:17–18

If you have been longing for healing and wholeness, it
is wisdom that you have been searching for. If you have
been looking for restoration in the love of God, wisdom
has been your driving force. Sweetness, gentle rest, and
refreshment exist in the presence of God. Deeper healing
for your soul exists in his embrace.

Wherever you find yourself on your journey, take
heart in the passion of God that pursues you relentlessly
today. It is the wisdom of Christ that is actively drawing
you into the place of your wholeness. There you will
find peace and prosperity and purpose. Eat the fruit of
wisdom and you will find that there are untold blessings in
partaking of her. There is no better place to look for your
healing than in the person of Christ, who is Wisdom itself.

**Christ, you draw me into your healing waters, and I am
brought to life from the inside out. Refresh my heart,
soul, and body in your beautiful presence. Thank you.**

FEBRUARY

BLUEPRINTS OF WISDOM

The Lord laid the earth's foundations with wisdom's blueprints. By his living-understanding all the universe came into being.

PROVERBS 3:19

Everything the Lord does, he does with wisdom. There is nothing that he set into place on the earth, no planet put into motion, that was without purpose. Do we trust that the living-understanding of the Lord that put the earth on its axis and set it into orbit around the sun is the same wisdom that guides us as we look to him? He radiates glory and shines revelation-light on all who ask for his perspective.

There is no problem that God cannot solve. No situation is too far gone that he cannot redeem it. No question can stump him. His perspective takes everything into account—all the details we would not even know to look for. Let's look to God for the blueprints of wisdom for our lives—every part of them. As he reveals his purposes, we will benefit from aligning with his ways rather than leaning on the limits of our own.

Master Creator, you laid the foundations of the universe with the detailed plans of your wisdom. I trust you to guide me as I yield to you.

LIFE GOALS

My child, never drift off course from these two goals for your life: to walk in wisdom and to discover your purpose. Don't ever forget how they empower you.

PROVERBS 3:21

What are the overarching goals for your life? Today is as good a day as any to consider what you are working toward, what impact you want to make on those around you, and the legacy you want to leave behind. There is tremendous power when you walk in true wisdom and discover your unique purpose. This purpose is something that only you can offer. No matter what it looks like, do it with integrity, love, and conviction.

Take some time to write down what you want to accomplish with your life. Dream big, and if the details seem fuzzy, think about how you want others to feel when they are around you. Your greatest impact will be in the lives of those you are closest to. How can you serve them in love? How can you reflect the generosity of the Lord to your community? The Lord, who is full of wisdom, will empower you by his Spirit as you look to him.

Faithful Father, refine my goals in the fire of your passion. May your kindness, generosity, and justice shine through my life as I follow your ways and wisdom.

GUIDING HOPE

They give you living hope to guide you,
and not one of life's tests will cause you to stumble.

PROVERBS 3:23

As you are inspired to do what is right, energized by
the refreshing healing your heart finds in walking in
wisdom's ways, you will find there is vibrant hope to guide
you. Though you walk through the valley of the shadow
of death, you will come out with a greater capacity to
empathize with those in pain. Though the cracks of
humanity may trip you up from time to time, the strong
arm of the Lord will hold you firm and fast.

Spend time in the presence of the Lord today
before you move on to anything else. Ask for the Spirit's
wisdom to reveal where your focus should be throughout
the day. Ask for his discernment to alert your senses when
you need to refocus on him. He is a ready help, and there
is a free-flowing fountain of living-understanding in
fellowship with him. Drink from it today and drink from
it often, for you will have your hope renewed as you do.

**Living God, thank you for the gift of your presence and
for the freedom to come to you whenever—no matter
the time of day or the circumstance. Thank you for
receiving me so lovingly. I look to you today.**

SHIELD OF PEACE

You will sleep like a baby, safe and sound—your rest will
be sweet and secure. You will not be subject to terror,
for it will not terrify you.

PROVERBS 3:24–25

No one is untouched by the anxieties of life. It is part of
the human experience to be struck by the question of
unknowns and what that could mean for our lives. It is
how we respond to these worries that tests our faith. Do
we ruminate, or do we turn to the Lord and release what
we cannot control to the one who never misses a detail?

The Lord is forever faithful, always caring tenderly
for his children. We do not need to worry about what
tomorrow will bring, for God is with us through it all.
He is our strength when we have none; he provides a way
when we are up against the walls of life. The peace of God
is available even now. He is ever so near, calming us like
a mother soothes her child to sleep. Even when terror
strikes, we need not be terrified, for the Lord God can
handle what we cannot on our own.

**Prince of Peace, calm me with your presence as I lean
on you. Be my shield and my strength, taking care of
me in the unknowns and in times of trouble.**

CONFIDENCE EVEN IN CRISIS

God is your confidence in times of crisis,
keeping your heart at rest in every situation.

PROVERBS 3:26

No matter what you are facing or how great the challenges, God is loyal, reliable, and victorious. Let his character be your confidence. Let your faith be rooted in his faithfulness. He will never stray from his redemptive heart, and you will never be left alone when you ask him for help. He is able to keep your heart in perfect peace in each and every situation.

Surrender your fears to the Lord today. Offer him your hopes and disappointments. Give him your trust and your apprehensions. He can handle it all! The faithfulness of God is not dependent on how you pray, what you say, or how you react. He will always be true to his word, never dismissing or forgetting a promise that he has made. Because "God is your confidence in times of crisis," you can rest assured that he will be with you through the hardest moments of your life.

Holy One, your redemptive power makes the blind see, the deaf hear, and the lame walk. Move in miraculous mercy in my life as I put all my trust in you.

Don't Delay

When your friend comes to ask you for a favor, why would you say, "Perhaps tomorrow," when you have the money right there in your pocket? Help him today!

PROVERBS 3:28

Instead of looking for excuses to hold off on doing what you can do today, lean into the present moment and embrace the day as all you have. Don't make allowances for putting off good deeds that you can quickly and easily accomplish now. You cannot do everything, and you cannot be the solution to every problem, but you know what you have to give. Let go of the responsibility to do it all, and instead do what you are compelled to do with compassion and follow-through.

May your actions speak louder than words as you yield to the leadership of your loving Lord. If you can help someone who needs it, offer assistance. If you can make headway on a project that will benefit those around you, do it. Embrace today, in all of its nuances and complexities, and simply show up and do your part. Why delay?

Loyal Lord, your example propels me to dig into the present moment and meet it with grace, compassion, and expectation. May I be a person of my word, following through on commitments and helping those I can along the way.

PEACEFUL PATHS

Why would you quarrel with those who have done
nothing wrong to you? Is that a chip on your shoulder?
Don't act like those bullies or learn their ways.

PROVERBS 3:30–31

We are in an age of division and disagreement. There is no
shortage of things to argue about, no lack of issues to use
as armor against one another. But this is not the way of
Christ. If we look for fights, we will find them. If we allow
defensiveness to be our first response, it will keep us from
trying to understand others in compassion. It is much
better to clothe ourselves in mercy and offer kindness to
others, no matter their beliefs.

Pursuers of peace don't prove their point while
putting others down. We caution children against
bullying, knowing its dangers in youth. And yet, it seems
so many of us align ourselves with powerful people who
act no better than playground bullies. May we reject the
ways of violence and embrace the merciful ways of Christ
instead. We reflect Christ best when we're clothed in
humility, kindness, and tenderness.

**Christ Jesus, I want to walk in your ways rather than
in the bullying tactics of this world. I want to remain
tenderhearted and passionate about truth, justice, and
mercy. May I choose peace instead of arguing.**

GIFT OF TRUTH

My revelation-truth is a gift to you,
so remain faithful to my instruction.

PROVERBS 4:2

As sons and daughters of the Father of eternity, we
grow stronger in our identity as we yield ourselves to
the wisdom and teachings of his Word. The revelation-
truth of Christ is a gift to us—priceless beyond gold,
gems, or any other earthly treasure. When we follow
the instructions of Christ, as laid out to us through his
life, ministry, and teachings, we submit ourselves to the
highest law—the law of his love.

Take the opportunity to read through this whole
chapter of Proverbs. Read it as though it were Jesus Christ
speaking to you personally. His Spirit is with you, and he
will reveal his permeating truth to your heart and mind
as you meditate on his Word. If you have even more time,
spend it in the Gospels, reading the words of Jesus to his
disciples. You can apply so much rich wisdom to your life
through his life-giving words.

**Jesus, your life and example are a picture of the Father's
matchless love, and I don't want to miss even one
nugget of wisdom that I could gain from you. Radiate
upon my heart and mind and speak to my soul as I
meditate on your Word.**

STICK TO IT

Stick with wisdom and she will stick to you, protecting
you throughout your days. She will rescue all those who
passionately listen to her voice.

PROVERBS 4:6

Listening to wisdom is an important step in growing in
our faith, but it's not the only one. We must love wisdom
and wholeheartedly incorporate her instruction into
our lives. First, we listen with an open heart, and then
we apply it in our lives. Without this, we do not actively
integrate or experience the extent of wisdom's benefits.

Consider how you can stick with wisdom today.
Is there wisdom that you have heard and have not yet
implemented even though you intend to do so? Choose
to go further than simply listening to the instructions of
wisdom and choose an action plan to incorporate it into
your life. You will not regret taking steps of consistent
action, for wisdom is like a shield that protects those who
put her ways into practice.

**Spirit, thank you for the wealth of wisdom I find
in your Word and in fellowship with you. Speak
to me today and give me insight into where I can
move forward in acting on your wisdom. The more I
experience your life-giving liberty, the more I want to
pursue you.**

INVEST IN WISDOM

Wisdom is the most valuable commodity—so buy it!
Revelation-knowledge is what you need—so invest in it!

PROVERBS 4:7

Wisdom is not simply a nice idea to grab hold of. It is not
relegated to the book of Proverbs, and it is not found only
within the confines of the Bible. It is found in the person
of Jesus Christ, in his Spirit, and in the representation
of the Father. Wisdom can help us with everything. It is
imperative that we get to know the qualities of wisdom
so that we can live full and vibrant lives in the light of
Christ's love.

As we give our time, attention, and hearts in open
fellowship with the Lord, we allow for his guiding truth
to lead us. As we become closer to the mercy of Christ,
embracing every lesson it has to teach us and allowing
its power to refine us, we get to know the heart of God.
There is no greater goal than to live in intimate fellowship
with the Father, and Jesus paved the way for each of us
to do this through his Spirit's work in us. How will you
invest in his heavenly wisdom today?

**Spirit, reveal the heart of the Father and make known
the qualities of your kingdom as I look to you.**

CLOTHED WITH GRACE

You will be adorned with beauty and grace,
and wisdom's glory will wrap itself around you,
making you victorious in the race.

PROVERBS 4:9

When we live by the insights of Christ's wisdom, we are wrapped in the glory of his presence. Our victory is not in our own efforts or merit but in the submission of our lives to the Prince of Peace. The All-Knowing Creator wraps us up in his glorious grace, signifying our victory in him.

First Corinthians 9:24 encourages us to "run the race to be victorious." With wisdom as our coach and self-control to keep us disciplined in our training, we will experience the breakthrough that every true athlete finds. Even so, let's not forget that mercy can restore us and strength can empower us when we are weak. Every day is a fresh opportunity to practice consistency, refine our focus, and submit to the love of Christ. His grace covers us completely, and his affectionate favor is all we need.

Loving Lord, thank you for both your wisdom and your grace. Thank you for providing insights to live with integrity and with the heart of a champion. You are my covering, and I look to you for all that I need today.

TAKE THE TIME

My son, if you will take the time to stop and listen to me
and embrace what I say, you will live a long and happy life
full of understanding in every way.

PROVERBS 4:10

It takes time, attention, and intentionality to grow closer
in our relationships. This is as true in our relationship
with the Lord as in any other. If we take time to listen
to the voice of our Father in the silence, we will be able
to recognize him even among the busyness of our lives.
When he speaks, we will feel the pull from the weight
of his words. Let's give him the start of our days and the
end of them, turning to him in prayer, reading his Word,
and fellowshiping with his Spirit. Then we will feel the
satisfaction of knowing him.

Rushing through our days won't offer us a feeling of
accomplishment or satisfaction. Let's take the invitation of
winter's gentler rhythm to slow down and dig deep. May
we take the time, no matter the season, to listen to the
words of wisdom that the Lord offers. He can change our
perspective in an instant.

**Father, I know that you are worth taking the time and
attention to listen to. Speak to me as I open my heart
to you.**

LIMITLESS POTENTIAL

Your progress will have no limits when you come along
with me, and you will never stumble as you walk along
the way.

PROVERBS 4:12

There is no limit to the fields of opportunity before you in
the realm of Christ's kingdom. You can always find more
to learn, greater joy to experience, deeper wells of love
to fill up on, and infinite ways to expand in the mercy of
God. When you feel stuck, breakthroughs are available.
When you come up against a wall, the Lord can break it
down and lead you into wide-open spaces.

Don't put limits on what God doesn't restrict.
Surely, you will reach the bounds of your own humanity.
You need to eat, hydrate, and rest. You need interaction
with others and to be known. You need relationships,
and you need something to work at. These things won't
change. You don't become superhuman by following the
Lord, but he does offer you more than you could ever
imagine. You can go further than you expect by leaning
on the Lord and persevering through the hard times.
Don't give up. There is more goodness to come.

**Father, thank you for the hope of your promise and
for the strength of your grace in my life. Expand my
expectation and experience as I open up to your love.**

EMBRACE CORRECTION

Receive my correction no matter how hard it is to
swallow, for wisdom will snap you back into place—
her words will be invigorating life to you.

PROVERBS 4:13

Being open and willing to receive correction requires a
humble attitude. Those who love us want what is best for
us. When they take the time to offer opportunities for
us to correct something that isn't quite working to our
benefit or the benefit of others, it is a gift to us. It is an
opportunity to consider someone else's viewpoint and
admit our own shortcomings.

The advice given in this chapter of Proverbs is from
a father to his son. It is from a parent to his child. This is
important to recognize. Not everyone in our lives has the
right or the role to correct us. However, we should readily
accept the wisdom of those we respect and who know
us well. The Father knows us best of all. He never steers
us wrong, and the wisdom of Christ will snap us back
into place when we need it. The kind correction of our
heavenly Father leads us to repentance.

**Loving Father, correct me with your kindness and lead
me to your truth. I give up the resistance I feel against
being wrong, and I choose to humble myself before you
and others today.**

LIGHT OF THE WORLD

The lovers of God walk on the highway of light, and their
way shines brighter and brighter until the perfect day.

PROVERBS 4:18

Where does this light—the highway of light—appear in
our lives? In John 8:12, Jesus said, "I am light to the world,
and those who embrace me will experience life-giving
light, and they will never walk in darkness." Christ is the
Light of the World, the sun around which we all orbit.
In him, we are never overtaken by darkness, for he is
radiant in glory, never dimming. The fears that lurk in the
shadows do not control us, for our God is with us, and
therefore, we have nothing to dread.

Jesus also said that we are reflections of his life-
giving light. In Matthew 5:14, he said, "Your lives light up
the world. For how can you hide a city that stands on a
hilltop?" As we walk in the light of Christ's life, taking up
our cross and surrendering to his leadership, we go from
glory to glory, the experience of his love shining brighter
and brighter until we come face-to-face with him.

**Lord, open my eyes to the wonder of your ways and
lead me in your mercy-kindness. I choose to follow the
path of your life-giving light, no matter what.**

RADIANT REVELATION

Fill your thoughts with my words until they penetrate
deep into your spirit. Then, as you unwrap my words,
they will impart true life and radiant health into the very
core of your being.

PROVERBS 4:21–22

Think of words that have impacted you greatly
throughout your life. There might be a mixture of great
words of encouragement and revelation as well as words
that brought shame and confusion. Not all words of
impact have the same fruit. When you fill your thoughts
with the words of Christ, the seeds of radiant truth are
planted deep within your spirit. They will produce a crop
of fruit that represents the Spirit's work within your life.

Colossians 3:16 advises, "Let the word of Christ
live in you richly, flooding you with all wisdom. Apply
the Scriptures as you teach and instruct one another." The
Word of Christ is rich with wisdom. The fruit of his Spirit
within you is found as you apply his Word to your life.
What wonderfully radiant revelations have shifted your
understanding of who God is and who you are in him?
Fill your thoughts with these things and remain open to
his life-giving teachings in every aspect of your life.

**Jesus Christ, thank you for the revelations of your love I
have already experienced. As I meditate on your Word,
reveal even more of yourself to me today.**

Soul Health

Above all, guard the affections of your heart, for they
affect all that you are. Pay attention to the welfare of your
innermost being, for from there flows the wellspring of life.

PROVERBS 4:23

When you think about your heart and all that it holds,
consider how it affects the way you live. What are the
guiding affections of your heart? How is the health of
your innermost being? When your spirit thrives, the rest
of your being will benefit. Like the purest mountain water,
the refreshing fountain of God's Spirit-life flows outward
from the secret place of your soul.

It is natural to struggle against your own
motivations from time to time. Get curious about the
motivations of your heart, and ask the Spirit to shed
light on the thoughts that do not align with his powerful
mercy. Pay attention to the pull of discernment that rises
within you, and take notice of the things that you are
drawn to. Feed your soul what it needs, and make space to
connect with the Life-Giver who brings fresh perspective,
clarity, focus, and strength whenever you need it.

**Healer, minister to the parts of my soul that desperately
need a touch from your restorative living water. I want
to live with intentionality for your kingdom's sake.**

WATCH WHERE YOU WALK

Set your gaze on the path before you. With fixed purpose,
looking straight ahead, ignore life's distractions.

PROVERBS 4:25

You have a divine destiny. God created you to live fully
and wholly surrendered to him, and he promises to
guide you along the path of life as you look to him. Your
journey is unique, and it requires courage and humility.
Fear not, for the Lord is with you wherever you go.
Humble yourself before the Lord and clothe yourself in
his merciful compassion. As you follow the path of his
laid-down love, you will find your purpose in choosing
the ways of Christ.

Let your eyes be fixed on Jesus, the one "who
birthed faith within [you] and who leads [you] forward
into faith's perfection," as Hebrews 12:2 says. Don't let life's
distractions keep you from looking to Christ. In him you
will find the satisfaction of your soul. You will find your
life's purpose in the simple ways you choose to love those
around you. Keep looking to Jesus! He will not fail you.

**Jesus Christ, you are the one I fix my eyes upon today
and every day. You are my vision. Give my heart hope
as I live by the strength of your presence. Revive me,
guide me, and keep me in your love.**

LISTEN TO EXPERIENCE

Listen to me, my son, for I know what I'm talking about.
Listen carefully to my advice.

PROVERBS 5:1

We choose wisely when we take others' lived experiences into account before jumping into big decisions. We don't have to rely on our own understanding; we can find a wealth of wisdom in the lives of those who have gone before us and those further down the path of their lives. Let's be sure that those we listen to are living according to the values that we want to emulate. Let's heed the advice of those who have tread the same paths we are starting out on. Their wisdom can encourage our hearts, sharpen our minds, and help refine our processes.

You don't have to figure out how to move ahead all on your own. Mentorship is important—not only in our spiritual lives but also in our relationships, businesses, and personal growth. We should listen to the elders who know what they are talking about, even as we step out in faith. Their wisdom can be a guide to keep us from making unnecessary mistakes and falling into the same pitfalls they found themselves in along the way.

Father, I know the benefit of listening to others, and I don't want to go it alone anymore. Connect me to the right people and give me discernment to know whom to trust.

CLEAR CONSEQUENCES

Why would you let strangers take away your strength
while the labors of your house go to someone else?

PROVERBS 5:10

Our choices do not affect only us. They also ripple into
the lives of those we are closest to. When we make
decisions, we must think more broadly than how they
affect us personally. When we choose hastily, without
much thought about the repercussions of our actions, we
choose foolishly. Instead of rushing into what feels good
at the moment but will not benefit us in the long run, let's
take time to be mindful about our choices.

When we are enticed into compromise, letting our
integrity falter, we will live with the consequences. As we
take the warning of this proverb under consideration,
we awaken to the power of our choices. We are the only
ones who can take ownership of our decisions. Let's not
give our autonomy away so easily to those who would
seek to manipulate and control us. Today, we can practice
self-control, sound-minded wisdom, and freedom in
the mercy of Christ. It does not matter what we chose
yesterday. We can choose differently today.

**Merciful One, thank you for the redemption of your
love. I want to choose wisely and in line with the
values of your kingdom as I go about my day. Give me
discernment and strength.**

STUBBORN PRIDE

Finally you'll admit that you were wrong and say, "If only I had listened to wisdom's voice and not stubbornly demanded my own way, because my heart hated to be told what to do!"

PROVERBS 5:12

Pride does not protect us. It keeps us from considering the scope of our actions and how they affect those around us. Pride builds a wall around our senses, keeping us from seeing beyond our own desires. There is a stark difference between selfish, stubborn pride and self-compassion. Pride rejects all forms of compassion and enters self-preservation mode.

Compassion toward ourselves is not a form of pride but grace. Humility recognizes our weaknesses and leaves room for mistakes. Pride pushes that possibility to the side. Think about the ways that wisdom has directed you before—what you knew you should do yet refused to do. Did your sentiments later on reflect today's verse? Consider clothing yourself in humility, receiving the mercy of Christ, and extending compassion to your less-than-perfect self.

Father, help me to show myself the same compassion that you show me. Grant me the grace to reject pride and embrace humility. Thank you.

LOYALTY AND LOVE

My son, share your love with your wife alone.
Drink from her well of pleasure and from no other.

PROVERBS 5:15

It is wise to protect the intimate union of our relationships. Doing so requires more than avoiding situations that cause us to physically compromise. We must be as careful with our thoughts as we are with our bodies. Jesus made this clear when he said in his Sermon on the Hillside, "If you look with lust in your eyes at a woman who is not your wife, you've already committed adultery in your heart" (Matthew 5:28).

Compromise begins in our hearts, and so does willpower. We should not be so lax with our thought life that we allow ourselves to imagine how we might sin and get away with it. Let's keep our "thoughts continually fixed on all that is authentic and real, honorable and admirable, beautiful and respectful, pure and holy, merciful and kind" (Philippians 4:8). When we do, our lives will reflect the bounty of the Spirit's life at work within us, and we will make choices that align with his kingdom.

Loyal Lord, thank you for your reliable and devoted mercy. I don't take it for granted, and neither will I act like my choice to love in heart as well as through my deeds doesn't matter. I fix my thoughts on you.

NOTHING HIDDEN

God sees everything you do and his eyes are wide open
as he observes every single habit you have.

PROVERBS 5:21

The Lord sees everything you do, think, and say. Nothing
is a mystery to him, including every motivation of your
heart. This isn't to scare you; he is full of mercy-kindness
toward you. There is not a wrong he can't right, a wound
he can't heal, a memory he cannot redeem. It is really
good news that nothing is hidden from him. He accepts
you as you are, covers you with the cloak of his mercy,
and calls you his own.

As you come alive in the compassion of Christ, you
will find grace to empower you in choosing the ways of
his kingdom. Instead of opting for ways of compromise
that will only lead you to shame and bondage to sin,
choose the better ways that Jesus laid out for us. You don't
need to hide from someone who knows you through and
through or cower when you live authentically and humbly
before him.

**All-Knowing One, I yield my life to your ways. I give
you access to every place in my heart and life, and I ask
for your wisdom, correction, and direction. Thank you.**

STAY ALERT

Beware that your sins don't overtake you and that the
scars of your own conscience don't become the ropes
that tie you up.

PROVERBS 5:22

When we live with intentionality, we don't simply
move through the motions of our lives. With mindful
consideration, we are aware of the pull of the world
and its deceptive lures. With discernment alerting our
hearts, we are in tune with the Spirit's invitation to live in
the expanse of his love. When we face the limits of our
humanity, we must not confuse it with the limits of God's
great grace, for there are none.

If there are areas of compromise in our lives that do
not line up with the heart and nature of Christ, let's deal
with them accordingly. Even this we do not do on our
own. The mercy of God covers and purifies us. His grace
is the strength that empowers us to choose to reject the
traps of the enemy and live in the light of his liberating
love. We get to take responsibility for our decisions even
as we leave room for restoration and redemption.

**Redeemer, thank you for the power of your mercy in
my life. I won't make excuses for compromise today.
I want to live in the freedom of your favor.**

FRUIT OF SELF-CONTROL

Those who choose wickedness die for lack of self-control,
for their foolish ways lead them astray, carrying them
away as hostages—kidnapped captives robbed of destiny.

PROVERBS 5:23

Self-control is one of the fruits of the Holy Spirit, and thankfully, it is not simply dependent upon our own willpower. It is the Spirit-strength of Christ within us. We partner with the power of the Spirit, who enables us to do far more than we ever could on our own. When we are weak, we lean on his strength. When we need help, he is there to pick us up, set our feet on the solid foundation of his Word, and lead us into his grace.

We can choose the wisdom of Christ today in all that we do. As we invite the mercy of his heart to cover us, the grace of his presence empowers us, and the power of his life infuses us with vision. We cannot choose what others will do or how they will live, but we can choose how we will approach the challenges that rise to meet us. May we walk in the light of wisdom, truth, mercy, and kindness.

Holy One, I choose to walk in the liberating light of your kingdom rather than the shadows of compromise. Help me to stay on the path of your love.

CONSIDER THE CONSEQUENCES

Rescue yourself from future pain and be free from it once and for all. You'll be so relieved that you did!

PROVERBS 6:5

There is a life lesson hidden in this passage. Even when we consider something that sounds good on the surface, we should take the time to ponder what partnering with that endeavor will mean for us. Unexpected consequences may be lurking beneath the surface that, if we take the time to discover them, may reveal that the risk is not worth the reward.

When we choose to invest in something or someone, we are wise to consider every aspect of that investment. Some will bring us pain in the future, leaving us bound to something that we no longer wish to be connected with. We cannot foretell the future, but we can certainly take all the possibilities into account before jumping into something big. Let's use wisdom in every area and consider the consequences, refusing to rush a big decision.

Lord, thank you for your wisdom that leads, guides, and corrects. May I refuse to act hastily and instead take the time to do my due diligence before jumping into the decisions in front of me.

DILIGENCE PAYS OFF

When you're feeling lazy, come and learn a lesson from
this tale of the tiny ant. Yes, all you lazybones, come
learn from the example of the ant and enter into wisdom.

PROVERBS 6:6

Diligence matters, and consistency yields results. If we
keep putting off what we don't want to do with the excuse
that we'll get to it later, later will never come. But doing
little things with consistency will produce a harvest in
time. Instead of leading with intensity, having to do
everything at once, let's look at the ways that we can
consistently make progress each day.

Animals know what they need to do, and they do
it. Squirrels do not harvest a winter's store in a day. They
do it for weeks and months leading up to the cold season.
In the same way, when we know what we need to do and
we work at it with consistency, we will have all we need
when the cold season sets in. Let's embrace the wisdom
of the natural world and be diligent in important, even if
small, ways.

**Lord, thank you for the reminder of your principles in
the natural world around me. Adjust my perspective
when I begin to go off course and procrastinate. Help
me to be consistent and build toward the vision and
goals you have given me.**

SEIZE THE MOMENT

If you keep nodding off and thinking, "I'll do it later," or
say to yourself, "I'll just sit back awhile and take it easy,"
just watch how the future unfolds!

PROVERBS 6:10

When we make endless excuses and put off what needs to
be done, we will reap the consequences of those decisions.
In the following verse, the author of Proverbs says, "By
making excuses you'll learn what it means to go without.
Poverty will pounce on you like a bandit and move in as
your roommate for life" (6:11). The language is strong, but
the message is effective.

Are there any areas of your life where you have
been making excuses for not moving ahead? Perhaps you
just keep avoiding some tasks. Do yourself a favor and list
them all out, and then ask for clarity from the Lord as to
why you have been avoiding them. Make a plan for action
and break it down into steps that are reachable as you
build a habit of following through. You will benefit from
knowing what you need to do and making the most of the
moment you are in.

**God, thank you for your kind correction. Help me to
resist burnout and endless work, but also give me clear
vision to move ahead in important areas that need my
attention and effort.**

PATH OF INTEGRITY

Here's another life lesson to learn from observing
wayward and wicked men. You can tell they are lawless.
They're constant liars, proud deceivers, full of clever ploys
and convincing plots.

PROVERBS 6:12–13

Here, we are given clear indicators for spotting those
who resist the path of integrity and who embrace their
own interests at every turn. It is not difficult to uncover
those who are "wayward and wicked." They lie constantly,
taking pride in their deceit. They are full of duplicitous
plots and ways to get ahead without doing the actual work
it takes to do it the right way.

As children of God, we should embrace the ways of
righteousness and follow Christ on his path of integrity.
We must be people of our word, honest and reliable. We
should do what we say we will do and, when we fail, own
up to our mistakes and seek forgiveness. We should be
people who look for ways to offer others an opportunity
at greatness, being generous with our resources and
encouraging others in the spirit of kindness, peace, and
joy. There is no better way to live without regret than to
use integrity as our shield.

**Powerful God, there is no deceit in you. You are faithful
to your word, always staying true to your nature. Help me
to resist the easy way and to embrace your path of truth.**

MARCH

SEWN INTO GRACE

When calamity comes knocking on their door, suddenly
and without warning they're undone—broken to bits,
shattered, with no hope of healing.

PROVERBS 6:15

Even when unexpected trials come knocking on our
door, we can rely on the grace of God to get us through.
He does not leave us without his presence, and we are
not abandoned in our pain. There is always hope for
healing for those who lean on the Lord. There is always
redemption available to those who look to him for help.

If we stubbornly refuse to rely on God's mercy, we
will suffer for it. The overwhelmingly good news is that it
is available to choose in every moment. We can resist the
pull to turn away from the steadfast love of the Lord and,
instead, live into it. Our lives are woven into the fabric
of God's great mercy. With that in mind we can clothe
ourselves in wisdom and live to our utmost potential.
Though it may seem like those who choose to follow
devious and cunning ways are getting ahead in life, they
will be undone and broken to bits in the end. Let's choose
the better way of Christ that leads to everlasting life.

**Merciful One, thank you for your saving grace that
guards my life. I choose to follow you.**

GODLY DIRECTION

Fill your heart with their advice and let your life
be shaped by what they've taught you.

PROVERBS 6:21

As we follow the life-giving wisdom of godly mothers
and fathers, we shape our lives into reflections of Christ's
abundant kingdom here on earth as it is in heaven. When
we choose to fill our hearts with righteousness and faith,
letting the advice of devout lovers of God inform our own
decisions, we choose wisely.

Every day, we have the opportunity to conform our
lives to the holy model of Christ and his ways. We must
be discerning about whose advice we follow. We need to
look at the fruit of others' lives much more than at what
they say. Integrity shines brightly, and the mercy-heart of
God radiates from those who choose to walk in Christ's
footsteps. Look for the peaceful, loving, and humble ones
who quietly live doing the right thing and who don't turn
others away in judgment. Follow their words and their
example, and you will be shaped by what they teach you.

**Generous Father, thank you for the practical help I find
in those who follow you and your ways. Give me greater
discernment as I submit my life to you and look to
learn from others who have gone before me.**

NEW MERCIES

Their wisdom will guide you wherever you go and keep you from bringing harm to yourself. Their instruction will whisper to you at every sunrise and direct you through a brand-new day.

PROVERBS 6:22

Wisdom never leaves us, so let's not abandon her. May we lean into the very present help that she offers. As we look to her in every question, every trial, and every intersection of our day, we find her guidance. We know the wisdom of God because it pierces our hearts and expands our spirits whenever we hear it. We learn to decipher wisdom within our beings, and we allow her perspective to shift our own.

Every morning dawns with fresh mercy and countless opportunities to receive greater grace. There is no lack of help in God's Spirit. There is not a problem we face that cannot be solved in the wisdom of Christ. Let's let go of the need to control outcomes and instead lean on the exceeding loyalty of God's mercy to refresh, renew, and redeem. We can trust him with every part of our lives.

Wise One, thank you for a new day to depend on your grace. Whatever comes, wherever I go, and whomever I meet along the way, keep me in line with your wisdom. Guide and direct me. Whisper to me throughout my day.

CONSISTENT CORRECTION

Truth is a bright beam of light shining into every area of your life, instructing and correcting you to discover the ways to godly living.

PROVERBS 6:23

We should not be discouraged when the Lord corrects us. We should not resist the instruction of those who love us either. Only we can choose how we will live, but that does not mean we should ignore the wisdom of others. Those who have walked the path we find ourselves on and come out wiser, full of love, and brimming with humility are people we can trust to advise us.

We must reject the bounds of perfectionism that require we appear put-together all the time, be proficient at new things, and that leave no room for improvement. Let's reject the false narrative that says we must be experts at life, for we are all just trying our best and constantly dealing with change. May we embrace the grace of God that corrects us. It does not mean that we are failures; it simply means that we are human. Even when we mess up, it does not change our worth. We are loved by a tenderhearted Father, and that is why he corrects us.

Faithful Father, thank you for your correction and kindness. Shift my perspective to reject perfectionism and embrace transformation. Thank you.

GUARDED AND STRENGTHENED

Truth will protect you from immorality and from the promiscuity of another man's wife. Your heart won't be enticed by her flatteries or lust over her beauty— nor will her suggestive ways conquer you.

PROVERBS 6:24–25

There are temptations all around us, seeking to persuade us to compromise our values. The world does not encourage us to extend compassion to those portrayed as our enemy. It may ridicule the choice to be faithful to a friend who does not seem to make time for us. It doesn't see the value in guarding our hearts against lust even though we haven't acted on it. Under the world's influence, we can weaken our resolve in many different ways if we are not careful.

In the presence of God, we find grace to empower us to stand strong in the values of Christ's kingdom. In the mercy of God, we find restoration and renewal for our souls. In the wisdom of God's Word, we find truth to protect us—mind, body, and soul. What strength there is in the wisdom of Christ's powerful truth!

Perfect One, as I meditate on your Word, may it go deep within and feed the soil of my faith. Strengthen my trust in you as I rely on the grace of your powerful presence. I lean on you, so grateful not to have to stand on my own.

CONSEQUENCES

Don't be so stupid as to think you can get away with your adultery. It will destroy your life, and you'll pay the price for the rest of your days.

PROVERBS 6:32

We cannot escape the consequences of our actions. This is a simple life lesson, and yet how many of us dive hastily into the deep end without considering the repercussions? We come face-to-face with the cost of our choices in life; this is true for everyone. The bigger the risks we take—including betrayal, deceit, and manipulation—the more devastating the results.

Of course, mercy will restore us whenever we repent. There is restoration for our souls. But we cannot expect the natural consequences of our choices to disappear. We reap what we sow. Let's choose today to turn to the one who guides us in righteous wisdom. His example of love is there to follow as we submit to the ways of his kingdom. We will not regret living surrendered to the Lord, for there is nothing to be ashamed of when we do.

Lord of Truth, I yield my heart to your leadership, and I invite your Spirit to guide me in all of my decisions—not only today but every day of my life.

LIVING WELL

If you do what I say you will live well.
Guard your life with my revelation-truth,
for my teaching is as precious as your eyesight.

PROVERBS 7:2

Who of us does not want to live well? We don't have to
hunt for hidden treasure in obscure places, and we need
not travel to the ends of the earth to find the secrets of
contentment. A good life is built, not found. With our
lifestyles and routines, we can put the wisdom of God
into practice. We can ask the Spirit to give us revelation
whenever we think of it. When he speaks, let's live out his
wise advice.

If we treat the wisdom of God with the honor
that it is due, submitting our lifestyles and shaping our
habits by its instruction, we will reap the benefits of soul
satisfaction and confident assurance in Christ's loyal love.
We don't have to do a grand overhaul of our lives at once.
Instead of focusing on intensity, let's look for small and
actionable changes we can make in the day-to-day that
will transform us all the same.

**Holy Spirit, shine the light of your revelation on my
heart, mind, and soul today. Open my eyes to simple
ways I can transform my habits and help me to be
consistent.**

PASSIONATE PURSUIT

Say to wisdom, "I love you," and to understanding,
"You're my sweetheart."

PROVERBS 7:4

If we were to approach our relationship to wisdom the same way that we pursue the objects of our affection, how would that shift our perspective? Perhaps we would find our connection to wisdom transformed. When we love something or someone, passion can be used to provoke us to action. We want to spend our time with loved ones. We think about doing the things that bring us joy, even when we are busy doing something else. In the same way, we can be motivated by our devotion to wisdom.

If we passionately pursue wisdom, our hearts will expand in their capacity to love. Our thoughts will become consumed with how wonderful wisdom is. If this all feels too indistinct to know how to go about it, look to Christ. He is Wisdom incarnate. Spend time getting to know him through the Gospels. Make time for prayer and deepening your intimacy with him through Spirit-to-spirit fellowship. When we pursue Christ, our attention will be easily redirected by his Spirit, who leads us in purity of purpose.

Wonderful God, I am eagerly approaching you today with an open heart and a ready mind to receive all that you have to offer. I want to walk in the ways of your wisdom all the days of my life.

Be Mindful

I noticed among the mindless crowd a simple,
naïve young man who was about to go astray.

PROVERBS 7:7

There is a difference between innocence and naivete.
Innocence comes from a purehearted and inexperienced
place. The verses that follow this verse in Proverbs explain
that this simple, naive man hurries to the house of a
harlot, someone he had planned to meet. His naivete did
not take wisdom's words into account; he simply followed
the pull of his desire, all the while thinking he would not
get caught.

We cannot be so mindless in our pursuits.
As people of God, we do not rely solely on our own
perspectives. We can gather counsel and look for advice
from those we respect. We must allow truth to penetrate
our hearts, even if it means that we cannot so blindly
follow our desires. When we are aware of our motivations
and allow the voices of others to speak into our lives, we
can make informed choices. Let's be thoughtful of this
even today.

**Wise God, you don't require my perfection, and for
that, I am extremely grateful. I don't want to be naive
in my decisions. Guide me in your wisdom and awaken
my heart in discernment as I follow you.**

STANDING STRONG

He was swayed by her sophistication, enticed by her
longing embrace. She led him down the wayward path
right into sin and disgrace. Quickly he went astray, with
no clue where he was truly headed.

PROVERBS 7:21–22

We must not give the power of our autonomy over to
those who do not have our best interest at heart. No
one but God deserves our full devotion. We can be
loving toward the people in our lives, laying down our
own preferences in order to meet others where they
are. However, this does not mean that we succumb to
another's will or desires. We are not to become enslaved
by anything.

Romans 6:16 says, "Grace frees you to choose
your own master...choose carefully, for you surrender
yourself to become a servant—bound to the one you
choose to obey. If you choose to love sin, it will become
your master...But if you choose to love and obey God, he
will lead you into perfect righteousness." We stand strong
in our faith by directing our focus to loving and obeying
God. When we do, we find ourselves able to resist the pull
of deceptive and destructive forces.

**Gracious God, I fix my eyes on you now. Shine your
light of love on my being, reviving me from the inside
out with your vibrant life.**

HOLY RESISTANCE

Control your sexual urges and guard your hearts against lust. Don't let your passions get out of hand.

PROVERBS 7:25

Lust is a trap that leads to bondage. Desire is natural. When we speak of longing, it is an expression of desire. Sexual desire is a gift from God that he imparted to us when he created us. Desire does not lead us to sin; lust does. When our thoughts are consumed by lust and it leads us to objectify others, our passions can cause us to sin.

Desire is a basic human function, so let's not demonize that. But in a world that says that everything we want is okay, let's not allow ourselves to mindlessly follow our passions. When the Bible speaks of lust, it is often associated with adultery. We need to protect our hearts against lust so that we will not undermine the intimate relationships in our lives. We get to choose how we fill our minds and what we listen to, watch, and read. What occupies our thoughts truly affects the passions of our hearts, and from our hearts, we choose how we live.

Holy Father, it is without shame that I ask for your help in this area. Fill my mind with your wisdom, my heart with love for you and others, and my body with peace. Help me to stand strong in resisting temptation and embracing integrity.

WISDOM SPEAKS

Can't you hear the voice of Wisdom?
From the top of the mountains of influence
she speaks into the gateways of the glorious city.

PROVERBS 8:1

Wisdom is personified throughout the book of Proverbs. She serves as a picture of God himself, by whose voice we are invited to receive the best way to live. The most excellent and noble way that she describes is the way of life found in Jesus Christ. It is no mystery that we find God's heart revealed through the life of Jesus. Let's not neglect the power that is available to us through fellowship with him.

Wisdom is found at the top of influential mountains and at the gateways of cities. She is present with us in the valleys of deepest darkness and in the overflowing fields of harvest. She is with us wherever we go, whispering her insights and revelations to our hearts. We have the opportunity to dig into the depths of her bounty as we fellowship with the Spirit of God. She is always speaking, always revealing the ways of God, and always leading us to life.

Holy Spirit, your presence is incomparably good. I am so grateful to be led by your love and to be empowered by your grace. Fill me, cover me, and uplift me as I listen for your voice.

LISTENING TO
LADY WISDOM

At the place where pathways merge, at the entrance
of every portal, there she stands, ready to impart
understanding, shouting aloud to all who enter, preaching
her sermon to those who will listen.

PROVERBS 8:2–3

Take time in the presence of God to listen for wisdom's
voice. Quiet your heart in his presence, and settle your
mind before him. Close your eyes, breathe deeply, and
allow your heart to open to his leadership. Ask the Holy
Spirit to meet you in power, to speak to you clearly, and
wait on the Spirit's response.

There are solutions for every problem you face.
God holds the keys to unlocking your destiny and
opening your understanding. Make it a priority every day
this week to spend time not only praying and in the Word
but also simply listening for the voice of the Lord. When
wisdom speaks, take notice. How does it feel in your
spirit? How does it feel in your body? Test the words you
hear against the nature of God and the truth of his Word.
There is revelation-light available today. Wait on the Lord.

**Lord, thank you for speaking to me. I wait on you, and
I'm not in a hurry. Even as I go about my day, continue
to speak to and strengthen my innermost being with
your wisdom.**

From the Inside Out

"Listen to me and you will be prudent and wise. For even the foolish and feeble can receive an understanding heart that will change their inner being."

PROVERBS 8:5

True transformation does not happen on the surface; it begins within. Anyone who looks to the Lord for wisdom can reap the benefits. Even the most foolish among us can be changed by the power of Christ at work in their lives. His revelations give us deeper understanding. His wisdom expands our comprehension and allows us to see from God's higher perspective.

Instead of overly focusing on what we can change in our exterior lives, let's be intentional about our soul health. We should take on not only practices that make us feel better but also those that allow the loving wisdom of Christ to soak deep into our psyches. How else can this happen other than by giving him our attention? Let's meditate on his goodness, looking for the fingerprints of his mercy in the details of our lives. What we look for, we will find, and what we focus on will consume us.

Pure One, as I turn my attention to you over and over again throughout my day, breathe life within the deepest parts of me. I want to be transformed by your love from the inside out.

RULING AND REIGNING

"The meaning of my words will release within you revelation for you to reign in life. My lyrics will empower you to live by what is right."

PROVERBS 8:6

As children of the Most High, we are nobles in his kingdom. We are princes and princesses. We belong to the house of the Lord, and he has given us his name. His authority covers us, and we walk in the confidence of his favor. We do not get to avoid the troubles of life, but we have God's help through every single one.

We have access to the King of kings, so we need not waste our time trying to get ahead on our own. As we learn his ways, we can represent him well. We are free to live from his love, following the teachings of Christ and allowing the Spirit to guide us into all truth. We do not simply hear the words of God, but they come alive within us, their meaning releasing revelation for us to live in the liberty of his love. Let's continue to lean on the grace of God to do what is right, just, and true.

Marvelous God, release the power of your revelation within my heart. Bring clarity to my confusion with your wisdom. Breathe peace into my soul as I follow your ways.

UNQUESTIONABLY RELIABLE

*"For everything I say is unquestionably true,
and I refuse to endure the lies of lawlessness—
my words will never lead you astray."*

PROVERBS 8:7

The wisdom of Christ will never lead us astray. When we choose to walk in the ways of his love, we can rely on him to empower us. When we follow in his footsteps, we can depend on his Spirit to help us along the way. Even when we walk through terrible times, he is with us. We must trust him when we cannot see the way ahead. We must rely on him to get us through the shadowy valleys of this life.

God is not a liar, and he never forgets a promise. He faithfully follows through on his Word. He does not abandon love at any point, for he *is* love. He is kinder than we give him credit for. He is more steadfast than we can imagine. He is better than the lifestyles of privilege and wealth. He is unquestionably true, and he is inherently trustworthy.

Lord of Lords, there is no one else like you. You are not a man, so you do not lie. You have no need to deceive or trick us. I trust you even when I don't understand what you are doing.

BETTER THAN ANY OTHER

"All the declarations of my mouth can be trusted;
they contain no twisted logic or perversion of the truth."

PROVERBS 8:8

It is hard to know whom we can trust these days. People in power tend to twist their words to suit their audience. But God is so much better than that. He does not change his message of mercy depending on whom he's addressing. He does not confuse or deceive. He is the source of all life, and his wisdom sets the captive free.

Do you trust God to do what he says he will? It is important to learn what his nature is truly like. If you are not undone in awe at the thought of his mercy, then there is more for you to discover in him today. He is undeniably good. His loving-kindness is more liberating than any other force on this planet. His peace is palpable, and his heart is undeterred in loyal love. Take him at his word today and dare to trust in his unfailing goodness as you let your hopes rise to meet him.

Loving Lord, I trust that you are better than I can imagine. Even so, expand my understanding of your goodness and blow my experience out of the water. Let hope arise within my heart as you meet me.

CLEAR-CUT

"All my words are clear and straightforward to everyone
who possesses spiritual understanding. If you have an
open mind, you will receive revelation-knowledge."

PROVERBS 8:9

We must remain humble and teachable, open to learning
the ways of God, no matter how long we have walked
with him. Pride tricks us into thinking we already have
the answers. Humility makes space for admitting that we
have so much more to learn. It allows us to change our
minds and do better when we know better. A humble
heart admits weakness and does not shy away from its
own humanity.

There is clarity in the revelation-knowledge of
God. We find deep understanding as we fellowship with
the Spirit. We must remain open-minded and willing to
adjust our understanding, not being so proud as to think
we have nothing to learn from others. So much growth is
ahead of us, so much grounding available, when we allow
the wisdom of Christ to expand our horizons.

**Spirit, I don't want to be a know-it-all, and I don't want
to be stuck in a mindset that limits who you are and
who I can be in you. Free me from the confines of pride
and lead me into your expansive mercy.**

PRICELESS

Wisdom is so priceless that it exceeds the value of any jewel. Nothing you could wish for can equal her.

PROVERBS 8:11

If we see wisdom for what it is, we will spend all we have to acquire it. We could never obtain anything more valuable in this life. It's time to set our focus on the wisdom-giver, Jesus Christ. Let's lavish our love upon him. He can be trusted with the deepest recesses of our hearts. When we align our lifestyles with his instruction, we walk in the light of his powerful presence.

Nothing can equal the value that wisdom brings to our lives. If we require assistance, wisdom is ready to help us. When we are running low on hope, wisdom gives us something to look forward to. No matter what it is we are deficient in, wisdom supplies in endless measure. Where there is defeat, wisdom paves the way for our victory. Where there is confusion, wisdom provides peaceful clarity. Where there is lack of vision, wisdom provides a joyful plan. As we spend time in the presence of God, we can receive all that we need for today.

Wise God, thank you for the endless wisdom you provide. I need your guidance, your help, and your strength. Move in me today and let joy rise within me as you do.

PURPOSEFUL PLANS

"I am Wisdom, and I am shrewd and intelligent.
I have at my disposal living-understanding
to devise a plan for your life."

PROVERBS 8:12

Many people struggle to know how to move ahead in life.
Perhaps you have made plans before only to find that they
did not turn out as you had hoped. We can start out with
dreams and follow through with consistency, and even
then, what we imagine and what actually happens are
not the same. We have to adjust our expectations, letting
ourselves still dream but letting the details of things we
could never anticipate unfold as they will.

God is with us through it all. The living-
understanding of wisdom is like a blueprint that we
can follow. Let's not allow far-off details to distract us
from what is ours to do now. We first have to build the
foundation before we can construct the frame. We need
to put walls up before we can think of furnishings. As we
lean into the wisdom of the Lord and trust his plans, we
can take each step as it comes.

All-Knowing One, thank you for the reminder that
there is purpose in your plans and that I don't have to
know every detail now. I give up the need to control
what is steps down the road, and I give myself to
following your directions now.

LIFE OF WORSHIP

"Wisdom pours into you when you begin to hate
every form of evil in your life, for that's what worship
and fearing God is all about."

PROVERBS 8:13

Worshiping the Lord is not about simply singing songs or
dancing before him. Sure, that's an expression of our love
for him. But we truly worship the Lord when we submit
our lives and apply his wisdom to our habits. When we
reject the evil ways of this world in favor of following the
Lord in righteousness, we truly honor God as our Father
and King.

As we worship him, he stands to fight for us and
defend us. He surrounds us with his presence and protects
us from the fiery darts of the enemy. Pompous pride has
no place in God's kingdom. Perverse speech does not
belong there. Let your mind be filled with the purity of
the fruit of the Spirit, feeding into every area of your life.
Worship God with your choices throughout the day.

**Worthy Savior, keep me from being deceived into
thinking that following you means that my life will be
perfect. You are worthy of my submission, adoration,
and trust. I reject pride and turn away from hatred
cloaked as concern. May I reflect your mercy and grace.**

UNIQUE DESIGNS

"You will find true success when you find me, for I have insight into wise plans that are designed just for you. I hold in my hands living-understanding, courage, and strength."

PROVERBS 8:14

No one can replace you. There is not another person on this planet, either living or dead, who could take your place in the kingdom of Christ. Even though there are many similarities among people, each is a unique reflection of his mercy. Every single person is worth our attention, for they are made in the image of God.

May you find compassion well up within you as you receive the overwhelming affection of God toward you. As you come to understand how thoroughly you are loved, may it compel you to love others in the same way. If you find yourself running low on peace, patience, or kindness, ask the Lord to fill you and spend time in his presence. He has all that you need. You will find in him all the understanding, courage, and strength you require.

Mighty God, I know that nothing is impossible for you. I realize that you love me as I am. I receive your mercy, and I ask for an expansion of my understanding as I do. Lead me on and encourage my heart in hope.

JUSTICE AND GENEROSITY

"I empower kings to reign and rulers to make laws that
are just. I empower princes to rise and take dominion,
and generous ones to govern the earth."

PROVERBS 8:15-16

Though we may live humble and simple lives in the eyes
of the world, God has made us kings and priestly rulers
by the grace of his redemption. Christ restored us to the
Father, making a way for full and total reconciliation.
His mercy covers us, and we come to the Father without
shame or fear. We will rule and reign with Christ in his
kingdom. What a glorious truth to take hold of!

God is concerned with justice. He does not ignore
the cries of the abused, overlooked, or rejected. He will
one day set right every wrong. Even as we wait for his
kingdom to come to earth as it is in heaven, we get to
partner with his nature and practice mercy, justice, and
laid-down love. Those who serve are greatest in the
kingdom of heaven, so let's not be overcome by the appeal
of comfort, privilege, or power. We reign with Christ
when we practice humble mercy-kindness and use our
influence to do good in our communities.

King of Kings, I want to reflect your kingdom values in
my life. May I always side with your mercy and reject the
pull of power that can distance me from you and others.

WHOLEHEARTED DESIRE

"I will show my love to those who passionately love me. For
they will search and search continually until they find me."

PROVERBS 8:17

Halfhearted cravings for wisdom will not lead to finding
it. We must love wisdom to gain it. We must love it
enough not only to listen but also to carefully follow
wisdom's ways. Wholehearted desire leads us to the
depths of wisdom's wealth. Superficial desire gets us only
superficial knowledge. This is the same in any area. We
will never reach profound intimacy with someone if we
do not put the work into getting to know them over time.
We won't become experts in any subject if we don't dig
deeper than the primary points on the surface.

What do you desire wholeheartedly? Where do
you spend your time and energy? What do you give your
attention to? As you consider these questions, evaluate
whether what you are spending your time on actually
serves the values that you want to be true in your life.
Choose today the areas where you want to move ahead
and keep searching for wisdom.

Merciful Lord, thank you for a fresh start in you every
time I approach you. I won't stop searching for your
wisdom, and I won't stop listening for your corrective
kindness. It is you I love.

Never without It

"From eternity past I was set in place, before the world began. I was anointed from the beginning."

PROVERBS 8:23

God possessed wisdom before he created the universe. Before a star was set into place, before the oceans were filled, or the Lord said, "Let there be light," wisdom was overflowing. The world has never been without it, and neither are we. When we do not know which way to turn, let us turn to the Lord. When we can't see our right from our left in the darkness of night, we can look to the light of the Lord that is always with us. We must listen for his still, small voice that directs us.

First Corinthians 1:24 states, "[Jesus] is God's mighty power, God's true wisdom, and our Messiah." Christ is the ultimate manifestation of God's power to save us from sin, to work miracles, and to defeat evil. He is the ultimate expression of wisdom, for he carries out the eternal plan of God, bringing it to completion. We know that we are never without Christ and his presence through his Spirit. Wisdom is always at hand.

Redeemer, you are the Anointed One, and you are worthy of my trust. I choose to follow your wise ways with my life. Be near and speak to me.

DELIGHTFULLY CREATIVE

"I was there, close to the Creator's side as his master artist. Daily he was filled with delight in me as I playfully rejoiced before him."

PROVERBS 8:30

The wisdom of God is not overly serious. There is joy and laughter in God's presence. There is light and life. It would be to our detriment if we believed that we have to be composed at all times. Jesus said that the kingdom of heaven welcomes those who are childlike. We don't have to be refined or put-together. We can let the joy and wonder that filled us as children lead us to the Lord, for he delights in us.

Wisdom is like an architect, knowing how to artfully and masterfully design things that last. When we have creative ideas, we can look to the Lord for guidance. We don't have to reinvent the wheel. As we look for places where wisdom is already at work in the industries we are a part of, we will find it. Let's work with integrity and build endeavors that will stand the test of time. There's inspiration in the presence of the Lord whenever we need it.

Creator, I am in awe of your masterful skill and creative expressions as I look at what you have made. Inspire me with your wisdom. Thank you for the creativity that is in me because I'm made in your image.

JOY IN THE WAITING

"If you wait at wisdom's doorway, longing to hear a word
for every day, joy will break forth within you as you listen
for what I'll say."

PROVERBS 8:34

All things are possible with the movement of God's Spirit.
We have only to wait on his timing. We are not stuck in
waiting rooms with nothing to do but twiddle our thumbs
and read up on the latest news. We continue to do what
is ours to do, following the rhythms of the Lord's leading
with expectancy and hope. There is joy in the in-between,
and there is delight in the overwhelming love of God that
covers us continually.

As we long to hear the Lord's voice every day,
making time to wait on him, we open our hearts and
settle our souls before him. As we practice making room
for him, we learn to embrace the peace of quiet moments.
In those moments, our souls come alive, and the depth of
our longing reaches out to the depth of God's great mercy.
What a wonderful exchange we find in his presence!

Wonderful One, the more time I spend before you,
the more expectant I become. I have tasted the
tremendously satisfying peace of your presence, and
I long for more. Let joy arise as I wait on you today.

LIFE-GIVING FOUNTAIN

"For the fountain of life pours into you every time that
you find me, and this is the secret of growing in the
delight and the favor of the Lord."

PROVERBS 8:35

When we experience the refreshing waves of God's
goodness, our delight grows. Our joy cannot be pinned
down, and our peace cannot be disturbed when the
fountain of Christ's life pours into us. This is not a one-
time experience. Every time we find him, we expand in
his love and our old understanding is overshadowed by
the incomparable goodness of who he truly is. Every time
the Spirit reveals an aspect of God that we did not see
before, we are filled with awe and wonder.

It is a worthy pursuit to give ourselves to beholding
the Lord. To encounter his life-giving fountain, we
can practice spending time turning our hearts and
imaginations over to him. When we focus on his
faithfulness, when we hear stories of his power, when we
remember the kisses of his sweet mercy in our lives, how
can we help but grow in increasing delight toward him?
The more we understand how limitlessly we are loved, the
more confident we become in our own pursuit of him.

**Lord, thank you for the fountain of your life that pours
over those who find you. Reveal yourself to me in a
fresh way as I look to you today. I love you.**

HEAVENLY ATTRIBUTES

Wisdom has built herself a palace upon
seven pillars to keep it secure.

PROVERBS 9:1

In the book of James, we find the seven components of
heavenly wisdom: "The wisdom from above is always
pure, filled with peace, considerate and teachable. It is
filled with love and never displays prejudice or hypocrisy
in any form and it always bears the beautiful harvest
of righteousness! Good seeds of wisdom's fruit will be
planted with peaceful acts by those who cherish making
peace" (3:17–18).

Spend some time today rereading those verses,
letting their truth sink deep. Read them aloud, slowly, and
pause whenever you are moved to meditate on a word or
phrase. As you consider the attributes of God's wisdom,
think through how you can apply them in your day.
How can you choose peace? How can you express love to
those around you? Where do you need to reject prejudice
or hypocrisy? The fruit of wisdom is easy to spot, and
anyone who is truly looking for it will find it. Allow
yourself to embrace the simplicity of God's ways and look
for places where wisdom is already at work.

**Spirit, as I feed on your revelation-truth, transform me
within. Not stopping there, help me to implement your
strategies and sow seeds of peace. Thank you.**

FEAST AT HER TABLE

She has made ready a banquet feast and the sacrifice has been killed. She has mingled her wine, and the table's all set.

PROVERBS 9:2

The table is set for you to feast with wisdom. She has prepared her banquet, and the abundance is overflowing. Come feed your heart on revelation-truth that will transform you. Implement the strategies you find at the feasting table. There is more than enough to feed you and everyone in your life. Be filled and then go share what you have consumed with others.

Even when you don't recognize your hunger, if you have gone long enough without eating, your body needs nourishment. In the same way, your soul needs to be filled with the wisdom of Christ. Even when you don't feel the hunger pangs, if it has been a while since you have eaten the fruit of wisdom's table, then your soul is in need. Come, fill up on the bounteous feast she has prepared for you. There is plenty more where it came from.

God of Wisdom, I come to eat from your table of plenty today. Fill me with the revelation-knowledge of Christ that nourishes my heart and soul. May every area of my life benefit from your incomparable insight.

OPEN INVITATION

She has sent out her maidens, crying out from the high
place, inviting everyone to come and eat until they're full.

PROVERBS 9:3

Wisdom is not reserved for the elite, and it is not
exclusive to those who grew up learning to hear her voice.
Wisdom invites everyone into her home, welcoming
them in to feast from the abundance of her table. Let's be
sure that we do not exclude anyone whom Christ himself
would not exclude from the table. In fact, we know that
Christ welcomes all who come to him. Who are we to do
any differently?

No matter what you chose yesterday, you have the
opportunity to choose differently today. Will you take
wisdom up on her invitation? Will you listen to her call?
The invitation is given from the high place so that it will
reach the ears of everyone below. Even as you heed her call
and come to her table, don't hesitate to bring others with
you. All are welcome! Whoever wants to receive wisdom is
encouraged to dine, and her door is always open.

**Gracious God, I'm so grateful that you never turn me
away when I come to you. May I be clothed in your
compassion, always welcoming others in your love.**

APRIL

RICHES OF RIGHTEOUSNESS

"Lay aside your simple thoughts and leave your paths behind. Agree with my ways, live in my truth, and you will find righteousness."

PROVERBS 9:6

When we refuse to leave our paths behind, unwilling to let the correction of truth redirect us, we resist what is meant to nourish us. Wisdom leads us in peace. Are we willing to let the love of God transform us so much that we lay down our rights to our offense? There is room for nuance in the mercy of Christ and space for more change than we often allow.

We find greater value in following the ways of Christ's kingdom than in following the winds of our own fleeting desires. The values of the Holy Spirit have plentiful purposes. When we feel stuck in our lives, whether it's through our own making or through what happens to us, we can find liberation in the love of God. There's always insight to help us know how to move ahead. Sometimes, we simply must wait for the season to change. As we look to the Lord today, agreeing with his ways and living in his truth, we find righteousness.

Righteous One, I lay aside my preconceived ideas of who you are and welcome your wisdom to transform my perception of you and others.

READY TO REDIRECT

Don't even bother to correct a mocker, for he'll only hate you for it. But go ahead and correct the wise; they'll love you even more.

PROVERBS 9:8

Stubborn hearts that refuse correction will not be changed by persuasive words. We cannot control the choices of others, but we can offer advice to those who are willing to hear it. It is not our job to correct everyone around us, so we should be wary of sticking our opinions in places where they are not welcome. Those who want to walk in the ways of wisdom will accept the opportunity to reflect and change.

King David eloquently put it this way in Psalm 141:5, "When one of your godly ones corrects me…I will accept it like an honor I cannot refuse. It will be as healing medicine that I swallow without an offended heart. Even if they are mistaken, I will continue to pray." *Even if they are mistaken*, we can take the healing medicine of correction and rebuke without becoming offended. We should simply take it to the Lord in prayer and let it be a lesson in consideration.

Great God, I will not resist the rebuke of others, and I will take every opportunity to pray and consider what they say even when they are wrong about me.

EXPANDED AND ALIGNED

Teach a wise man what is right and he'll grow even wiser.
Instruct the lovers of God and they'll learn even more.

PROVERBS 9:9

We are constantly changing, adapting to the shifts in our
world. Whether we use the opportunities to transform
and expand in wisdom or to resist and make our own way
is up to us. When we are offered new wine, we should not
put it into an old wineskin, as Jesus explained in Mark
2:22: "The wine will be spilled and the wineskin ruined.
Instead, new wine is always poured into new wineskins."

Let's take the opportunity to put new wisdom into
practice, not forcing it to fit into our worn-out ways.
There is increase available as we align ourselves in the
wisdom that moves us from glory to glory. When we
learn a better way, we don't need to hold so tightly to the
way we've done things before. In fact, it serves us best
when we redirect and shift ourselves according to our
expanded understanding.

**Jesus, I don't want to resist change when you bring
it. I don't want to stay stubbornly stuck in limited
understanding. I choose to follow the extension of your
wisdom.**

CONSUMED WITH AWE

The starting point for acquiring wisdom is to be consumed with awe as you worship YAHWEH. To receive the revelation of the Holy One, you must come to the one who has living-understanding.

PROVERBS 9:10

As we set our hearts on the Lord, offering him our attention and affection, we prepare ourselves to receive from his gracious and generous wisdom. When we look for the Lord, we will find him. When we search for hints of his mercy, we will uncover where he is at work within the cracks of our lives.

Christ has all the living-understanding we could ever need. Instead of chasing empty promises of men, we can go straight to the one who is full of wisdom's secrets. David was consumed with awe as he danced before the Lord with great abandon (see 2 Samuel 6:14). We must abandon our pride to allow awe to move us to worship the Lord in the same way. We cannot worry whether it seems undignified to others. Whatever it looks like, when we become overwhelmed with wonder, we offer the Lord our unhindered worship.

Awesome God, there is no other like you. You are worthy of my devotion and of my liberated worship. I come to you freely, with a heart overflowing with praise. Pour your wisdom into me today.

FRUITFUL INCREASE

Wisdom will extend your life,
making every year more fruitful than the one before.

PROVERBS 9:11

Through the ebbs and flow of our lives, we will experience times of great rejoicing, and we will experience times of great sorrow. The fruit of the Spirit is not dependent on our happiness or lack of trouble. It blossoms and grows even in the harshest climates. As we follow wisdom, we cannot expect perfect lives, but we can expect the overwhelming satisfaction of God's mercy meeting us wherever we are.

The Spirit-fruit of overflowing joy, subduing peace, enduring patience, active kindness, prevailing faith, wholehearted gentleness, and Spirit-strength come from lives yielded to the wisdom of Christ. We attain a virtuous life as we partner with the kingdom values of Jesus. We experience the increase of his bountiful goodness as we apply his wisdom to every area of our lives.

Holy Spirit, may my life be filled with your fruit as I continually surrender to your ways. I choose to walk in the path of peace, to practice the law of love, and to endure trials with patience. Thank you for your strength and overwhelming goodness.

ADVANTAGES FOR YOU

It is to your advantage to be wise. But to ignore the counsel of wisdom is to invite trouble into your life.

PROVERBS 9:12

The counsel of wisdom keeps us on the right path. It keeps us from chasing fantasies that never materialize, abandoning our inheritance in the process. Scripture uses the imagery of someone leaving behind his own vineyard to wander in barren wilderness. Why would we forsake our fields when there is plenty to nurture and grow in the fortified soil of our lives?

It is to our advantage to pay attention to wisdom. It is to our benefit when we listen to the counsel of Christ and follow his ways. Let's not walk away from his never-ending mercy into the barren realm of false promises. What a treasure it is to stay close to him, leaning in to hear his voice, know his presence, and fill up on his wise offerings. There is abundant life in Christ, far beyond the simple ability to get by.

Christ, I choose to listen to your counsel and follow your ways. I don't want to go chasing after fantasies that trade the abundance that is already at my fingertips for wandering in the barren wilderness. I choose you, for I know you know what's best for me.

COMPETING VOICES

There is a spirit named Foolish,
who is boisterous and brash;
she's seductive and restless.

PROVERBS 9:13

We know that wisdom's influence is found around us, but hers is not the only voice calling out. We cannot assume every piece of advice we receive is from the well that wisdom draws from. Some voices will feel chaotic and brash. Other advice you've been given may feel restless and impatient. It is important that we are cautious when deciding whose advice to take. We must be discerning with the calls we answer and the opinions we heed.

May you find yourself rooted in the grounding wisdom of Christ. There is no confusion in his call. He gives you clarity to move ahead in simple and manageable ways. He's always inviting you to clothe yourself with compassion, to trust the Father with what you cannot control, and to live with integrity in all of your decisions. Don't abandon your values because of the pressure others may put on you. Find peace in the presence of God through wisdom's understanding.

Peace-Giver, give me discernment to turn aside from foolish distractions, to resist the pull of easy outs and shortcuts, and to hold steadfastly to your truth.

GENERATIONAL RIPPLES

The wisdom of Solomon: When wisdom comes to a son,
joy comes to a father. When a son turns from wisdom,
a mother grieves.

PROVERBS 10:1

When we live, learn, and apply the wisdom of God to
our lives, not only do we benefit, but the breakthrough
we experience also brings joy to the ones who raised us.
When we yield our lives to the Lord and take ownership
of our mistakes and give God honor for our successes,
those who taught us the value of right living experience
immense delight. Even if we did not experience this in our
natural family systems, there are spiritual mothers and
fathers who rejoice with us as they take us in as their own.

It is wise to consider how our own choices will
affect those who come after us, just as they echo back to
those who have gone before. There is a wealth of wisdom
to continually draw from, and the well never runs dry.
May we honor our caregivers and their influence through
our submission to the Lord and offer them gratitude for
their own laid-down love that paved the way for us to run
to the Father.

**Father, thank you for the power of generational
blessings and for the strong connection of family. I'm
so glad I have found myself at home in your family.**

HONEST HAPPINESS

Gaining wealth through dishonesty is no gain at all.
But honesty brings you a lasting happiness.

PROVERBS 10:2

When we live with honesty as a prevailing value, we have nothing to hide. Whether it is our work, our family lives, or what we do in times of leisure, we don't have to fear being found out when we are honest. This is not to say that every person is privy to our most personal experiences—surely not. There is a difference between privacy and dishonesty.

When it comes to how we make a living, we have no excuse for dishonesty or corruption. We will not be able to experience true and lasting happiness knowing that at any moment someone could discover our compromise. Let's be sure to apply this lesson to every area of our lives, including our relationships. Our souls thrive when we are living in the light of truth. Our hearts have peace when we are at peace with our decisions. When we lean into the grace of God, we find strength to empower us, correct us, and lead us into the satisfaction of his ways.

Faithful Father, there is nothing I have need of that you do not already know. I reject the temptation to compromise your values for my own gain, and I choose to walk in the light of integrity.

TRUE FULFILLMENT

The Lord satisfies the longings of all his lovers,
but he withholds from the wicked what their souls crave.

PROVERBS 10:3

True and lasting fulfillment is found in the presence of
God. He welcomes us with open arms whenever we turn
to him. He never prevents a hungry heart from eating
at his table of grace. He covers us with the garments of
his mercy, and he liberates our hearts with the powerful
tenderness of his love.

If you find yourself questioning whether you are
counted as a lover of God, know that he receives you with
the incomparably kind and generous love of a faithful
Father. Open your heart to him, and he will fill you with
the light of his glorious countenance. His Spirit will give
you the peace you long for, and you will find satisfaction
in his delight. Romans 3:21–22 says that the righteousness
of God was made visible through Jesus Christ. All who
believe in him receive the gift of it. Turn to him and
receive his gift of righteousness today.

**Jesus, I turn to you with an open and willing heart. I
want to walk in the light of your righteousness, so fill
me with your liberating mercy today. I long to know
you more.**

SEASONAL RHYTHMS

Know the importance of the season you're in and a wise
son you will be. But what a waste when an incompetent
son sleeps through his day of opportunity!

PROVERBS 10:5

There is incredible importance in recognizing the seasons
that we are in. What is required of us in the winters of
our lives is very different from the summers. When we
learn to embrace the rhythms of the seasons, we find
satisfaction in knowing that we are fulfilling what is
necessary at the time.

Are you in a winter trying to live as though it were
summer, or vice versa? You will inevitably be frustrated
if you fight the natural rhythms of life. Ask for clarity
and perspective to see what is required of you here and
now. When you can recognize the season you are in, you
will be able to harness the goodness in it. Tilling soil and
planting seeds is hard work, and so is harvest. But they do
not last forever. Neither does the seeming barrenness of
winter. Embrace the season you are in, and you will reap
the fruit in the next.

Creator, I want to learn from the cycles of nature that
you so intentionally set in place. May I not resist the
rest of winter nor the hard work of reaping. Show me
where I am and what you require of me now.

MEMORIALS OF RIGHTEOUSNESS

The reputation of the righteous becomes a sweet
memorial to him, while the wicked life
only leaves a rotten stench.

PROVERBS 10:7

When we treat people with respect, kindness, and honor,
we have nothing to fear when others spread lies about us.
The truth will be known, and the fruit of our lived-out
love will be heralded by those who know us well. Let's be
sure that we are living in the light of Christ's compassion,
reaching out in loyal love in all that we do, with nothing
to hide from others.

Integrity is a shield for those who live by its
standards. When we are freely ourselves, we can admit
when we get it wrong and when we fail others. We must
not be afraid to let our understanding be transformed by
the expansive love of Christ. We need to be honest about
the learning curves of life, with ourselves and others.
There is no need to "fake it until we make it." Let's live
empowered by the righteousness that grace offers and live
in the light of mercy, going from glory to glory.

**Righteous One, it is your righteousness that covers me.
I choose to live openly, without fear of the future, for I
trust you to guide me. I choose to follow your pathway
of peace.**

TAKE TIME TO LISTEN

The heart of the wise will easily accept instruction.
But those who do all the talking are too busy to listen
and learn. They'll just keep stumbling ahead
into the mess they created.

PROVERBS 10:8

Many lessons repeat themselves throughout the book
of Proverbs, and the above verse happens to be a main
theme threaded throughout. If we take the time to listen
and learn, remaining humble and teachable, we make
room to grow in the understanding of God's mighty
mercy. Everyone's voice matters, and every person has a
unique perspective on life. May we spend as much time
listening to those around us as we do sharing our own
ideas, stories, and opinions.

We need to take the time to truly hear those
who differ from us. It is one thing to open our hearts to
those we love and trust for correction, but it is an even
greater act of humility to consider the points of those
who don't agree with us. Let's not shut our hearts against
the opportunity to listen to those with differing views
and lived experiences. It may just be what causes our
breakthrough in understanding Christ more than we
already do.

**Christ Jesus, help me to remain humble and open,
feeding on your truth, no matter who it comes through.**

FEARLESS CONFIDENCE

The one who walks in integrity will experience a fearless
confidence in life, but the one who is devious will
eventually be exposed.

PROVERBS 10:9

There is hope for those who walk in the footsteps of
Christ's righteous path of love. When we know the heart
of the One we trust to lead us, turning at his voice, and
shifting our gaze with his directives, we walk in the
fearless confidence of faith. Nothing surprises him, so we
can take courage when we encounter difficulties, knowing
that he will get us through every single one.

Consider your level of hope today. Ask the Holy
Spirit to reveal any area of your life where you can trust
him more. Let his kindness lead you to the truth behind
your quaking fears. Perhaps you resist pain when it rises
within you. Maybe you resist conflict at the expense of
reconciliation. Perhaps you feel the fearless confidence
that Solomon speaks of, but it shifts depending on
the circumstances in your life. Don't be afraid to face
the feelings within. There is so much to learn as you
compassionately present your heart in full to the Lord.
He is the healing balm, the empowering strength, and the
discerning wisdom you need.

**Spirit, reveal where I can align more fully with your
kingdom today.**

PROMOTERS OF PEACE

The troublemaker always has a clever plan and won't look you in the eye, but the one who speaks correction honestly can be trusted to make peace.

PROVERBS 10:10

When you think about the people you trust most in your life, what qualities do they have that cause you to go to them time and again? Perhaps they are level-headed and clear, reliable and trustworthy. Even when they correct you, you know it is from a place of loving-kindness, wanting the best for you. If you don't have anyone who fits that description, don't be discouraged. The Holy Spirit is full of wisdom and is with you, and he will guide you to relationships that are grounded in truth and love.

Look to the pursuers and promoters of peace. Find the advisers that unite rather than divide. Look for the trusted gatekeepers who practice what they preach. Find those who, no matter what they profess to believe, live with compassion, kindness, and a commitment to truth. They will be a good landing place for you. May you resist the shifty-eyed appeals of those who resist integrity, and may you also give honest and kind feedback to those who ask for it.

Prince of Peace, I want to be a person of peace, just as you are. Transform me in your loving-kindness and give me courage to stand firm.

SHELTER OF LOVE

Hatred keeps old quarrels alive, but love draws a veil over
every insult and finds a way to make sin disappear.

PROVERBS 10:12

It is not hard to imagine what stirring up offense leads to
these days. It is all around us! We see it clearly in media,
politics, and our own homes. The choice to humble
ourselves in love leads us to peace, but it is not an easy
choice to make when our own ideas of what is right and
wrong are triggered. We must choose to look beyond the
concepts and choose to see the person behind them.

Love will cover up offenses against us. We can
extend love to those who harm us, no matter what it is
that they have done. We free ourselves as much as we free
them when we do. We must be careful to never use love
as an excuse, however, for why someone should forgive
us. This is not our place. Love is not manipulative or
controlling. When we hurt someone, we have no right
to demand forgiveness. We can only repent and offer the
love of our own hearts.

**Father of Love, may I never use your love as an excuse
to resist humble repentance. Thank you for your mercy.
In your love, I find freedom.**

TREASURE IT WITHIN

Wise men don't divulge all that they know, but chattering
fools blurt out words that bring them to the brink of ruin.

PROVERBS 10:14

There is wisdom in not talking for the sake of having our
voices heard. Part of practicing wisdom is knowing when
to speak and when to be silent. After the shepherds had
visited Mary, Joseph, and baby Jesus, they told all about
the miraculous sign that had led them to the Christ. It is
interesting that Luke recorded Mary's reaction, saying,
"Mary treasured all these things in her heart and often
pondered what they meant" (Luke 2:19).

Do you take time to treasure the words and signs
of God that have touched your life? It is good practice to
ponder what they mean. Some things need time and space
in our hearts and minds before we speak about what we do
not yet see in full. Ask the Spirit to reveal the things that
you can hold close while letting him bring clarification
with time and perspective. Don't do as others do, sharing
more than is necessary with any who will listen.

**Holy Spirit, thank you that I don't have to figure out
your wonders on my own. Give me clarity to know what
things you are stirring need time to breathe in my heart
and life. Thank you.**

WISDOM IN RESTRAINT

If you keep talking, it won't be long before you're saying something really wrong. Prove you're wise from the very start—just bite your tongue and be strong!

PROVERBS 10:19

Have you ever known someone who seemed to put their foot in their mouth on a regular basis? Perhaps as you got to know them more, you could more easily overlook their slips. But think of how much they could have been spared offense and strife if they had learned to regulate their words.

It takes strength and self-control to not bite back at those who take digs at you. Make it a practice to refrain from saying more than is necessary, especially to those who don't know you well enough to realize your intentions. Wisdom is found in restraint. May you not disregard the power of self-control to avoid needless offenses. God knows your heart, he sees things for how they truly are, and you cannot offend him. The same cannot be said for others.

Jesus, thank you for the reminder that restraint can benefit my relationships. I have nothing to prove, so I won't overexplain myself. I trust you to defend me when the need arises.

REDEMPTIVE WORDS

The teachings of the godly ones are like pure silver,
bringing words of redemption to others,
but the heart of the wicked is corrupt.

PROVERBS 10:20

The fruits of our words reflect what is in our soul. None of us is perfect, and every single one of us has areas to grow in love, truly. It is still important that we not ignore what our speech is sprinkled with. Are we offering encouragement that is backed up by the support of kindness and service to others? When we offer advice, we should encourage the listener to stand in their strength and the power of God's grace. We must refrain from directing them away from themselves and from the standards of Christ's kingdom.

May the words we speak reflect the redemptive wisdom of God. James 3:17 says that "the wisdom from above is always pure, filled with peace, considerate and teachable. It is filled with love and never displays prejudice or hypocrisy in any form." As we display this wisdom in how we speak to others, our words will be pure, honoring, and filled with peace. May our speech be filled with consideration and humility.

Redeemer, I want to reflect your mercy-kindness not only in the way I live my life but also in how I speak about and to others.

MULTIPLY MERCY

The lovers of God feed many with their teachings,
but the foolish ones starve themselves for lack
of an understanding heart.

PROVERBS 10:21

Another way to translate the beginning of this verse from
the Aramaic is "the lips of the righteous multiply mercy."
When we are so covered in the compassion of Christ that
our lives are transformed by his living love, we cannot
help but display it in our words, our actions, and our
relationships. Let's steer away from the wisdom of this world
that says we need to fight those who disagree with us. That is
not, and has never been, the way of Christ or his kingdom.

When we put our devoted faith into practice, we
cannot ignore the continual maturing of our souls. We
must remain teachable, just as we hope others will. We can
look for ways to grow in our understanding not only of how
Christ's kingdom works but also of compassion. Let's take
time to really try to understand where others are coming
from, especially those we don't agree with. We multiply
mercy by being openhearted rather than shut off from the
world. Today is the day to embrace the pursuit of God's love
that will lead us in our pursuit of understanding.

**Father, thank you for the wisdom I have already tasted.
I want to be moved by your mercy to understand
others. I submit to you.**

ANCHORED IN CHRIST

The wicked are blown away by every stormy wind.
But when a catastrophe comes,
the lovers of God have a secure anchor.

PROVERBS 10:25

The wicked are like the foolish man who built his house
on the sand. When winds and waves rushed in, his home
was destroyed. The wise are like the man who chose the
right place to build a house and then did the work to lay
a deep and secure foundation. Even when storms and
floods raged, the house stood strong and unshaken. Jesus
described it this way in Luke 6:47–48 and then went on
to add that those who hear his teaching and put it into
practice are wise while those who do not are foolish.

What kind of a builder are you? Are you tethered to
the anchor of Christ, which is securely fastened? We are
true lovers of God when we hear what he says and live it
out in our day-to-day lifestyles. As we put our faith into
practice, we honor the Lord with our very lives. When the
storms come, we will not be lost in the tempest.

**Christ, my Anchor, you are the one who holds me fast
and secure. I trust you with my soul, and I show it with
my yielded life. I am yours.**

SANCTUARY OF REST

The beautiful ways of God are a safe resting place
for those who have integrity. But to those who work
wickedness the ways of God spell doom.

PROVERBS 10:29

God is much wiser than we can imagine. Nothing he
does is without purpose or redemption. He is made up
of limitless and loyal love, and his ways never fail. Those
who go against God's mercy—who oppress the vulnerable
and abuse their power—are not walking in the light of
God's ways. If someone professes to be a Christ follower
and yet does not display his values in their choices, then
they are liars.

May we not be fooled by the glitz of power that
promises more than it can deliver. We must resist the
temptation to put others down in order to get ahead.
Integrity guards our hearts, souls, and minds in the peace
of Christ, and it is a safe resting place for those who live
by its standard. Integrity is not perfection, but it is the
commitment to mercy, holiness, and justice. We get to
choose how we will reflect these values today.

God of Peace, forgive me for when I have lost sight of
your powerful love and instead sided with those who
would tear down anyone who disagrees with them.
I choose to follow you, for you are my resting place.

PERFECT STONE

Dishonest business practice is something that YAHWEH
truly hates. But it pleases him when we apply the right
standards of measurement.

PROVERBS 11:1

Deceptive balances and hypocrisy have no place in the
kingdom of God. He is pure, full of mercy-kindness for
all who look to him. He does not offer varying amounts
of mercy, depending on who you are. He offers the same
generous love, grace, and power to all who look to him.
He is a faithful and exceedingly good Father. He does
not play favorites because there is no need. His love is
extravagantly better than we can imagine, and there is
room for all to swim in its limitless depths.

Knowing that we don't have to compete for our
Father's favor frees us up to live in his image. We can be
generous because we have more than enough in him.
We can be gracious because he offers to fill us with more
grace. Love is not a limited resource, so let's never be
fooled into thinking we need to be stingy with it. The
perfect measurement—the perfect stone—is Christ, and
Christ is expansive, welcoming, and pure.

**Lord, may I live with integrity, not hypocrisy. You are
generous, and I will move in that same spirit.**

CLOTHED IN HUMILITY

When you act with presumption, convinced that you're right, don't be surprised if you fall flat on your face! But humility leads to wisdom.

PROVERBS 11:2

Have you ever witnessed someone whose pride kept them from admitting they were wrong? Consider what impression that left on you. It is not a strength to be a know-it-all. It isn't in our best interest to pretend that we know more than we do. Humility is one of the most valuable traits a leader can have. If you want to lead well, then follow the example of Christ. He was a servant to all, and yet he was pure in heart and powerful in love.

Don't move too quickly with your assumptions. Take time to really get curious about them. When you presume that you know something that you have not taken the time to investigate, you may find yourself needing to backpedal. Lead with wisdom and take time and space to uncover what lies beneath the assumptions. Have honest conversations that seek to understand. Walking in humility helps you to make wise decisions, so don't neglect its power.

Servant of All, I choose to follow your lead and humble myself. Give me patience and perspective to take time with information before jumping to conclusions.

PATHS OF RECONCILIATION

Those with good character walk on a smooth path, with no detour or deviation. But the wicked keep falling because of their own wickedness.

PROVERBS 11:5

The value and depth of our character truly matter. It affects everything we do, how we interact with others and the paths we choose to take. When Samuel was sent to anoint the next king of Israel, God warned him not to judge the sons of Jesse based on their outer appearance. The Lord looks at the heart, not at what people see. This is incredibly important because our heart is where character is developed.

Don't despair if you feel you have failed in this area. If you have a willing and humble heart, God will use it. He will shape it with his generous grace and mercy, teaching you his ways and offering you the strength of his own power. In David's confessionary psalm, he proclaimed, "You will not despise my tenderness as I bow down humbly at your feet" (Psalm 51:17). We know that God restored David after his repentance from sin, and he will do the same for all who come to him in humble surrender.

Faithful One, no matter how many times I mess up, I keep coming back to you. Thank you for your restoration and the power of your forgiveness.

SEEDS OF BLESSING

The blessing that rests on the righteous releases strength and favor to the entire city, but shouts of joy will be heard when the wicked one dies.

PROVERBS 11:10

The blessing of the righteous does not only affect the righteous ones, but it also reaches into the communities where they are planted. Your blessing becomes seeds of blessing to those you interact with. When you sow into the places where you dwell and work, not just through relationships but also through your resources, you get to share your own breakthrough with others.

We know this to be true about wealth. When those with great resources give back to the community, they open pathways for others to benefit from their blessing. Let's try to outdo one another in generosity. We can reflect the love of Christ as people who sow into our communities—not only with our taxes but also with our time, our profits, and our active participation and service. There is so much goodness to share.

Righteous One, thank you for the blessing that releases from my life. I want to become an active partner with you in sowing seeds of blessing in my community. Show me ways I can increase my impact and honor you in the process.

WISE RESERVE

To quarrel with a neighbor is senseless.
Bite your tongue; be wise and keep quiet!

PROVERBS 11:12

When we live at peace with our neighbors, we promote atmospheres of understanding. Think of your physical neighbors—those who live on your street. How well do you know them? Do you have a good rapport? Perhaps neighbors are fighting with each other, or maybe you know the struggle of conflict yourself. Tension surely affects the neighborhood dynamic.

There is no sense in arguing with our neighbors. In fact, it could just make life more complicated and perhaps a bit miserable. This applies to those we work with and live with as well. May we be wise, keep quiet, and show the sense of our own reserve. We have nothing to prove in winning an argument, and it can damage relationships that would have otherwise blossomed. We don't have to be best friends with everyone in our lives. We won't like everyone. But that is okay; love does not require it. We can honor others even when we would not choose to be their close friend.

Loving Lord, your standards are perfect, and you back them up with marvelous mercy. Help me to show restraint with my speech and give me strength when I feel like engaging in a senseless argument.

TRUSTED FRIENDS

You can't trust gossipers with a secret; they'll just go blab
it all. Put your confidence instead in a trusted friend,
for he will be faithful to keep it in confidence.

PROVERBS 11:13

You probably would not share a deep secret with a
stranger, and you would not expose your vulnerabilities
to those who haven't proven their trustworthiness.
Perhaps this is a lesson you learned the hard way. Honesty
and integrity do not require vulnerable admissions to
everyone. In fact, it is wisdom that helps us to know who
can be trusted with our secrets.

Don't feel pressure to share a part of you with
someone you don't feel safe with. Manipulation and
control are not fruits of the Spirit. Even when you are
struggling to know whom you can trust in your flesh
and blood relationships, know there is one whom you
can always turn to. May you flourish in your relationship
with the Spirit, offering him access to the places you keep
hidden. Nothing can shock him, and he won't expose
you. He is full of loyal love, and he accepts you as you
are. Being built up in his love, he will be your confidence.
From this place, you can have the confidence to find
trustworthy friends to build into your life.

**Spirit, thank you for your wisdom and friendship.
I love you.**

GOOD COUNSEL
LEADS TO VICTORY

People lose their way without wise leadership,
but a nation succeeds and stands in victory
when it has many good counselors to guide it.

PROVERBS 11:14

We should be wary if we feel pressured to take a leader's advice just on the merit of his or her own word and relationship with the Lord. This is a form of spiritual manipulation, and it does not reflect the heart or will of God. There is a reason why kings, presidents, and other powerful leaders have councils and not just one person whom they trust to offer advice, direction, and wisdom. As today's proverb says, "A nation succeeds and stands in victory when it has many good counselors to guide it."

Do you have good counselors you can go to in your life? Choose wisely—those who walk in integrity, who are humble and knowledgeable, and who lead with servant-heartedness. Don't be afraid to spread your net wide, but also be sure to connect with the Holy Spirit, who is our best Counselor and wise director. There is victory in his wisdom.

Great God, thank you for the practicality of your wisdom that counsels me. Help me to gather good counsel in my life. I rely on your discernment to do it.

GRACIOUS GENEROSITY

A gracious, generous woman will be honored with a splendid reputation, but the woman who hates the truth lives with disgrace and is surrounded by men who are cutthroats, only greedy for money.

PROVERBS 11:16

The heart of a gracious woman is like gold. She can offer from the well of compassion that the overflowing fountain of the Lord feeds within her. She is generous with what she has, feeding her family first and then offering out of the overflow to those who are without. She offers security, safety, and reliable help in trouble.

We probably all know women like this—those who work hard and who offer the generosity of what they have with their communities. It is important that we honor these women. We should also venture to be like these women—not for the sake of our reputation but for the honor of serving others well. This is what it means to be Christlike. This is love in action—gracious generosity intentionally poured out.

Gracious Father, I aspire to be a person of great generosity, just as you are generous. As I look for ways to expand in this practice today, open my eyes to opportunities right before me. Thank you.

MAY

LIVING ABUNDANTLY

A son of righteousness experiences the abundant life,
but the one who pursues evil hurries to his own death.

PROVERBS 11:19

Jesus said, "I have come to give you everything in abundance, more than you expect—life in its fullness until you overflow!" (John 10:10). The abundant life we are looking for is found in Christ, and it is so much greater than we could expect to receive. His wisdom is practical and gives us insight into how to best live. His Spirit fills us with overflowing mercy, grace, and peace.

Come to Christ and receive the overflowing fullness of his heart and purposes for you. There is rest for your soul, clarity for your decisions, and comfort for your pain. Pursue his heart, and you will find an unending source of goodness. All that you need comes from him. Instead of trying to make it through on your own, lean on the everlasting arms that uphold you. Trust the words of life that Jesus speaks and put your faith in his faithfulness. He will not fail you.

Eternal One, I know that I can find abundance of life in you. Instead of trying to find a better way, I will look to you today, for you are the limitless source of wisdom I need.

PURE PATHS

The Lord can't stand the stubborn heart bent toward evil,
but he treasures those whose ways are pure.

PROVERBS 11:20

When we consider what it means to be pure, perhaps a
few descriptors come to mind—clean, wholesome, and
virtuous. The Lord looks at the purity of our hearts, and
he does not judge us on our outer appearances. We are no
less pure of heart when we've been working in the fields,
covered with dirt and sweat, than we are after we have
freshly bathed.

It is imperative that we not judge others based on
how they appear to us but instead take the time to get
to know them. In the mercy-flow of Christ's love, we are
clean. Let's not stand in judgment against another, for
that is the opposite of what God wants for and from us.
He created us in love to love one another. We get to offer
compassion, kindness, and peace from hearts deeply
rooted in the kingdom of Christ. Psalm 139 was dedicated
by King David to "the Pure and Shining One." He is the
purity we seek. Christ knows our hearts, and he sees right
through us. Let's follow on his pure paths of peace.

**Jesus, I know that you are the Pure and Shining One.
No one compares with you. As I meditate on your
incomparable goodness, reveal deeper truths of who
you are and who I am in you.**

PLEASANT WISHES

True lovers of God are filled with longings for what is pleasing and good, but the wicked can only expect doom.

PROVERBS 11:23

We can inspect the fruit of our thoughts, wishes, and longings in the light of the eternal values of God's kingdom. We don't need to over-spiritualize our longings. Some of our wishes in our earthly life will be unique to us and, if they do not bring harm to ourselves or others, are no less pleasing or good than those that fit the script of our spiritual understanding.

When our wishes are to better the world around us, to love others well, to be pursuers of peace and sharers of joy, to uphold justice and bring liberty to the oppressed, we can be sure that we are partnering with God's heart. Let's not overcomplicate the longings we have. Instead, we can invite the Spirit to show us where we can move ahead, even in waiting seasons, in hope, practicality, and service. God's wishes for us are pleasant. In light of that beautiful truth, why would we wish for another's harm?

Good Father, your love is so much purer than my own. You always uphold mercy when I would be quick to render judgment. You are better than the fairest judge, and you are more powerful than any nation. May my wishes, hopes, and longings align with your loyal love.

SATURATED WITH FAVOR

Those who live to bless others will have blessings heaped
upon them, and the one who pours out his life to pour
out blessings will be saturated with favor.

PROVERBS 11:25

It is not a waste when we live to bless others. What a
reflection of God's heart we become when we look for ways
to serve others in love. May we all be challenged to stretch
our capacity for compassion more than we have. Just like
building physical endurance, it takes time and effort, but
there is always room for strengthening this muscle.

As children of the living God, we are saturated
with his favor. We have the abundance of his resources
to share with others. We must not be stingy or become
comfortable in our little worlds. Instead, we can look
for creative opportunities to impact our families,
communities, and the larger world with abundant
kindness. There is always something to offer with our
time, attention, and resources. It does not have to be all
or nothing. In fact, the most sustainable growth happens
with little changes over time. What is one thing you can
do today to bless someone?

**Glorious God, thank you for endless growth potential
in your kingdom. Give me creative vision to see where
I can meet the needs of others and where I can bless
others as I have been blessed.**

SOCIAL CONSCIENCE

People will curse the businessman with no ethics, but the one with a social conscience receives praise from all.

PROVERBS 11:26

In our businesses and in our personal lives, we must conduct ourselves with a greater social awareness. If we put profits above people, we may make money, but we won't win praise from others. Our lives should promote the values of empathy and kindness while promoting the importance of our shared humanity.

Reflect on the values you want to be known for. Are they revealed in your work life? Consider if the way you do business is in line with the way you would treat family. The importance of showing practical care not only through your personal life but also through your work is paramount. If you do not know where to start in building a social conscience, look at the life and ministry of Christ. Pinpoint the values you see presented in his priorities. May you follow his example and find actionable steps to move in that direction.

Jesus, I know that you challenged the religious narrative of your day, and you broke the mold of who Israel thought God was. Do the same for me as I choose to live radically for your kingdom.

HARBINGERS OF GOOD

Living your life seeking what is good for others brings
untold favor, but those who wish evil for others
will find it coming back on them.

PROVERBS 11:27

When we live mindful of what is good for others, we
follow the golden rule that Jesus set forth in his teachings.
In Matthew 7:12, Jesus said, "In everything you do, be
careful to treat others in the same way you'd want them to
treat you, for that is the essence of all the teachings of the
Law and the Prophets." This truth is echoed throughout
the Scriptures, and through the lens of Jesus, we can spot
it here.

What you spend time thinking about and planning
for will ripple into your life. If you look for ways to bless
others, you will find them. If, instead, you look for ways
to undercut others, you will also find them. We are prone
to confirmation bias. This is why it is so important to
recognize the root of our thoughts, our motivations, and
our intentions. We must let the Spirit of Christ reveal
where we are out of line with his values so that he can set
us straight in his wisdom.

Good Father, I choose to look for ways to share your
love with others today. Help me to choose kindness
when I would rather choose criticism. Thank you.

SPRING UP

Keep trusting in your riches and down you'll go!
But the lovers of God rise up like flowers in the spring.

PROVERBS 11:28

When we put our trust in things that change almost
constantly, how will we stand when those things shift like
a rug being pulled out from beneath us? We cannot take
a thing from this world with us to the next. We cannot
control whether stocks will rise or fall. It is foolish to put
our confidence in our earthly resources, for even the most
valuable will rust and decay.

Jesus instructed instead to "stockpile heavenly
treasures for yourselves that cannot be stolen and will
never rust, decay, or lose their value" (Matthew 6:20). Our
hearts pursue what we value as treasure, so we must be
sure to get our priorities straight. Let's set our intentions
on loving God, on knowing him more, and on reflecting
his love in this world. When we do, we rise up like flowers
in the spring.

**Holy One, I choose to put my trust in you over every
other thing. You never change. You are always loyal in
mercy-kindness, and you will not change your mind
about a single promise you have made. Thank you for
being faithful and steadfast.**

TEACHABLE HEART

To learn the truth you must long to be teachable,
or you can despise correction and remain ignorant.

PROVERBS 12:1

When the wise are corrected, they appreciate the
value that correction brings. If we want to grow in our
understanding, we must remain teachable. We are all still
learning more about God and his kingdom. Each of us
is still learning about the world and its ways. There is so
much more to discover, and this will always be the case.
The universe is still expanding, so why would we be so
foolish as to think that we know all there is to know?

A humble and teachable heart is a wise person's
strength. The proud refuse to hear differing perspectives,
but the wise take the time to listen in order to understand.
We must choose the path we will take. The exceedingly
good news is that no matter how resistant we have been
before, we can choose at any moment to quiet ourselves
and learn from others. Correction is humbling, but it is an
opportunity to expand our own world.

Wise Teacher, I do not presume to have it all figured
out. In fact, I admit how much more I have to learn.
May I remain open to learning from your Spirit and
from others today.

FIRMLY ROOTED

You can't expect success by doing what's wrong. But the lives of his lovers are deeply rooted and firmly planted.

PROVERBS 12:3

We must not neglect the importance of soul care within our lives. We need to nourish our hearts, spend time with those we love, and give ourselves time to refresh in the presence of the Holy Spirit. It is beneficial to us when we read the Word, along with works of writers, speakers, and thinkers who inspire us to love God more.

Where we plant the seeds of our time and attention, life will grow. The living water found in Christ feeds the seeds we plant, and they blossom and thrive under his tender care. As we partner with him in nourishing our souls, he teaches us how to best take care of our inner world. He is the Master Gardener, and we are his apprentices. He is the Vine, and we are the branches. He is the Sun, and we are planets orbiting around him.

Wonderful One, my life is rooted and grounded in your love. Thank you that no one has the power to pluck me from your hand. Hold me close, and may I bloom under your magnificent light.

INFLUENTIAL ALLIANCES

The integrity and strength of a virtuous wife transforms
her husband into an honored king. But the wife who
disgraces her husband weakens the strength of his identity.

PROVERBS 12:4

We are intricately connected by our associations. Our close
friends, family members, and partners, as well as how
we are perceived by others, can influence our well-being.
This is a fact of life. Think of someone whom you highly
respect. Now consider how your esteem for that person
may affect how you view those to whom they are close.

We cannot choose what families we are born into,
and we do not always know how to react when we see
our family members making harmful choices. Even so,
we do not need to reject them because of their mistakes.
Life and relationships are much more nuanced than
that. We can choose our close friends, business partners,
and spouses. Even then, they may make choices we do
not agree with. Let's ask the Lord for wisdom when this
happens. We must choose how we will respond. Will we
make excuses for bad behavior, or will we stand on truth
and seek restoration?

Jesus, I want my relationships to reflect your mercy as
much as any other part of my life. May I be a person of
integrity, standing in that strength even when others
don't. Help me to choose wisely those I align myself with.

BRILLIANT IDEAS

The lovers of God are filled with good ideas that
are noble and pure, but the schemes of the sinner
are crammed with nothing but lies.

PROVERBS 12:5

When you are looking for creative solutions, seek first the
kingdom of God. His presence releases divine revelations
that will guide you in clarity. The inspiration of God's
Spirit will offer you good ideas that are noble and pure.
You are probably familiar with the fruit of the Spirit and
how to test what is good, pure, patient, loving, and true. If
not, take a deeper dive into Galatians 5.

You need not rely on your own understanding,
trying to conjure ideas out of thin air. When you give
yourself space to breathe, quiet your soul and mind, and
make room for rest and inspiration, creativity has a place
to bloom. Brilliant ideas are sourced from the Father of
Creation, but they may come through various sources. A
walk in nature, a conversation with a friend, or an idea
before you fall asleep may spur you to pursue what you
had not previously considered. Wherever you are, the
Spirit is with you. Ask him for his wise insights to help
you today.

Magnificent Father, resonate within my soul and give me
discernment to know your voice when you speak today.

DEFENDERS OF THE VULNERABLE

The wicked use their words to ambush and accuse,
but the lovers of God speak to defend and protect.

PROVERBS 12:6

Our heavenly Father is the Defender of the weak, and
he bids us to represent him in the same way. Psalm 82:3
advises that we "Defend the defenseless, the fatherless and
the forgotten, the disenfranchised and the destitute." We
are "to deliver the poor and the powerless; liberate them
from the grasp of the wicked" (v. 4). When we consider
how we live, do we side with the marginalized, or do
we align ourselves with the wealthy and powerful who
distance themselves from the vulnerable and oppressed?

Proverbs 29:7 states, "God's righteous people will
pour themselves out for the poor, but the ungodly make
no attempt to understand or help the needy." May we
take this opportunity to humbly and openly measure
where our lives align in this regard. We must refuse to
over-spiritualize this matter and look at the practicality
of our lifestyles. As we put into practice the defense and
advocacy of the vulnerable, we can look for ways to make
actionable movements of mercy.

**Merciful One, I know that you are practical in your
mercy. Give me eyes to see where I have made excuses
for my lack of advocacy. Show me where I can move to
meet needs and defend vulnerable people.**

BE TRUE TO YOU

Just be who you are and work hard for a living,
for that's better than pretending to be important
and starving to death.

PROVERBS 12:9

Our importance and influence in the kingdom of heaven
have nothing to do with how much power we have on this
earth. Instead of reaching for the highest accolades, let's
consider what we actually want in life. We are free to just
be who we are. What liberation! We get to show up with
our quirks and humor, our strengths and weaknesses, and
work hard at what we do.

   We don't have to pretend that we have the best
experience, education, or accolades when we don't.
Instead of complicating our lives by wondering what we
aren't doing enough of, we can simplify our expectations
and put our hands to the plow, so to speak. There is
work for us if we will work hard, and hard work pays off.
Joseph was a hard worker and a trustworthy servant. He
rose through the ranks from novice servant to household
manager by being faithful in what he did. Let's do the
same and trust God with the rest.

**Jesus, thank you for the freedom to be me. Just me.
I won't neglect the work that is mine to do, and
I won't pretend to be somebody that I'm not.**

CONSIDERATE ACTS OF KINDNESS

A good man takes care of the needs of his pets,
while even the kindest acts of a wicked man are still cruel.

PROVERBS 12:10

No creature is insignificant to a person of integrity. This proverb states that a good man not only takes care of his household but also cares for the needs of his pets. God does not overlook any living thing, and neither should we. Let's take a cue from this lesson and extend our care beyond the obvious. What needs are we discounting in our homes or even in our communities? Perhaps we are already taking care of all that is ours, but we notice neighbors who are struggling to water their plants because they cannot move as well as they once did.

When we walk in the light of Christ, we become transformed by his miracle of mercy. His kindness moves us in kindness. His tender love pushes us out of our habitual complacency and into creative expressions of care. We have the privilege of looking for ways to expand our reach and to take care of all living things, no matter how small.

Merciful One, your kindness is unmatched. You don't overlook any living thing, and I want to notice what you take note of. Give me eyes to see where I can meet needs that have gone unmet.

BENEFITS OF
HARD WORK

Work hard at your job and you'll have what you need.
Following a get-rich-quick scheme is nothing but a fantasy.

PROVERBS 12:11

When we resist the temptation to compromise in our
work, we can focus on what is ours to do here and now.
We don't need to look for ways to garner wealth quickly
when we can build a foundation of wise choices with
integrity, honesty, and transparency. We cannot control
the outcomes that are unforeseeable, but we can certainly
put our effort into what we can do today to move closer to
our dreams and visions of the future.

Start with where you are. That's all you can do. Ask
the Holy Spirit to give you clarity and soundness of mind,
grounded in his mercy and truth, if you are struggling
to know where to begin. You don't have to know the
end from the beginning, but you do need to start with
what you have. Don't put off for another day what you
can begin today. As you consistently build habits of
productivity, you will reap the benefits that are developed
over time.

**Master Builder, I trust you with my future, and I ask for
your wisdom and endurance in creating habits of hard
work in my present. Thank you.**

UNFETTERED TRUTH

The wicked will get trapped by their words of gossip,
slander, and lies. But for the righteous,
honesty is its own defense.

PROVERBS 12:13

When we practice discernment and self-control in what
we communicate to others, we build a shelter of honesty
around ourselves. This is not to say that we won't ever
cross lines or make mistakes. Even the wisest among us
errs. It is with repentance and honesty that we can repair
relationships and restore reputations.

Think about the fruit of the conversations you have
been engaged in recently. Do the people you spend time
with often slander others or gossip about things that are
none of their business? If this is the case, you may want
to either distance yourself or make it clear that you won't
participate in disparaging others. Let your honesty stand
on its own, even if it rubs others the wrong way. You can
be kind and clear, and others may still balk. Stand in the
strength of integrity and align yourself with others who
do the same.

**Faithful Father, forgive me for the ways that I have
compromised the honor of others' humanity in my
conversations and judgments. I know that you are
the only wise and true judge. I ask for your grace to
empower me to stand in truth even when it costs me.**

SATISFYING FRUIT

There is great satisfaction in speaking the truth,
and hard work brings blessings back to you.

PROVERBS 12:14

As you choose to speak the truth and work hard at your job, simple satisfaction will nourish your soul. The fruit of satisfaction is yours to feast upon today as you do what is within your grasp to accomplish. Life is a partnership with the Lord. You have work to do, just as God gave Adam and Eve dominion over the garden of Eden. He blesses the work of your hands.

Trust the Lord with what you cannot control, and do not get too far ahead of yourself in your mind. That only leads to worry. There is incredible encouragement in the satisfaction that a job well-done brings, and it is amazing what progress can do to bolster our hearts in hope. There is tremendous strength and help in the presence of God to give us clarity and perseverance. May we look to him often throughout the day, leaning on his wisdom and asking for his perspective.

Faithful One, you are the gardener of my soul, and I pick up the tools you have given me to do my part in tilling, sowing, and reaping. I trust you to do what I cannot, and I am privileged to partner with your purposes in doing what I can.

RESIST OFFENSE

If you shrug off an insult and refuse to take offense, you demonstrate discretion indeed. But the fool has a short fuse and will immediately let you know when he's offended.

PROVERBS 12:16

We cannot control how others speak to or about us, but we can certainly regulate our own responses. There will be times when loved ones hurt us—either intentionally or because of carelessness. In relationships that matter to us, we should take the time to honestly share hurts that we cannot simply shrug off. But when it comes to little offenses or even insults those who do not know us may throw at us, we should learn to let go and move on.

We are wise when we resist allowing offense to construct walls around our hearts that will close off our ability to see from different perspectives. We learn to resist offense best when we are able to give others the benefit of the doubt. Most people are doing their best with the tools that they have been given in life. Instead of seeking revenge or a quick comeback, we should remain soft and secure in the loving identity we have in Christ.

Gracious God, I don't want to let someone else's ideas of me ruin my confidence in you. Love me to life in your kindness, and I will have more compassion to offer others.

WORDS OF HEALING

Reckless words are like the thrusts of a sword,
cutting remarks meant to stab and to hurt.
But the words of the wise soothe and heal.

PROVERBS 12:18

We can be sure that reckless and harmful jabs against others are not rooted in the loving wisdom of Christ. Psalm 119:103 says, "How sweet are your living promises to me; sweeter than honey is your revelation-light." God's words are full of life-giving light, bringing refreshing hope and encouragement to the hungry soul.

The words of the wise soothe and heal, but this does not mean that they soften the hard realities that we face. We don't have to shrink away from the truth of pain, suffering, or heartbreak in our lives in order to speak words of life that bring comfort and healing. In fact, the Holy Spirit is known as the Comforter because he meets us in the midst of our mess and pain. He is our Advocate and our help. As he speaks his healing words over us, we learn to do the same for others.

Healer, thank you for being with me in my great confusion, suffering, and grief. As you soothe and heal my soul, may I find grace to offer your words of healing to others.

PLANS OF PEACE

Deception fills the hearts of those who plot harm,
but those who plan for peace are filled with joy.

PROVERBS 12:20

When we find ourselves wishing for another's defeat
or demise, we should humble our hearts in God's
presence. We already know that God looks at our hearts,
and he sees our intentions. When we make plans to
harm another, even if we never follow through, God
understands the state of our hearts. Instead of letting the
hostile root of bitterness grow, we have the opportunity to
invite the love and peace of God to uproot and cleanse the
soil of our hearts.

As lovers of God, may we be known by our pursuit
of peace in relationships and in our communities. As we
reflect God's nature, we become counselors of peace to
those in trouble and safe places of refuge for those who
are struggling in life and in their faith. Jesus is described
as the Prince of Peace. There is no lack of mercy-kindness
in his kingdom.

**Prince of Peace, I humble myself before you and ask for
your revelation-light to shine on the deepest spaces of my
heart. Drench me in your mercy and clothe me in your
compassion, and I will dwell in the light of your peace.**

No Need to Impress

Those who possess wisdom don't feel the need to impress others with what they know, but foolish ones make sure their ignorance is on display.

PROVERBS 12:23

Jesus, the Son of God, did not live to impress the religious elite or try to win their favor. He had nothing to prove to them. His ministry was a reflection of the Father's love. He did not shy away from displaying God's power through miraculous signs and wonders. Even so, he never acted from a place of pride or insecurity.

As sons and daughters of the living God, we also have no one to impress. Though it is extremely normal to want to gain favor from those we love, the truth is that we are set free in the liberty of the Father's love. We don't ever have to prove ourselves to God. In light of this truth, why would we try to impress others from a sense of striving? Let's live in the freedom that is ours and be wonderfully ourselves. That is what Christ did, and it is what he desires for us.

Liberator, I lay aside the need to impress others and instead focus on who you say that I already am. I shift my focus to what I can do today to grow even more securely rooted in your kingdom.

LIFE-GIVING ENCOURAGEMENT

Anxious fear brings depression, but a life-giving word
of encouragement can do wonders to restore joy
to the heart.

PROVERBS 12:25

When you belong to the Lord, the Word of God lives in
you. There is perpetual encouragement dwelling within
you by the presence of the Holy Spirit. It is the Spirit who
brings the Word of Christ alive within you. Sometimes,
instead of finding encouragement through a friend, you
will find it within your own heart. It will rise up and fill
your heart with hope. This is overwhelmingly good news
for each one of us.

When we shift our focus from that which causes
anxiety and worry to rise within us (mostly the things
in life we have absolutely no control over), we are able
to hone in on the everlasting joy we have in Jesus Christ.
He is our portion every moment of every day. He is near,
ready to speak whenever you tune in to him, and he is
working things together for your good. Trust him and
listen to his voice today.

**Hope of my heart, speak your words of wisdom within
my being today. Bring hope and let it rise within my
heart until it expands in your encouraging kindness.
I love you so.**

WISE STEWARDS

A passive person won't even complete a project,
but a passionate person makes good use of his time,
wealth, and energy.

PROVERBS 12:27

How can we put our passion into more efficiently pursuing growth in our lives? We must first have an idea of what our guiding values are. We discover these values as we consider what we want to be known for in our relationships and how we want people to feel around us. Other considerations include what we want to achieve in our work and what values we are unwilling to compromise. We are wise stewards of our time, resources, and energy when we pair intention with consistent practice.

Passivity is a quality that does not lead to success. When we are apathetic about an endeavor or relationship, we lose interest quite quickly. However, we can align our passion with our purpose when we get clear on what is most important to us. We leave the status quo behind when we pursue what matters with diligence and reliability. As we do, we can be sure that we are being wise stewards of what we have while pursuing growth at the same time.

Generous Lord, thank you for your Spirit that gives me strength in my weakness. Help me to take responsibility for what is mine to do and to move into what you are calling me toward.

LOVING TRUST

A wise son or daughter desires a father's discipline,
but the know-it-all never listens to correction.

PROVERBS 13:1

No matter the strength of the relationships we have with our caregivers, we can experience the overwhelming kindness of our heavenly Father's correction. Perhaps we had heavy-handed parents who did not leave space for our emotions. Maybe we had caregivers who were uninvolved with our decisions, leaving us to figure it out on our own. Whatever the case may be, our Father disciplines us perfectly and with kindness. He is not abusive, nor is he controlling. He is not passive, and he does not withhold guidance when we ask for it.

The more we know the love of our Father, the deeper trust is embedded within our hearts. He proves his goodness to us time and again through his faithful love. Even when he is brutally honest, our hearts know his good intentions and feel the kindness of his affection. He will never use our past against us or shame us into change. He picks us up in love and calls us forth in generosity. May we press into the presence of his goodness and find our hearts coming to life in his discipline.

Loving Father, I have experienced your delight, and I want to know the kindness of your purehearted correction. I am yours. I trust you.

DRENCHED IN KINDNESS

The words of the wise are kind and easy to swallow,
but the unbeliever just wants to pick a fight and argue.

PROVERBS 13:2

If we spend our time looking for ways to dissect others'
beliefs and experiences while promoting our own, we
should not be surprised when people don't want to talk
to us. If, instead, we can talk about hard things with grace
and kindness, there is nothing off-limits in conversation.
We should never allow our eagerness to be right overrule
our willingness to be open and listen to others.

We cannot go wrong when we approach
conversations with compassion and kindness. No one
wants to be dishonored or dismissed. When we feel heard,
our hearts open to build bridges of trust. Vulnerability
is a gift that the kindhearted and compassionate will be
given time and again, for others see them as someone
they can trust. It is important that we be intentional with
our conversations and choose to speak the truth with
tenderness, allowing others to share their views with grace.

Jesus, the kindness you showed in your life and
ministry is something I aspire to. May I be a safe
harbor for the vulnerable, and may my words drip with
your compassionate kindness to everyone I speak with.

PASSIONATE PERSEVERANCE

The slacker wants it all and ends up with nothing,
but the hard worker ends up with all that he longed for.

PROVERBS 13:4

Even the harshest nuggets of wisdom exist to instruct us
for our good. Though we may long for breakthrough in
our lives, if we do nothing about it but dream, we will not
taste the fruit that we so desire. Consistency builds paths
of success, but simply wishing for change will do nothing
but disappoint. We should never forget the power of
persistence or the benefit of passionate perseverance.

When there is nothing we can do to move ahead
practically, an invitation is still available for us. We can
follow the example of Hannah, who prayed relentlessly
for her longings to be born. She wanted a child, and
she prayed fervently for one. When God heard her and
answered her prayer, she dedicated her son to serving the
Lord and his temple (see 1 Samuel 1). She passionately
persevered in prayer for something that she could not
make happen on her own. Pair your passion with prayer
and action and watch God come through for you.

Faithful One, you hear the cries of your beloved ones,
and you answer them. You give me strength to persevere
in practical ways and to trust you with the things I
cannot achieve on my own. Be glorified in my pursuit.

NOTHING TO BE ASHAMED OF

Lovers of God hate what is phony and false, but the wicked are full of shame and behave shamefully.

PROVERBS 13:5

If there are any areas of your life cloaked with shame, take a breath and focus on the truth of God. If you feel the sting of regret that goes beyond your actions into the depths of who you are, it is likely affecting your identity. Romans 8:1 states, "There remains no accusing voice of condemnation against those who are joined in life-union with Jesus." Case closed; no further evidence necessary. If Christ will not condemn us of the very things he has forgiven, why would we hold them against ourselves?

In Christ's compassion, he has trampled our sins under his feet and thrown them into the depths, never to retrieve them. Psalm 103:12 says, "Farther than from a sunrise to a sunset—that's how far you've removed our guilt from us." If you have yielded your heart to Christ, there is no guilt or shame that he will ever hold against you. He has removed every bit of it, even the things that others still remember. In light of this truth, we can walk in the glorious goodness of his liberating love over us.

Redeemer, thank you for removing the guilt of my sins. I want to walk in the freedom of your affection with joy and delight.

OPEN FOR MORE

Wisdom opens your heart to receive wise counsel,
but pride closes your ears to advice and gives birth
only to quarrels and strife.

PROVERBS 13:10

Wisdom instructs you to receive counsel from those
around you. Utilize the people you trust to help guide you
in decision-making. Spend time with wise friends whose
advice you can take into consideration before moving
ahead in new ventures. Lead with openness and look for
trusted input. Your choices are your own, but wisdom keeps
your heart open while pride closes the door to counsel.

We are not meant to go it alone in life. God created
us for family and community. We need relationships
not only to thrive but to survive. The wisdom of trusted
friends cannot be overstated, and the loving support of
those who know us well is a gift and a foundation from
which to grow. First, let's open our hearts to the Lord, and
then let's keep our hearts open to receive the wise counsel
of others.

**Spirit, thank you that I do not have to search high and
low for wise counsel and that I don't have to follow the
advice of everyone willing to give it. Speak to me, lead
me, and fill me with your discernment.**

SLOW AND STEADY

Wealth quickly gained is quickly wasted—easy come, easy go! But if you gradually gain wealth, you will watch it grow.

PROVERBS 13:11

There are many stories out there of people winning a big sum of money only to have none of it left a few years later. It is said that up to 70 percent of lottery winners end up broke within seven years. This illustrates today's proverb particularly well. We can apply the wisdom of the Lord at any point and change our trajectory, but wealth quickly gained is often quickly wasted.

Consider the things in your life that you have had to work for. How have they grown and expanded with your effort? Think about the personal value of that growth. Perhaps you have learned lessons through the years to help you treasure what is most important and to refine your goals in accordance with what works and what is wasteful. Don't despise the time it takes to build a legacy that is worth leaving to future generations. Slow and steady will bring a bounty when you sow with wisdom and refine your process as you learn lessons along the way.

Wise God, thank you for the gifts of time and of perspective. Help me to refine my vision and to put your wisdom and values into practice as I slowly build toward the future.

SATISFYING SWEETNESS

When hope's dream seems to drag on and on, the delay
can be depressing. But when at last your dream comes
true, life's sweetness will satisfy your soul.

PROVERBS 13:12

When we find ourselves in seasons of waiting and
deferred hopes, it can be difficult to not give in to despair.
Though it would be wonderful if we could manifest our
dreams simply by wishing them into existence, none of
us can speed up the timing of the Lord. His heart for us
is good and undeterred, so let's embrace trust as we wait.
The satisfying sweetness of a dream come true is like a
wellspring of life. Our souls will be filled.

We can trust the loyal love of our God and believe
him for the promises that he has given. He is faithful
and true, and he will not fail. Even when our dreams are
laboring long, when our hope is anchored to the mercy
of God, we will experience the breakthrough of newness.
Let's rejoice in hope, even as we welcome the Spirit of
comfort into the ache of our longing.

**Promise Keeper, I trust you to do what only you can
do. Revive my heart in hope and fill me with the
inexplicable goodness of your affection. I look to you.
Hold on to me as I put all my trust in you.**

TRUSTWORTHY MESSENGERS

An undependable messenger causes a lot of trouble,
but the trustworthy and wise messengers release healing
wherever they go.

PROVERBS 13:17

As God's sons and daughters, we are peacemakers,
healers, and faithful deliverers for others. We are
messengers of the good news of the kingdom of Christ.
When we serve others in laid-down love, we have no
trouble to stir up. Though many will dismiss our attempts
at peace, we must never give up the good fight of faith.
It is our calling to be peacemakers and liberators where
others seek to stir up trouble and create division.

As trustworthy messengers of the gospel, we
release the healing life of Christ in our relationships, our
workplaces, and our communities. When we live with
mercy-kindness overflowing our hearts and moving us
into action, we spread the compassion of Christ. The love
of God is powerful enough to propel us to help those in
need, uplift those who are beaten down, and elevate the
voices that have been overpowered. There is healing and
wholeness in the overwhelmingly sufficient love of Christ.

**Christ Jesus, I want to be known as a trustworthy and
wise messenger of your kingdom, bringing peace,
healing, and deliverance wherever I go. You are better
than anyone could dream.**

JUNE

EASILY CORRECTED

Poverty and disgrace come to the one who refuses
to hear criticism. But the one who is easy to correct
is on the path of honor.

PROVERBS 13:18

When the Pharisees pressed Jesus on the law of keeping
the Sabbath, Jesus offered a different way of looking at
it. The letter of the law is not greater than the Creator.
In Matthew 12, when Jesus' disciples were hungry on
the Sabbath, Jesus did not require that they refrain from
picking and eating grain from the field they were walking
through, even though the Torah forbade harvesting on
the Sabbath.

Instead of listening to Jesus and considering the
truth of what he spoke, the Pharisees went away with
offense in their hearts and a resolve to get rid of him.
True poverty and disgrace come to those who refuse to
hear criticism because they look for ways to silence those
who disagree with them. When their power is being
challenged, they fight back instead of humbly considering
if there is truth in what is being offered. May we follow
Christ on the path of honor—the way of his righteousness.

**Righteous Jesus, may I not be so full of pride that I am
unwilling to consider a perspective different from my
own. May I remain humble and open in your love not
only for you but also for others.**

TURN TO HIM

When God fulfills your longings, sweetness fills your soul.
But the wicked refuse to turn from darkness to see their
desires come to pass.

PROVERBS 13:19

Can you remember a time when you experienced the
fulfillment of a deep longing? Take some time with the
Lord, prayerfully asking for his Spirit to bring to mind the
sweetness and satisfaction you felt. Remember the feeling
of hope in your heart, the gratitude that overflowed from
the depths of your soul in response. Connect once again
to the experience of your desire being fulfilled and the
growth that happened in your heart as a result.

Turn to the Lord today, looking to his glorious
light of truth to expand your awareness of his goodness.
There is more to hope for than you could imagine. More
goodness awaits you in his presence. More satisfaction
is coming. Turn your attention to where his Spirit meets
you today, no matter how ill-equipped you feel to stand in
hope. Let his love lead you as it will. You do not need to
make anything happen. Just turn to him and let his light
shine on you.

**Jesus, let the rays of your loving light revive my heart
in hope today. I cannot force your hand, and I cannot
control your timing. But I trust your loving-kindness.**

CHOOSE WELL

If you want to grow in wisdom, spend time with the wise. Walk with the wicked and you'll eventually become just like them.

PROVERBS 13:20

The wisdom of the Lord is incredibly practical and simple, though it is not always easy to choose. If we want to grow in wisdom, we should spend time with those who are wise. The same principle applies to any area where we want to experience growth. If we want to learn how to build houses, then we need to spend time with architects and contractors. If we want to play an instrument, then we need to listen, observe, and learn from those who are proficient.

If we choose to spend the majority of our time with friends who do not live how we aspire to, then we will end up being influenced to settle into ways that we never intended. What we give our time and attention to, we will learn to emulate. We must be wise about how and with whom we invest our time if we truly want to grow in wisdom.

Wise Father, thank you for your practical lessons of wisdom that I cannot complicate with my own ideas. You are worth following, and your wisdom is worth putting into practice. I choose the ways of your kingdom.

LEAVING A LEGACY

The benevolent man leaves an inheritance that endures to
his children's children, but the wealth of the wicked
is treasured up for the righteous.

PROVERBS 13:22

Even though we cannot control the tide of events that
will happen in life, wise parents work to build a life that
will bless their children. Foresight is required to leave
a legacy. It takes planning to live with the intention
of passing on the blessings that we incur in life as an
inheritance to those who come after us. May we not lose
sight of the importance of the treasures we have to pass
on. Our successes become the building blocks for future
generations to go further than we could.

There is tremendous value in being intentionally
generous with our resources, and it is a wise person who
does not neglect the spiritual heritage that he or she
can pass on. When we talk openly about the benefits of
loving the Lord and how we can apply those values to our
practical lives, we offer insight into intentional integrity.
As we have unguarded, deep conversations about the
Lord, we can invite our children into them. They learn
from what we model, and they will carry that example
with them.

**Faithful Father, give me the keys to building a legacy
for my family and for the future as I partner with you.**

BRICKS OF ENCOURAGEMENT

Every wise woman encourages and builds up her family, but a foolish woman over time will tear it down by her own actions.

PROVERBS 14:1

No family is without its troubles. A wise person does not dismiss the challenges that arise, but they offer encouragement to others. They are able to find ways to build hope, secure trust, and offer loving support within their relationships. Is there a person who comes to mind when you read this verse? Perhaps there is a nurturer in your life who has become a safe landing place for you. Even if she is not bound by blood relation, she can serve as a mother figure in your life.

When we open our hearts to encourage others in love, calling them up to their potential rather than diminishing their worth according to their mistakes, we take on the role of nurturers. God is the greatest of them all. He is a loving Father who welcomes his children home when they are still far off but turned toward him. He wraps us up in the royal robes of his mercy. As we turn to him, he becomes our example of how to rise up in loyal love.

Good Father, thank you for your kindness and attention. You encourage my heart in hope, even in correction. You are my Rock of refuge; may I be a shelter for others as well.

DON'T BE AFRAID
OF THE MESS

The only clean stable is an empty stable. So if you want
the work of an ox and to enjoy an abundant harvest,
you'll have a mess or two to clean up!

PROVERBS 14:4

We cannot avoid the unpleasant aspects of work, life,
or relationships. As long as we live in this world, we
will have messes to clean up. Instead of being taken by
surprise at the challenges that come our way, we can meet
them head-on with the tools already at our disposal.
There is more than enough wisdom to guide us through
every trial.

Instead of avoiding the messes in our lives, we can
benefit from them if we only accept them. We cannot
avoid conflict or fatigue after a hard day's work, but we
can navigate through trying circumstances with kindness
and humility. Whatever it is that we feel we shouldn't be
experiencing, we have the choice to see it through the
light of Christ. If we want to enjoy an abundant harvest,
we will have to embrace the need to clean up messes
along the way.

Advocate, thank you for not hesitating to get into the
messiness of life with me. Help me to see my trials
through the lens of wisdom rather than through the
lens of inconvenience. Thank you.

More than Information

The intellectually arrogant seek for wisdom, but they never seem to discover what they claim they're looking for. For revelation-knowledge flows to the one who hungers for understanding.

PROVERBS 14:6

When we hunger and thirst for righteousness, we will be filled. When we search for understanding the way one searches out treasure, we will find what we are looking for. God reveals himself to those who sincerely seek him. Let's take God at his word when he says that he answers those who call on him. There is no need to hold back, for God has limitless resources of wisdom, grace, and mercy.

Wisdom is not simply ingesting information. It does not seek to know everything but to understand what can be known. It goes beneath the surface knowledge that we find at our fingertips to the heart of a matter. There is no need to remain satisfied with pat answers when we can dig into the depths of understanding more of God's heart and his kingdom.

Wise One, I don't want to be satisfied with superficial information or knowledge. Reveal the insights of your kingdom truth as I search for wisdom and broaden my understanding of your limitless love.

ON THE RIGHT TRACK

The wisdom of the wise will keep life on the right track,
while the fool only deceives himself and refuses
to face reality.

PROVERBS 14:8

When we refuse to face reality, we only deceive ourselves.
Others have an easier time seeing through our resistance.
We need not stay stuck in glass castles of our own
building because God offers us the liberating love of his
wisdom to keep us on the right track.

When our loved ones try to bring to our attention
ways in which we may be avoiding reality, we should stay
openhearted and soft to their suggestions. Let's not dig in
our heels out of stubbornness but willingly look at their
critiques with openness. We certainly don't need to take at
face value everyone's ideas of who we are, but we must be
willing to humbly listen to the wise voices in our lives. It
will be to our benefit if we do.

Jesus, I don't want to stay stuck in false narratives
or cycles of destruction when you offer a better way.
May my heart remain humble when others offer their
differing perspectives. Give me discernment to know
what I should heed and what I should shrug off.

MANAGE EXPECTATIONS

Don't expect anyone else to fully understand both the
bitterness and the joys of all you experience in your life.

PROVERBS 14:10

There is rich beauty in shared experiences with those
we love. We must recognize, however, that no one, apart
from the Lord, who sees and knows everything, can
know the depths of our souls. We all long to be seen
and known, and there is a deep sense of satisfaction in
belonging. Just as no other person can read our thoughts
or hearts, no one else can know the breadth and nuances
of our experience of life—not even those who live with us
through it all.

As we grow in our understanding, we can have
greater grace for others as we recognize that we each react
uniquely to the same stimuli. We may experience the
same event and come away feeling completely differently
about it than others. It is a practice of fellowship to listen
to others, to ask questions that dig below the surface, and
to give space for each of our individual experiences. As
we let love cover our hearts, as well as our expectations, it
will generate greater grace, mercy, and kindness.

**Spirit, only you know the nuances of my unique soul.
Thank you for loving me so well. May I love others well
by leaving room for them to experience and express
themselves in unique ways.**

CONFIRMATION IS CRITICAL

A gullible person will believe anything,
but a sensible person will confirm the facts.

PROVERBS 14:15

Faith is not synonymous with gullibility. Faith requires a loving trust in God, whose nature never wavers. He is loyal to his Word, and he will never change. What God says, he will do. We take him at his word. This is not the same thing as believing anything we hear. There are many opinions out there about every subject under the sun. The wisdom of God does not call us to abandon reality. We should not simply take all that religious leaders say as our own opinion but fact-check what we hear.

We do not have to abandon logic in order to follow God, though we do need to leave room for mystery. The Lord confirms his Word, and he does not speak only through special messengers. "Remember, it is the same Holy Spirit who distributes, activates, and operates these different gifts as he chooses for each believer" (1 Corinthians 12:11). We have the same Holy Spirit, and he breeds the same fruit in the lives of all his loyal lovers.

Holy Spirit, even as I lovingly trust you, may I not be ignorant to the realities we face in this world. Help me to seek confirmation while looking for the bridges you build instead of the walls that people put up.

EMBRACE THE TIME IT TAKES

An impulsive person has a short fuse and can ruin everything, but the wise show self-control.

PROVERBS 14:17

We apply the power of self-control not only to the things we say yes or no to but also to the things we are willing to endure. When we refuse to be set off by the emotions that others trigger in us, we practice wise and patient endurance. Wisdom has no need to rush in to things. It can allow space for things to unfold in whatever time they take. Habitual impulsiveness is not a sign of maturity but of shortsightedness.

When we learn to embrace the process that it takes for seeds to grow into fruit-bearing plants, we can appreciate the importance of progression. We need to be aware of when we hurry headlong into situations that would benefit from a more measured and prolonged approach. When we recklessly rush in with anxiety that can so easily accompany anticipation of the future, we may ruin something that needed time to bloom organically. There is so much wisdom in a patient approach coupled with self-control.

Father, give me grace to be patient when my problems take longer to resolve than I would prefer. I trust your ways more than my own.

SECURE PLACES OF REST

Confidence and strength flood the hearts of the lovers of God who live in awe of him, and their devotion provides their children with a place of shelter and security.

PROVERBS 14:26

When we live as passionate lovers of God, the benefits do not end with us. They also pass to future generations. Our children inherit the shelter of homes built upon the foundation of Christ's peace. They experience the security of his mercy. We must look beyond the scope of our own comfort to the possible goodness that awaits our households as we commit to loving God with all our hearts, souls, and strength.

In the day of our trouble, God hides us in the secret place of his presence (see Psalm 27:5). The testimony of God's faithfulness is not ours alone, but it is power to all who hear it. When we share with the younger generations the miracles of God's mercy revealed within our lives, we give them a framework of expectation that they, themselves, can build upon. May we embrace the beauty of generational blessing that is shown through God's Word. As we do, we can expand our vision to see the impact we can have not just in our own lives but on future generations.

Lord, thank you for your power and rest. May I honor you as I interact with different generations.

SLOW TO ANGER

When your heart overflows with understanding you'll be
very slow to get angry. But if you have a quick temper,
your impatience will be quickly seen by all.

PROVERBS 14:29

The heart of an understanding person is slow to anger
not because they are perfect but because they are able to
see what is behind a person's actions. When we take time
to graciously consider why others act the way that they
do, we are more able to extend compassion to them. This
does not mean that the most gracious of us will never get
angry—for even the anger of Jesus was tested.

As we broaden our perspective of the world
through fellowship with God's Spirit, we grow in our
capacity for endurance. Patient endurance is bred through
walking with the Lord in the light of his righteous truth.
As we yield our lives to his leadership, he does not
remove our trials or pain, but he meets us in the midst
of them, offering us grace to empower us in each and
every trouble. He is with us, and his love rejuvenates and
strengthens our resolve.

**Lord, I know that you are tenderhearted and kind and
so very patient with me even when I fail you. May my
own capacity for endurance grow as I remain rooted in
the rich soil of your love.**

HEALING PEACE

A tender, tranquil heart will make you healthy,
but jealousy can make you sick.

PROVERBS 14:30

Jealousy is not simply the act of wanting what others have.
The Greek word implies an obsession to promote oneself
at the expense of others. When we become preoccupied
with how we can be better than others, it affects our
behavior, which then affects those around us. James 3:16
says, "Wherever jealousy and selfishness are uncovered,
you will also find many troubles and every kind of
meanness."

Envy breeds chaos, whereas tenderness and
compassion produce peace. Consider if you are reaching
to prove yourself at the expense of others even if only in
your own heart and mind. Life is not a competition, and
you don't need to put others down to get ahead. There
is room for all of us to help each other reach our best
potential without sacrificing our integrity to do so. Let
the tenderness of Christ propel your own heart in loving
acceptance as well as ambition.

**Loving Jesus, thank you that I don't have to compete
for my place in your family or kingdom. May I rest in
confident trust of your affection and champion the
success of others instead of letting their success drive
dissatisfaction with my own life.**

HONORING ACTS

Insult your Creator, will you? That's exactly what you do
every time you oppress the powerless! Showing kindness
to the poor is equal to honoring your maker.

PROVERBS 14:31

Every person on this planet is made in God's image. There
are no exceptions. The poor and powerless, the privileged
and wealthy, the forsaken and forgotten, the embraced
and beloved all find their beginning in the Creator's hand.
There is no excuse for us to overlook or use others. We
cannot oppress others—nor can we support systems or
people that do—and still claim to honor the Lord with
every part of our lives. We honor God when we honor
others, no matter their station or situation.

Jesus said, "When you cared for one of the least of
these, my little ones,…" (the sick, imprisoned, hungry,
naked, and homeless) "you demonstrated love for me"
(Matthew 25:40). We show our love and care for the Lord
by loving and caring for the most vulnerable around us.
When we turn to help the poor and needy, when we offer
true compassion and mercy, we honor the Lord well.

**Worthy One, people need and deserve kindness simply
because they are made in your image. Open my eyes to see
where I have been avoiding showing kindness to others.**

GENTLE RESPONSES

Respond gently when you are confronted and you'll defuse
the rage of another. Responding with sharp, cutting words
will only make it worse. Don't you know that being angry
can ruin the testimony of even the wisest of men?

PROVERBS 15:1

Gentleness can soften the anger of another. Perhaps you
have already experienced this. When we are in the throes
of frustration, it can be difficult to see beyond our own
defenses. But when someone else responds with humility
and gentleness, it can totally disarm our anger and help us
regulate our inflammatory responses.

Instead of fighting fire with fire, let's allow the
living water of Christ to be the tool we reach for over
and over again. Paul instructed Timothy this way when
he advised, "A true servant of our Lord Jesus will not be
argumentative but gentle toward all and skilled in helping
others see the truth, having great patience toward the
immature" (2 Timothy 2:24). This advice remains for
us today. As servants of Christ and representatives of
his kingdom, it is love that propels us in kindness and
humility.

**Jesus, help me to respond with the gentleness of your
Spirit as I encounter difficult people today. May the
peace of your living water quell the flames of anger in
others as I submit to your humble love. Thank you.**

ENCOURAGERS OF HOPE

When you speak healing words, you offer others fruit
from the tree of life. But unhealthy, negative words do
nothing but crush their hopes.

PROVERBS 15:4

Healing words can be a balm of refreshment to the heart,
offering perspectives that can shift hearts in hope. Gentle
truth spoken through someone else can even change the
way we approach certain aspects of our lives. Revelation-
knowledge comes through the Spirit of the Lord, and it
can come through any vessel imaginable. If God could
speak through a donkey, he can certainly use us.

We can be builders of faith and encouragers of
hope to the people in our lives by speaking words that
heal. Let's do our best to resist sweeping platitudes and
positive-thinking clichés. As we allow the Spirit of truth
to pierce our hearts with his incredibly liberating wisdom,
we can offer what is true, what is admirable, and what
is life-giving. From this place, we are able to offer the
healing power of words drenched in the love of Christ.

**Spirit of God, reveal your heart to me through the
revelations of the incomparable goodness of God. I
want to be a builder of your kingdom, encouraging
others in hope that is rooted in your mercy. Be glorified
in what I say and how I speak to others.**

YIELDED AND PLEASING

It is despicable to the Lord when people use the worship
of the Almighty as a cloak for their sin, but every prayer
of the righteous is pleasing to his heart.

PROVERBS 15:8

Our yielded hearts are the most pleasing sacrifice we can
offer God. When we submit our lives to his leadership,
following his wise guidance, our whole lives become an
expression of true worship. Those who claim to know
God and yet do not allow his truth to penetrate their
hearts or change their habits are only cloaking their
lifestyles in a superficial identity.

Romans 12:1–2 says, "Surrender yourselves
to God to be his sacred, living sacrifices. And live in
holiness, experiencing all that delights his heart. For
this becomes your genuine expression of worship…Be
inwardly transformed by the Holy Spirit through a total
reformation of how you think." We are transformed by the
mind of Christ when we offer our whole beings as living
sacrifices to the Lord.

**Righteous One, I offer you leadership over my whole
being. Cover me in the complete mercy-kindness of
your love and set me free to walk in the light of your
truth. I yield my heart and my life to you, for I know
you are wise and kind and that you have my best at
heart. I love you.**

PURSUE PURITY

The Lord detests the lifestyle of the wicked,
but he loves those who pursue purity.

PROVERBS 15:9

Pursuing purity is much more than appearing
uncorrupted. Purity is a heart issue, and it is
deeply rooted in righteousness. Thankfully, Christ's
righteousness becomes our own when we yield our lives
to him. As Romans 3:22 says, "We are made right with
God by placing our faith in Jesus Christ. And this is true
for everyone who believes, no matter who we are" (NLT).

When we put our confident trust in Christ, his
righteousness covers us. First John 3:3 says that "all who
focus their hope" on Christ appearing and returning "will
always be purifying themselves, just as Jesus is pure."
We don't depend on our own strength, and yet we have
the opportunity to partner with Christ's purposes and
receive his empowering grace to endure in love, to remain
steadfast in mercy, and to choose to stand for justice. This
kind of lifestyle reflects the kingdom of our great God.

**Gracious Father, thank you for your wonderful love
that liberates me to walk in your ways. I choose
to follow in the path of your loyal love, offering
compassion and kindness and standing on the truth
of who you are. This is how I will remain pure—by
pursuing you.**

EVERYTHING EXPOSED

Even hell itself holds no secrets from the Lord God,
for before his eyes, all is exposed—
and so much more the heart of every human being.

PROVERBS 15:11

There is nothing hidden from the gaze of God—not on
the earth, in the heavens, or in the far reaches of the
universe. He sees everything clearly. This knowledge can
either bring relief or anxiety, depending on how we view
God. Whatever this evokes in us today, may we turn to
the loving light of Christ, which already shines as bright
as day. He accepts us in love, and he offers us grace upon
grace to turn from the things that hinder our freedom.

As you turn to Christ, the glory-light of his
presence will shine upon your heart. He will not shame
you, nor will he hold your past against you. Even in
correction, he is incredibly kind. He will not pacify you
in deception but will call you into his liberated love with
the truth of his mercy. Allow his kindness to lead you to
repentance as you accept his perspective, letting it shift
your own. He is a tender Father, ready to restore you.

**Lord God, thank you for your love that covers every
one of my mistakes and failures. I won't hide from your
voice or your truth today. Shine on me and set me free.**

Choosing Cheerfulness

Everything seems to go wrong when you feel weak and depressed. But when you choose to be cheerful, every day will bring you more and more joy and fullness.

PROVERBS 15:15

We cannot avoid stressors in life, and we certainly cannot sidestep grief. There will be seasons of great loss and others when we are overworked and grasping for extra time. How can we choose cheerfulness when we are overtired and the demands of life do not give up? We must remember the importance of rhythms of rest in our lives. We need to build boundaries of Sabbath, trusting that the Lord knew what he was doing when he established a day of rest in the beginning. He still knows that we need dedicated time to be restored and to delight in lightened loads.

Choosing to be cheerful has less to do with rejecting reality and more to do with being open to hope and joy in their simplest forms. Consider what brings delight to your heart. What are the simple joys that refresh your soul? Make it a priority to incorporate and mindfully engage those things. As you do, you will experience reprieve in a hard world.

Joyful Jesus, I am overwhelmed with the thought that you delight in me. May I embrace joy when it comes, and may I remain open to hope as it springs up.

GOOD ADVICE

Your plans will fall apart right in front of you if you fail
to get good advice. But if you first seek out multiple
counselors, you'll watch your plans succeed.

PROVERBS 15:22

Anyone can make a plan and then follow through on it,
but not every plan will succeed. It is to our benefit to seek
out the wisdom of trusted counselors, especially those
within the field that our plans pertain to. The wisdom of
multiple counselors can balance our approach, and it can
help us to refine our vision and make our plans succeed.

We live in a very individualistic society that
perpetuates the notion that we should be able to succeed
on our own. But this is utter and complete foolishness.
We thrive in community, and we grow strongest in the
company of others. So much good advice exists out there,
so let's not neglect the supports already in place to help
us succeed. We must reject the idea that we need to figure
things out on our own. Find strength in the company of
wise people and wisdom in their counsel.

Wise God, open my heart to receive the advice that
others offer as well as the discernment to know whose
counsel to trust. I remain open to the wisdom that
comes with time, perspective, and experience.

PERFECT TIMING

Everyone enjoys giving great advice. But how delightful
it is to say the right thing at the right time!

The right word at the right time can turn the tide of our
hopelessness into a field of opportunity. May we be so
yielded to the leadership of the Lord that we hear his
goodness in even the most unlikely of spaces. As we
surrender to the wisdom of Christ, we become able to
recognize the imprints of his mercy in the dust of the
world as readily as we do in the halls of sacred places.

The timing of the Lord is perfect, and we can trust
his heart as well as his hand. He is loyal to his Word.
Every promise spoken is a vow that he has made. He
cannot break it because it would go against his very
nature. We can accept the wonders of God's loyal love,
even as we wait on him. As we look for where he is
already at work, we will see how he is weaving together
the strands of our lives into the wonderful tapestry of his
great grace.

**Faithful Father, I trust you with the timing in my life,
and I invite you to use me to bring delight to others as
I yield my heart, speech, and life to you.**

POWERFUL PRIORITIES

The one who puts earning money above his family will
have trouble at home, but those who refuse to exploit
others will live in peace.

PROVERBS 15:27

When our priorities are straight, we can live without the
pull of guilt playing on our anxieties. The peace of God
belongs to those who rest in his presence. Those who rest
in his presence practice the compelling compassion of
his heart as they go about their days. There will always
be pressure from the outside world to do more than we
could possibly offer, but when we have a grounded sense
of what our priorities are, we can put healthy boundaries
into place.

What are the priorities that drive your choices?
Be brutally honest. First, look at what you want your
priorities to be, and then look at what your actions reflect
about which priorities you are actually living out. With
this information, do not let shame keep you from moving
forward. Ask the Lord for loving wisdom on how to align
your values with your lifestyle. There is power in our
priorities.

**Powerful One, I won't wallow in guilt or failure. I ask
for your help to move forward in the freedom of your
love, and I ask for the peace of your presence to guide
me in my decisions.**

THINK FIRST

Lovers of God think before they speak, but the careless blurt out wicked words meant to cause harm.

PROVERBS 15:28

It is incredibly important to consider what we say before we say it, especially in situations when we lack a bridge of trust with those around us. It all begins with our hearts. We must think through our intentions and the ideas we want to present. We need to be considerate about which opinions are strong and yet divisive. We do not have to hold back truth when it is appropriate, but we must be careful in how we talk about things. Just as gentleness can turn away wrath, humility can keep others from remaining walled off in offense.

How often do we think before we say something? It is wise to consider the possible repercussions of our choices as well as our off-handed remarks. How do we speak about others when they are not present? If we are not careful, we may break the trust of those who confided in us. If this is the case, others will not feel confident speaking freely. Let's not be those who are careless with our words. Even in our imperfection, there is grace. Still, we should take the time to think first before we speak.

Jesus, you were so wise with your words. You did not use words to harm or hurt others, and I don't want to either. Help me.

REFRESHING NEWS

The Lord doesn't respond to the wicked,
but he's moved to answer the prayers of the righteous.

PROVERBS 15:29

The Lord not only listens to our prayers, but he also is moved to answer them. Perhaps you question whether he hears you. If you struggle to know who is wicked as opposed to righteous, consider the fruit of the Spirit and simply look at the opposite fruit. A wicked person wishes harm to others, has a disregard for justice and righteousness, and looks for ways to exploit others for his or her own gain. Wicked ones think of themselves more than they think of anyone else, and everything—including their prayers—reflects that.

The Lord alone knows our hearts. He alone discerns our motivations and longings. He will never answer a prayer that causes him to act outside of his character. Instead of us worrying about how God perceives us and disqualifying ourselves, let's invite his Spirit to speak his perspective of us over our hearts today. He brings light, life, and freedom. He gives peace and joy. How refreshing!

Lord, I come to you with a heart open to receive and a hunger to know you more. As I pray, I trust you to answer according to your nature. Thank you.

CONSTRUCTIVE CRITICISM

Accepting constructive criticism opens your heart to the path of life, making you right at home among the wise.

PROVERBS 15:31

There are different kinds of criticism that we can offer as well as kinds that others can offer to us. Criticism that tears down another's identity and hopes without any type of solution is pointless. Criticism that produces condemnation is not helpful to anyone. Criticism that disparages only destroys. Constructive criticism, however, offers the challenge along with a helpful push. When we are offered a different way, it can be liberating to know we have opportunity for change rather than the belittlement of our identity in Christ.

We should be careful to offer critiques with compassion and encouragement to take a different path. If we have nothing helpful to add, let's withhold our judgment. If we have no wise words to help redirect in a loving way, then we should keep our opinions to ourselves. Just know this is not an excuse to be apathetic. We have so much wisdom to offer and accept if we are open to it.

Creator, you are a builder, not a destroyer. When I am tempted to criticize others while offering nothing in return—not even the recognition of my own faults— may I embrace your better way.

ULTIMATE LEADER

Go ahead and make all the plans you want,
but it's the Lord who will ultimately direct your steps.

PROVERBS 16:1

There is nothing wrong with making plans. In fact, we will not go very far in life if we don't. It is the posture of our hearts—how much we trust the Lord—that will determine how we move ahead. We can make all the plans we want, but the Lord is the one who ultimately directs our steps. We don't have to worry about making a "wrong" choice when we are surrendered to the Lord. He will continue to guide us.

God goes with us in our moves, and he stays with us in our hibernation. He is with us. May we trust him to have his way. No matter which plans succeed and which fail, he is still the Redeemer. He can restore what the locusts have eaten. He can revive a weary heart. He can do it all. Accept the invitation to lean into the very present mercy of Christ today and to trust him, for he is our confident hope.

Lord Jesus, I trust you to do what I never could on my own. I trust you to lead me through the winding road of this life. Direct me, and may I rest in loving and hopeful trust.

TESTED AND PROVEN

We are all in love with our own opinions, convinced they're correct. But the Lord is in the midst of us, testing and probing our every motive.

PROVERBS 16:2

It is the human condition to think we know what is best. We are prone to bias, and unless we purposefully challenge our way of thinking, we stay stuck in very narrow ideas about the world, others, and God. "The Lord is in the midst of us, testing and probing our every motive" so that we will not be stagnant in our faith or understanding.

Colossians 3:12 instructs, "Robe yourself with virtues of God...Be merciful as you endeavor to understand others, and be compassionate, showing kindness toward all. Be gentle and humble, unoffendable in your patience with others." As we endeavor to understand others with compassion and kindness, we allow our hearts to remain open to expanding in the wisdom of God. May we allow the Spirit to examine our hearts and challenge our understanding today and every day.

Wise God, thank you for your perfect perspective in a world filled with narrow ones, including my own. I want to grow in understanding and in grace, for I know that they go hand in hand.

Commit Your Business to God

Before you do anything, put your trust totally in God and not in yourself. Then every plan you make will succeed.

PROVERBS 16:3

Whatever it is that you do for a living, commit your business to God, and he will help you succeed. Whatever creative endeavors you have, if you put your trust totally in God, he will guide you to bring your plans into being. Broaden your definition of success to include being rooted in the kingdom of Christ, and turn away from narrow views that say you must make a lot of money in order to be effective.

Verse 4 of this same chapter in Proverbs says, "The Lord works everything together to accomplish his purpose." He will take your choices, your giftings, and even sometimes your failures, and use them for his glory. Whatever you have to offer is useful. God uses even the smallest things to effect change for his kingdom when we are submitted to his loving leadership.

God, I put my complete trust in you—in both the new and the habitual parts of my day and life. I trust you to lead me in your goodness and to establish your mercy as I follow your guidance.

JULY

SURRENDERED AND SET FREE

You can avoid evil through surrendered worship and the
fear of God, for the power of his faithful love removes
sin's guilt and grip over you.

PROVERBS 16:6

The power of God's loyal love completely and irrevocably
removes sin's guilt and grip over us, his yielded children.
Jesus echoed this when he said, "If the Son sets you free
from sin, then become a true son and be unquestionably
free!" (John 8:36). When we surrender to Christ, he
liberates us in his strong love.

Think about how your surrendered worship of God
has moved you into greater freedom. Have you tasted the
goodness of knowing how incredibly delighted the Father
is over you? Have you experienced the peace of God that
transcends understanding and seeps into your very soul?
The incredible power of God's love that sets the captive
free and makes the lame dance in unabashed joy before
him is yours to experience. May you worship and honor
the Lord with the grateful heart of someone caught up in
the wonder of his marvelous mercy.

**Joyful Jesus, in your love, I come alive. I want to know
even greater freedom in your presence and in my lived-
out spirituality. Transform my guilt into the testimony
of your goodness. I love you.**

ACTIVATED GRACE

When the Lord is pleased with the decisions you've made,
he activates grace to turn enemies into friends.

PROVERBS 16:7

In the gracious love of the Lord, we have the ability to turn enemies into friends. It is not magic or wishful thinking. The grace of God is incredibly powerful in paving the way for this possibility. Jesus instructed his disciples in his Sermon on the Hillside to love their enemies. "I say to you, love your enemy, bless the one who curses you, do something wonderful for the one who hates you, and respond to the very ones who persecute you by praying for them" (Matthew 5:44).

It is through prayer, humility, intentional kindness, gentleness, and purposeful acts of love that we build bridges of grace to turn enemies into friends. We certainly cannot control whether someone else's heart will soften in love, but we can choose how we will act toward them. Christ's instruction was to love others, even our enemies, with practical and, frankly, astonishing kindness. There is grace in the presence of God to do this.

Gracious God, your ways are so different from the world's. Your love is overwhelmingly good, and I choose to partner with it. Help me to build bridges of grace with those I like and with those I have a hard time with. Soften my heart.

FAIR MEASURES

The Lord expects you to be fair in every business deal, for he is the one who sets the standards for righteousness.

PROVERBS 16:11

We cannot separate our work lives from our spiritual lives, just as we cannot separate our family lives from our personal lives. We live with integrity when our values are aligned in every area—no separation or distinction. God, the one who set the standards for righteousness, is the measure by which we should hold everything.

We must not overlook little compromises in the workplace, expecting them to amount to nothing. We need to be people of our word, honest and fair in the way we do business. As representatives of Christ, we get to offer our hard work coupled with firm values rooted in his kingdom. As we follow the lead of the Lord in everything we do, we can trust him to help us when challenges arise. We will have nothing to hide when false accusations are directed at us, and we will have no reason to fear when people look under the surface.

Perfect One, you are righteous, just, and true in all that you do. When I am faced with the opportunity to compromise, may I resist it, knowing the reward of standing on righteousness is far better than anything I would stand to gain.

KISS OF TRUTH

Kings and leaders love to hear godly counsel,
and they love those who tell them the truth.

PROVERBS 16:13

There is a reason why wise leaders love to hear godly counsel. When people have different roles and levels of power, almost everyone sees an opportunity to try to garner the favor of their leaders. However, when we trade the truth for favor, everyone loses. Wise leaders love those who tell them the truth even if it is not what they want to hear. They know truth-tellers can be trusted.

Maybe you have already experienced this. Perhaps you have known someone who would tell you what they thought you wanted to hear only to find out later that it was not their truthful opinion. It can be incredibly frustrating. We must resist the urge to placate others and stand on the truth. The wise among us will see it for the beautiful opportunity it is to be challenged and grow. Only the foolish resist the truth and want their egos sustained.

Righteous One, I choose to stand on the truth and be a person who tells the truth whenever asked. I will not trade favor for my integrity. I choose your ways. Kiss me with your truth today—whether it is hard to swallow or like honey to my soul.

BEWARE OF OVERCONFIDENCE

Your boast becomes a prophecy of a future failure.
The higher you lift yourself up in pride,
the harder you'll fall in disgrace.

PROVERBS 16:18

It is not a sin to be self-assured and confident in who
you are. However, if you let pride elevate you above
others in your own estimation, you'll find that when
reality humbles you, it will be a hard fall. Confidence and
overconfidence are not the same. You can be confident
and still be extremely humble. If you need an example,
look at Jesus.

Jesus was extremely humble and compassionate,
yet he never wavered in his confidence of who he was. He
knew the Father loved him and chose him, and that did
not keep him from reaching out to others with incredible
patience and mercy. It is the pride of overconfidence that
can keep you from letting compassion direct your actions.
Instead, choose to walk in the humble confidence of
who you are in Christ and offer incredible compassion,
knowing who others are in him.

**Jesus, you are so loving and kind, and yet you never
wavered in your identity. May my confidence grow
strong in who you are and who I am in you. I love you.
I humble myself before you, and I choose to clothe
myself in your compassion.**

SMALL WONDERS

It's better to be meek and lowly and live among the poor than to live high and mighty among the rich and famous.

PROVERBS 16:19

No one can argue that a wealth of resources leads to an easier life. Yet, in this proverb, we are told that it is better to be meek, humble, and to live among the poor than it is to live high and mighty among the rich and famous. This has nothing to do explicitly with resources and more to do with the attitude of our hearts. We could be poor and proud or rich and humble. Wealth and humility are not mutually exclusive. However, it is a wise heart that does not seek wealth and status over the simple satisfaction we can find in a humble life.

When we live with the values of Christ's kingdom, we don't choose to elevate ourselves over others. We do not lord our knowledge, our appearance, our identity, or any other thing over another human being. We don't pretend to be something that we are not. We do not seek superficial connections with others to bolster our own egos. Let's be sure that, no matter our current economic situation, we are right in our hearts and motivations.

God, help me to find satisfaction in the simple joys that are available to me. May I find peace right where I am.

MOTIVATED

Life motivation comes from the deep longings of the heart,
and the passion to see them fulfilled urges you onward.

PROVERBS 16:26

Motivation does not happen out of thin air, and it usually
cannot be something that we are pressured into. True
life motivation—motivation that is long-lasting and
effective—comes from the deep longings of our heart.
From this place, coupled with the passion to see our
desires fulfilled, we are moved to action.

Take some time to consider the deep longings of
your heart. Which have motivated you to take action, and
how has that worked for you? You do not need to feel the
emotion of motivation in order to make movement in any
area. You can do necessary and even hard things when
you feel unmotivated. But your efforts to move forward
may not last if you are not passionate about the goal. Be
sure that your actions match the desire and let the loving
freedom of the Lord compel you when you are stuck.

**Lord, even when I do not feel passion, may the deep
longings of my heart move me to action. I want to build
consistent action coupled with a heart of trust in my
life. You are my greatest motivation.**

MATURE WISDOM

Old age with wisdom will crown you with dignity and honor, for it takes a lifetime of righteousness to acquire it.

PROVERBS 16:31

Old age does not guarantee wisdom. Just because time passes does not necessarily mean we have learned valuable lessons. The wise allow their experiences to expand their understanding, challenge their biases, and change their minds when they find better evidence. The Lord is constantly moving in loyal love, and we can learn so much from how God has worked in the lives of those who have gone before.

It is important to look for the fruit of righteousness, of wisdom, and of the Spirit in the lives of those around us. As we have conversations with the mature among us who have lived longer than we have, may we be open to their perspective and advice. There is tremendous gain when we lean on the generations for growth, expansion, and understanding.

Wise Father, I admit that I have not learned to honor the wisdom of the elderly, and I don't want to miss out on their lived lessons because of my own pride. Give me grace to expand my own perspective as I honor those who have lived longer than I.

GODLY AMBITION

Do you want to be a mighty warrior? It's better to be known as one who is patient and slow to anger. Do you want to conquer a city? Rule over your temper before you attempt to rule a city.

PROVERBS 16:32

This is such a powerful proverb. It is not bad to want to be a mighty warrior, but it is much better for others to see us as one who is patient and slow to anger. Mighty warriors are not known for their restraint or peacemaking abilities. It is much wiser to learn to rule over our passions and tempers before we aim to lead others.

This is sage advice for every age. It helps check the ambitions of our hearts. If you want to be a great leader, think through your reasons. If you want to build a business empire, what is the purpose of it? If your goals are focused on your own achievements, then you have a bit of growing to do before you are equipped to lead many people successfully. Learn patience and endurance, kindness and equity, for these are the building blocks of wise and successful leaders whose impact reaches further than their own interests.

Great God, help me evaluate the ambitions you have set inside of me. May I not be too quick to take control when I need to first learn the surrendered and humble life of serving others.

PEACE IN THE HOME

A simple, humble life with peace and quiet is far better than an opulent lifestyle with nothing but quarrels and strife at home.

PROVERBS 17:1

Have you ever looked at the life of someone else and wanted to trade places? Consider what it was you would trade. Perhaps it was the house they lived in, the car they drove, or the person they were partnered with. Though, on the outside, the life of opulence may be appealing, it is hollow if there is nothing but conflict at home. It is better to have fewer resources and have peaceful, satisfying relationships than it is to have more and not have stable, safe relationships.

God calls us to be people who produce atmospheres of peace within our homes, no matter how much or how little we have. We can be safe harbors for those in our lives, and we should surround ourselves with people who can do the same. We must not overlook the importance of peace in our homes. More than wealth, harmony is a wellspring of life and joy.

Holy God, I crave the satisfaction of simple peace. I don't want to be focused on the superficial things of life, overlooking what generosity I can find in the simplest of things. Thank you.

PURIFIED BY FIRE

In the same way that gold and silver are refined by fire,
the Lord purifies your heart by the tests and trials of life.

PROVERBS 17:3

The refining process of gold and silver is not a gentle thing. The flames of a hot fire melt the impurities away and leave the pure substances behind. In the same way, our hearts are refined by the trials of this life. As we go through the fires of testing, the impurities melt away—our false mindsets, pride, and shame. When we are brought to our knees, we can lean more readily on the gracious love of our Savior.

Let's not fight the transformative power of process. We should not try to resist the changes that inevitably come through the shifts in our lives. Instead, may we embrace the process and allow what does not serve us or the kingdom of God to melt away. The heat of the fire will not kill us, but it can make us shine brighter as we come to understand that under pressure, our pain can turn to beauty.

Loving Lord, I know that you do not bring harm to my life. I trust that you will use even the most painful circumstances to refine me in your love. I want to be transformed by you through it all.

HONEST INTEGRITY

It is not proper for a leader to lie and deceive,
and don't expect excellent words to be spoken by a fool.

PROVERBS 17:7

In our value of truth, we should consider whether we are willing to hear honesty, even when it comes to us through vessels and people that we would normally not listen to. Are we able to keep open hearts, listening for wisdom's voice in the world around us? No one has a monopoly on wisdom, and there is no person, group, or ideology that has a perfect understanding of God or his plans. We need to lean in to the truth of God's Word and guidance and let him propel us into action.

Liars and deceivers are found out, for they build traps with their words that they will eventually fall into. We should never make excuses for leaders who get caught in their web of lies. Instead, we need to be willing to call for accountability and stand on justice. Do we expect more from our leaders than they have proven they can offer? This is often the case. We must instead put our trust completely in the Lord and remain rooted in his mercy, truth, and justice.

Father, you are steadfast and true, and I stand upon the foundation of your kingdom. May I never make excuses for deception, and may I embrace your loving wisdom in my expectations of others. Thank you.

OVERLOOKING FAULTS

Love overlooks the mistakes of others,
but dwelling on the failures of others
devastates friendships.

PROVERBS 17:9

It is to our own glory when we overlook the mistakes of others, especially those who are dear to us. To maintain love in our relationships, we cannot carry offense in our hearts. Offense will eventually erode the connection we have by cutting off true communication and vulnerability. We must learn to overlook the mistakes of others when they are not worth confronting.

When someone has made a mistake that is too significant to overlook, we should bring it to them in love, not holding something against them or refusing to offer them the opportunity to speak. We can overlook small offenses and still hold others accountable when they hurt us. It is important to know the difference. Either way, loving-kindness that easily forgives should flood our hearts. Our relationships will be better for it, and our own hearts will know the freedom of not trying to control another.

Father, you are the King of overlooking offenses. May I not let pride or hurt keep me from loving others in my life. Give me discernment to know what to simply let go of and what to confront. I depend on you.

REAPING WHAT IS SOWN

The one who returns evil for good can expect to be
treated the same way for the rest of his life.

PROVERBS 17:13

A pretty simple concept is put forth in this proverb. We
reap what we sow, and those who return evil for good can
expect to be treated that way in their own interactions.
We do no one any favors—ourselves included—when we
choose to treat others in a way that is unkind.

Jesus described this concept in a parable about an
unforgiving servant (see Matthew 18:21–35). This servant
owed money to his king, and knowing that he could not
pay his debt, he begged his master to have mercy on him.
The king was gracious and forgave the servant's entire
debt. Now, instead of acting in the same manner, this
servant hunted down someone who owed him money
and demanded repayment. Instead of extending the same
mercy he'd received, the servant had the other person
thrown in jail. When the king heard, he ordered that the
servant be thrown in jail and suffer until he repaid his debt
in full. Let's take this as our cautionary tale to offer mercy
whenever possible and to do good whenever we can.

**Merciful Father, thank you for your gracious heart of
forgiveness. May I be gracious to others in the same way.**

UPHOLDERS OF JUSTICE

There is nothing God hates more than condemning the one who is innocent and acquitting the one who is guilty.

PROVERBS 17:15

God never rejoices when the wicked are acquitted of their crimes, and he does not delight when the innocent are condemned. Do we view justice in the same way that God does? Let's ask him to expand our understanding in his perspective. Not stopping there, may we press in for a greater glimpse of his mercy in action. It is not our duty to condemn those whom God declares free, and we should be careful when we judge those whom we know little about.

It is always a good idea to err on the side of the vulnerable and oppressed. It is a gift when we lead with mercy. Will we be swayed by the biases that others try to push on us in fear, or will we openly allow the mercy-kindness of God to lead our opinions? Most of us are not ruling as judges, but many of us act that way when we talk about others. We must be careful to let compassion have room and let God be the true judge.

Advocate, I want to lean toward mercy with my whole heart. Help me to stand on the foundation of your justice and allow your compassion to change my heart.

THROUGH THICK AND THIN

A dear friend will love you no matter what,
and a family sticks together through all kinds of trouble.

PROVERBS 17:17

It is a beautiful thing to have dear friends who love us no matter what. No matter the changes we go through, the losses we experience, or the ways in which we fail to meet their expectations, a dear friend sticks with us through it all. A family built on love stays through the troubles of life, offering support, reprieve, and strength.

Do you have friends who are like family or family members as dear to you as a friend? Count yourself blessed if you do. If you have not known the love of a person who sticks with you through the ups and downs of life, don't let discouragement cloud your mind. You can find your strength in the greatest and most faithful friend—Jesus Christ. His Spirit is yours, making his home in you. You are never without the love of Christ, and he will never leave you alone. He makes connections for you where there seem to be none. He will open your eyes to the gift of friendship that is right at your fingertips.

Spirit, thank you for your incomparable friendship, and thank you for the dear friends who are family to me. I cannot express my deep gratitude enough.

WISE INVESTMENTS

It's stupid to run up bills you'll never be able to pay or to cosign for the loan of your friend. Save yourself the trouble and don't do either one.

PROVERBS 17:18

It is wisdom that advises us to live within our means. It is foolish to run up bills on frivolous things that we do not need and cannot pay off. When wisdom says to resist the consumerism of our culture, it is for our own benefit. There is blessing in restraint, which is not mutually exclusive with generosity.

It is important that we be wise with our investments, taking the sage advice of those who have paid off their debt and who live while building legacies for their future and family. It is not advisable to rush into cosigning loans for people we don't trust. We cannot let our hopes of potential overshadow the probabilities in line with a person's character. If we give anything, we should do it as a gift, with no expectation of return. It will save us trouble if we are intentional and wise with how we both spend and invest our money.

God, I trust that your wisdom always has my best at heart. I trust your guidance and the godly instruction of those who walk in your ways. Help me shift my perspective on spending to be in line with your kingdom.

JOYFUL HEARTS
OF HEALING

A joyful, cheerful heart brings healing to both body and soul. But the one whose heart is crushed struggles with sickness and depression.

PROVERBS 17:22

We cannot avoid the pain and losses of life. Heartbreak is not a lack of faith, and suffering is not a sin. It is part of the human experience. When pain weighs us down, we can look to the Lord for relief. It doesn't help us to pretend the pain is not there. We must acknowledge it before we can be healed of it. As we give ourselves permission to feel it all, let's be sure to never lose sight of the comfort of God's healing hope.

If we are experiencing a difficult time in our lives, let's remember that the sun will rise again. We will experience the joy mingled with relief of the dawning of a new day. We don't need to despair, and we also don't need to pretend everything is fine. True joy and cheerfulness come from the delight of God's heart. As we look to him, we can rely on his love to carry us through. As he does, we will experience the healing of his jubilance and pleasure over us.

Healer, you are the one I rely on. Your joy is much deeper than feigned happiness. Your delight is the well of life that I drink from. Revive me in your living waters again today.

Cool under Pressure

Can you bridle your tongue when your heart is under pressure? That's how you show that you are wise. An understanding heart keeps you cool, calm, and collected, no matter what you're facing.

PROVERBS 17:27

Wisdom does not break under pressure. When we can control our responses when our hearts are triggered, then we know that we have attained a depth of wisdom that no one can take from us. When we know that another person's reaction has more to say about them than it does about us, it takes the pressure off to defend ourselves.

We can learn how to remain cool, calm, and collected in the face of frustration. There are available tools for us to harness that help us maintain our autonomy and regain compassion for others. We are allowed to take breaks when we need to, breathe deeply, disengage from the trigger, and calm ourselves by reminding our hearts that we can process it later in trusted spaces. Remaining cool and collected does not mean that we are perfect. It just demonstrates that we have learned ways to control our responses—and there is wisdom in that.

Wise One, thank you for the tools that you have given me to practice patience and self-control in the face of frustrations. I want to grow in wisdom; help me.

STAY CONNECTED

An unfriendly person isolates himself and seems to care
only about his own issues. For his contempt of sound
judgment makes him a recluse.

PROVERBS 18:1

Not every isolated person is unfriendly, and not all who
find themselves alone are resistant to wisdom. Instead
of judging those who are alone, we should practice the
mercy-kindness of Christ. Perhaps everyone they loved
has gone, and they are left on their own, not knowing how
to make new connections.

The importance of human connection and
companionship cannot be overstated. We were created
for family, community, and relationship in general. This
is not to say we should not be comfortable being alone.
Jesus spent time alone. And if he did, we should feel no
guilt about needing to get away for a while. We can have
alone time and still come back and connect to our loved
ones. As we press into the power of community, we will
find there is deeper healing in our shared experiences
than we could experience on our own.

Jesus, I trust that you created humanity for connection.
I long to know you more in the context of community.
Expand my understanding as I choose to reach out and
connect more with others.

DEEP SPRINGS

Words of wisdom are like a fresh, flowing brook—
like deep waters that spring forth from within,
bubbling up inside the one with understanding.

PROVERBS 18:4

When wisdom touches our hearts, it feels like a fresh,
flowing brook reaching the deepest spaces of our souls.
Understanding bubbles up, and we perceive what we
could not before. Revelation is expansive and intoxicating
when we taste it. It is like deep calling to deep, resonating
within the recesses of our souls.

May you drink deeply from the springs of the
Spirit's living waters within you. There the humble and
seeking heart can find more understanding, and those
seeking wisdom's light can encounter more clarity. Open
up and receive from the overflowing fountain of mercy
that anoints you today as you look to Christ. He can give
you refreshment for your soul and wisdom to revive your
deepest hopes. May you catch a glimpse of the glorious
affection your Father feels for you and be loved to life in
his presence.

**Creator, speak your words of wisdom and revive my
heart in your love today. I long for a fresh revelation,
a new understanding, of your goodness. I am ready to
receive from you.**

HEALED PEOPLE OFFER HEALING

The words of a gossip merely reveal the wounds of his own soul, and his slander penetrates into the innermost being.

PROVERBS 18:8

We can either tear down others with our words, or we can build them up. What we offer is a reflection of our own hearts. If we are carrying around gaping wounds of rejection, shame, or fear, then what we say to others will reflect that. If we have experienced healing in our hearts, releasing forgiveness, mercy, and kindness through the acceptance of Christ's love, then we will also reflect that with our words.

If we are prone to tearing others down, we should look within and ask the Lord what is behind it. Instead of blaming others, we have the opportunity to humble ourselves before him and allow him to speak to the deep places of our pain. Without using our hurt as an excuse, let's choose to build others up in encouragement. The kingdom of God is one of abundance, not of scarcity. There is no need to hold back mercy when there is a never-ending supply available to us.

Merciful King, thank you for the healing power of your love in my heart and life. Touch the places that I did not even realize were still waiting to be healed as I look to you.

RUN INTO HIS HEART

The character of God is a tower of strength,
for the lovers of God delight to run into his heart
and be exalted on high.

PROVERBS 18:10

It is a delight to run into the heart of God because that is where we find ourselves loved to life time and again. In him are an endless mercy and a generous supply of wisdom, understanding, and kindness. He provides comfort for our pain, clarity for our confusion, and the warm embrace of a loving Father whenever we turn to him. The character of God is full of vibrant life, for he is the source of it all. He never changes, and he never will.

God is love. All that we are looking for can be found in him. He is the perfect expression of all that we desire. He does not lie or manipulate, and he will never shame or fool us. He is better than we can imagine. How could we not be delighted to run into his heart again and again? There we find grace to empower us, affection to assure us, and truth to challenge us. What an amazing Father he is!

Marvelous God, I want to experience the delight of your presence in refreshing and life-changing ways today. I run into your heart. Transform me in your presence as I do.

LISTEN FIRST

Listen before you speak, for to speak before you've heard the facts will bring humiliation.

PROVERBS 18:13

It is wise to listen carefully and understand the full scope of an issue before jumping to conclusions. If we jump in too fast with our opinions, we are doing nothing more than trying to bolster our preconceived notions by proving we are right. Let's approach conversations, complex issues, and situations with a learner's heart and open mind. Instead of trying to win an argument, we should try to understand where others are coming from.

James 1:19 echoes this when it says, "Be quick to listen, but slow to speak." We practice patience, wisdom, and humility when we keep our hearts open to learning from others. We grow in wisdom when we listen—we know this is true from the Scriptures. If we listen to the Lord and apply his instruction to our lives, then we will also learn to listen to those around us, for it is an act of love to do so.

Jesus, I don't want to be foolish in thinking that listening to you and rejecting the need to consider others is the wise way to live in your kingdom. May I remain humble in your love rather than rushing to conclusions in pride.

HUNGRY FOR MORE

The spiritually hungry are always ready to learn more,
for their hearts are eager to discover new truths.

PROVERBS 18:15

When we crave food, we are motivated to look for
nourishment. Who does not go looking for sustenance
when their stomach growls with hunger? It is the same
with spiritual hunger. We need the nourishment of God's
Word and Spirit to satisfy us. If we ignore the cues of our
souls, we will find ourselves malnourished in spirit.

Take some time with the Lord today as you examine
your heart. Consider if there are areas where you are
deficient. What do you need to strengthen your spirit? Ask
the Spirit to nourish you with his overwhelming goodness
and to satisfy you with the generous grace of his truth. You
can find all you need in him. Feast on his presence and
find yourself revived in your innermost being.

Father, I know that you are the only one who can truly
satisfy the longings of my soul. Every time I hunger,
you feed me. I won't stop coming to you, and I will not
neglect the hunger that reaches out for you.

CONSIDER BOTH SIDES

There are two sides to every story. The first one to speak
sounds true until you hear the other side and they set the
record straight.

PROVERBS 18:17

Just as a court case presents both sides, we should not get
too swayed by one account before we hear the other side.
It is foolish to jump to conclusions before all the evidence
is presented. Only after we hear both sides can we make
a sound judgment. Look for ways that you can apply this
wisdom to your life. Perhaps there are issues in which you
have avoided listening to the other side because you are
already convinced that you've heard the truth.

It is wisdom that lends patience and the willingness
to hear the story in full. It is wisdom that recognizes that
there is more to an account than one person's view on it.
As we follow the loving lead of wisdom, we will consider
the full scope, not just one aspect of the story.

Wise Judge, only you know the full account of every
situation and circumstance. Only you can see through
our very souls to the root of our intentions. Help me to
practice patience and wisdom as I consider more than
what feels or sounds true in the moment. May I remain
open in your grounded mercy.

SPEAK LIFE

Your words are so powerful that they will kill or give life,
and the talkative person will reap the consequences.

PROVERBS 18:21

When we are careless with our words, we may end up
hurting those we don't mean to hurt. When we practice
discernment with our speech, we can choose what we
do with our words—whether we build people up or tear
them down. We must not overlook the importance of our
intentions and the power that our words have over others.

Can you think of a time when a careless or straight-
out demeaning comment stuck with you? Perhaps it
was something a parent or teacher said. Maybe it was
a schoolmate, friend, or sibling. If something comes to
mind, you know the experiential power of someone else's
words. Perhaps you remember someone giving you a
timely word that gave you courage and perspective. This,
too, is powerful. Let's be purposeful with our words,
practicing grace and mercy when we get it wrong, as we
seek to make it right as quickly as possible.

Giver of Life, I don't want to harm others with careless
words. Help me to be wise and discerning with what
I say, building others up in love, challenging them in
mercy, and offering grace whenever possible. Thank you.

CLOSEST FRIEND

Some friendships don't last for long, but there is one loving friend who is joined to your heart closer than any other!

PROVERBS 18:24

Even when our friendships shift and change, there is a friend who never leaves. He always knows our hearts, and he does not misunderstand our motivations. He sticks closer than family, is more faithful than a loyal lover, and will never abandon us. There is grief in the loss of relationships—whether it is because of a breakup, a death, or a move. Even in our heartbreak, God is with us. He won't ever leave us.

What a gift it is to have close friends in this life. What an even greater gift it is to be known by the Creator of the Universe, the Maker of our souls. Even when our closest friends cannot understand the choices we make, God does. Even when others don't trust our transformation, God never wavers in love toward us. We are secure in his mercy.

Great God, thank you for never leaving me or misunderstanding me. You don't threaten to cut off our relationship when I ask hard questions, and you are not threatened by the expansion of my understanding. In fact, you encourage it. Help me to be a loyal and faithful friend to others, just as you are to me.

CHOOSE HONESTY

It's better to be honest, even if it leads to poverty,
than to live as a dishonest fool.

PROVERBS 19:1

There is tremendous power in living in the light of truth.
When we refuse to compromise the honest truth, we are
free to let others react how they will, but we will not live
in the regret of what-ifs. It is much better to have nothing
to hide, living in the conviction of our values and beliefs,
than it is to pretend to be something that we are not.

In 2 Timothy 2:15, Paul instructs, "Always be
eager to present yourself before God as a perfect and
mature minister, without shame, as one who correctly
explains the Word of Truth." Maturity leads us to honesty,
which leaves us without shame in the face of whatever
comes. Remember that we can only control our own
actions and reactions, not anyone else's. Instead of
trying to manipulate a best-case outcome, let's show up
in authenticity and be honest. It is always the best way
forward.

**God, may I choose honesty over the easy way out
or over trying to conform to others' ideals at every
juncture. Keep me steadfast in your truth and covered
in your mercy as I do.**

TAKE RESPONSIBILITY

There are some people who ruin their own lives
and then blame it all on God.

PROVERBS 19:3

We cannot avoid the responsibility we bear for the choices
we make. Only we can account for our actions before
God. Not everything that happens in life is a result of our
own making, and not everything that happens to us is in
direct result of our choices. But there are circumstances in
which we make choices that lead to suffering. Whenever
we abandon integrity and lie, cheat, or steal, we will face
the consequences.

We must resist the temptation to blame others for
the effects of our foolish choices. In particular, we should
not blame God for the things that we have caused or
the suffering that we inflict upon ourselves, and we also
should not blame ourselves or others for the troubles that
cannot be avoided. Let's be very careful here not to judge
others based on the trials that they are going through.
This is a good test for our own hearts and souls.

**Lord, I don't deny the power of my choices, and that's
why I choose to walk in the ways of your kingdom.
Where I am prone to blaming others, may I instead see
where compromise has led to pain.**

GENEROSITY IS BETTER THAN FAME

Everyone wants to be close to the rich and famous,
but a generous person has all the friends he wants!

PROVERBS 19:6

As far as influence goes, a generous person has stronger
reach than the rich or famous. It is better to be generous
with what we have than to measure our worth against the
wealthy. No matter how vast or limited our resources, we
can live charitably and humbly.

The lesson of the widow's offering is a beautiful
example of giving God our best. Luke 21:1–4 recounts
how a widow "dropped two small copper coins in the
offering box" at the temple. Jesus drew his disciples'
attention to it, saying, "This poor widow has given a larger
offering than any of the wealthy. For the rich only gave
out of their surplus, but she sacrificed out of her poverty
and gave to God all that she had to live on." May we be
as generous with our own offerings as well as the gifts
we extend to help others. God is a faithful Father who
will supply all our needs, so there's no need to withhold
anything from him.

**Source of Life, I want to reflect your wonderful
generosity in the way I live. Be honored in my giving.**

AUGUST

Keep Learning

Do yourself a favor and love wisdom. Learn all you can,
then watch your life flourish and prosper!

PROVERBS 19:8

When we align our lives in the kingdom of Christ and
apply his wisdom to our lifestyles, we will prosper in the
fruit of his Spirit. Our lives flourish in his mercy when
we are focused on living with integrity and walking in
righteousness. We turn away from anything that keeps
us from living in the liberty of his love, and we learn to
generously offer his mercy-kindness to everyone around
us. As we plant seeds of peace, we sow an orchard of
God's goodness.

Keep learning, and you will find yourself going
from glory to glory. Keep applying the wisdom of Christ
as it is revealed to you, and you will be refined by his
faithful love. Don't hold too tightly to old vessels or ways
of doing things. He is doing something new, and he is
providing a new wineskin to pour yourself into. Allow
yourself to expand with new understanding, and don't
resist the kind correction a wise person offers to you.
There is so much more to learn and so much space to
grow in his kingdom knowledge.

**Wonderful Savior, help me to let go of old ways and
embrace the expansion your revelation brings.**

OVERLOOK INSULTS

An understanding person demonstrates patience, for
mercy means holding your tongue. When you are
insulted, be quick to forgive and forget it, for you are
virtuous when you overlook an offense.

PROVERBS 19:11

It is easier said than done to overlook an offense. But
Scripture says it is to our glory—it is honorable—to be
quick to forgive and forget. How easily we can let go
is a reflection of our own hearts, not of the person we
forgive. Especially when it comes to small offenses, let's
be quick to give the benefit of the doubt and move on. In
instances where we need to confront someone, we can
still approach it with a heart of humility that is ready to
forgive.

Think about the kind of insults can you choose
to overlook. Consider what kind of offenses you are not
willing to put any emotional energy into. When we grab
on to insults and let them affect our worth, it has the
potential to devastate us. Instead of going that route, we
can choose to let go of offenses for the sake of our own
hearts. Let's forgive and forget for our own well-being.
What wisdom there is in doing so!

**Jesus, you are the King of overlooking insults. What
you would not hold against another person, may I also
learn to let go of. Help me.**

HONORING GOD

Honor God's holy instructions and life will go well for you. But if you despise his ways and choose your own plans, you will die.

PROVERBS 19:16

Choosing our plans while yielding to the wisdom of Christ and following his ways and leadership will not lead us astray. When we submit our lives to him, that includes our choices. He will direct us in which way to go, and when we begin to go astray, he will redirect us. Despising his ways means that we reject living under his mercy, we let pride and self-protection be our motivators, and we refuse to love others the way that he loves us.

Do not get so caught up in the particulars of your decisions that you become stuck in fear of which way to move. Gather wise advice from trusted sources, pray and ask for God's direction, and then move ahead. He will help you every step of the way. He can easily direct you as you move, but he will never force your legs to go in any direction. Life is a partnership with him, and you need not fear making a wrong decision when you live by his instructions. He will direct and redirect you as many times as necessary.

God, thank you for guiding me. I am yours.

LOANING TO THE LORD

Every time you give to the poor you make a loan to the Lord. Don't worry—you'll be repaid in full for all the good you've done.

PROVERBS 19:17

How many times have we stopped ourselves from giving to the poor because we felt we needed to know how they would spend that money? That is not our responsibility. We cannot control how they will use the resources given to them, but the Word of God says that every time we give to the poor, in whatever way we do, we make a loan to the Lord, and it is he who repays us in full.

As we trust God to care for the needy, we should also join his heart and his purposes to provide for those who have less than we do. Let's not turn blind eyes to those begging to feed their families. We must not look over the ones, even in our midst, who struggle to make ends meet. We have the opportunity to give to the poor as if we are giving it to the Lord, trusting him to do with it what needs to be done. There's no need to worry or try to micromanage our gifts. They belong to the Lord, after all.

Lord, thank you for the permission to let go of trying to manage my gifts to others. I allow them to be loans I make to you, and I trust you with it.

WISE PARENTING

Don't be afraid to discipline your children while they're still young enough to learn. Don't indulge your children or be swayed by their protests.

PROVERBS 19:18

Most of us know the power of discipline and how it can influence our choices going forward. Let's be wise, leaning into the mercy and grace of God in all things—including instructing younger generations. Discipline is not a one-size-fits-all endeavor. We must recognize that an honest conversation can be enough to steer one person, while someone else may need to feel the consequences of privileges revoked.

We should not be afraid to offer discipline, and we should also not be afraid to offer grace. May we lead with curiosity and compassion, as Christ always does. His kindness leads us to repentance, so we should also be gentle, even in our discipline. We need to make sure that those whom we discipline know we love them. Instead of being swayed by the protests of our children, let's stand strong in our values and decisions, for only then will they know the boundaries they cannot cross.

Merciful Father, thank you for your kindness, even in discipline. I want to be able to direct my dependents in love and integrity even when they don't understand. Help me to stand strong in both compassion and conviction.

PEOPLE OF OUR WORD

A lover of God who is poor and promises nothing is better than a rich liar who never keeps his promises.

PROVERBS 19:22

Following through on our promises is as important as the vows we make. In fact, it is even more valuable. If we do not faithfully do what we promise, then our word means nothing to others. Instead of building bridges of trust, we tear at the fabric of our own character. We cannot forget the power of keeping our promises. It is not too late to do what we said we would. Importantly, we should also consider how we can transform going forward. Instead of overpromising and underdelivering, we can ask God to help us be discerning in the yeses we offer.

When we are honest about what we can do and don't offer an inflated idea of our potential, we are able to take the small steps toward rebuilding trust. When we realize that we've overpromised, let's be honest about it and ask for forgiveness. Honesty is the critical first step in restoration. And when others fail to meet our expectations, we can also offer compassion and tender mercy to them, giving them the chance that we hope for.

Restorer, thank you for the permission to say no to things without feeling guilty. Help me be selective about the promises I make so that I have the ability and resources to meet them.

KEYS TO ABUNDANT LIFE

When you live a life of abandoned love, surrendered before
the awe of God, here's what you'll experience: Abundant
life. Continual protection. And complete satisfaction!

PROVERBS 19:23

What a wealth of abundant life is found in the love
of Christ! When we make mercy our priority, greater
treasures than we could ever imagine are available to us.
The way of the cross is the path of laid-down love. The
way of Christ is worth following at every turn. When
we are tempted to give up, take a side, or wall ourselves
up in our comfort zones, let's instead choose the greater
though harder path: to continue to extend compassion
and mercy-kindness.

Surrendering our lives before the awe of God is
not foolishness; it is wisdom. There is more to gain in
the satisfaction of his illuminating presence than any
temporary pleasure we experience in the world. We must
not give up pressing into the presence of God and living
yielded to his loving leadership in our lives, for there in
his presence is all that we seek—abundant life, continual
protection, and complete satisfaction.

**Awesome God, thank you for the beauty of your
wonderful character that transforms my life from the
inside out. I trust you more than I trust any other. I live
for you.**

HONORABLE PEACEMAKERS

A person of honor will put an argument to rest.
Only the stupid want to pick a fight.

PROVERBS 20:3

It is much better to keep a friend than it is to win a fight.
When we prioritize relationship and connection over
the need to be right, we promote the peace of Christ in
our midst. If we truly value the relationships in our lives,
we will not compromise closeness to elevate our own
opinions. This does not mean we cannot disagree, for it is
inherently human to have differences of opinion. The goal
isn't sameness; it is intimacy.

Beware of those in your life who simply want to
argue. Surround yourself with those who promote peace
even when you disagree. Disagreement does not have
to mean disconnection. The people with whom you can
agree to disagree while continuing to be yourselves are
relationships to be treasured. People of honor will put
arguments to rest without forcing agreement. Compassion
leads us to consider others' perspectives. As we grow in
that, we also grow in our peace-making abilities.

**Jesus, you are the ultimate peacemaker. I want to be like
you—unafraid of differences or diverse opinions. May I
live with peace as my portion, and may I be a promoter
of your love in all things and all relationships.**

DISCERNABLE CHARACTER

All children show what they're really like by how they act.
You can discern their character,
whether they are pure or perverse.

PROVERBS 20:11

Just as children clearly display their character through
their actions, so can you discern the fruit of an adult's
character through his or her choices. Pay attention to how
they treat others—how they talk about them when they're
not around and how they speak to them when they are.
Notice whether they are reliable to follow through on
what they said they would do. Consider how you feel after
spending time with them.

We should not be quick to judge a person based on
one interaction, but let's be sure to not ignore the signs of
bad character as they are revealed. A house is built with
many parts. Pay attention as you get to know others, and
you will notice what materials make up their nature. It is
wise to discern what kind of people you grow close to.

Wise Spirit, help me to pay attention to important
markers of character in others. May I listen to others'
experiences and impressions, and may I proceed with
both compassion and discernment.

DO THE WORK

If you spend all your time sleeping, you'll grow poor.
So wake up, sleepyhead! Don't sleep on the job.
And then there will be plenty of food on your table.

PROVERBS 20:13

Have you ever felt the pull of procrastination keeping
you from moving ahead in an area of your life? Consider
with curiosity what is keeping you from stepping ahead.
Whether it is fear of failure, perfectionism, or competing
demands that keep you from moving forward, dare to take
a deeper look. But remember that burnout is not laziness,
so don't confuse the two. Rest is important and necessary.
It is not laziness to take breaks without the pressure of
having to perform—there is always more to be done.

The idleness suggested here is the avoidance of
necessary parts of life. You don't have to do everything and
do it well. If you don't have the capacity to do more than
your job and care for your dependents, don't feel guilty.
Instead of throwing your hands up in surrender, make a
list of what you *must* do, and let everything else fall away
without feelings of guilt if you don't get to it today.

**Jesus, thank you that I don't have to strive for your love.
Help me to let go of what I cannot control and embrace
what I can accomplish today.**

SKILLFUL STRATEGIES

If you solicit good advice, then your plans will succeed.
So don't charge into battle without wisdom,
for wars are won by skillful strategy.

PROVERBS 20:18

Notice that the advice this proverb alludes to is *good* advice—not simply any advice from any source. There are a few ways to know if someone has given you good advice. It will resonate in your soul and challenge you in the same way Christ challenges you—to take courage. It will direct you in loving trust toward God and yourself, and it will not lead you to overly depend on it. Good advice is guidance, not micromanagement.

When you are making plans that you hope will succeed, be sure to go to those who have already achieved what you are looking to do. Learn from their mistakes, and let their wisdom help shape your strategies. It is good to get advice from many good sources so that you can build your own plan of action with tried-and-true wisdom. In the end, you cannot avoid all challenges, but you can prepare for many of them.

Skillful Master, you are full of strategic wisdom for every question I have. Help me to make plans that will succeed, and even when some plans fall apart, may I heed the wisdom of others who will help redirect me toward your purpose for me.

GRACIOUS ENDURANCE

Don't ever say, "I'm going to get even with them if it's the last thing I do!" Wrap God's grace around your heart and he will be the one to vindicate you.

PROVERBS 20:22

Vengeance is a foolish pursuit. We will ruin our own lives while trying to exact revenge on someone else. The obsession will tear us apart, and no good will come of it in the end. Paul said in his letter to the Romans, "Don't be obsessed with taking revenge, but leave that to God's righteous justice. For the Scriptures say, 'Vengeance is mine, and I will repay,' says the Lord" (12:19).

When we surrender the need for revenge, we can rest in the trust that our faithful and merciful God will have *his* way with his perfect justice. Let's do what we are called to do—forgive. We do this as much for the freedom of our own souls as we do for the people we release. Even so, let's go above and beyond in extravagant love, winning over even our enemies with kindness. With God's grace wrapped around our hearts, we can do anything.

Faithful One, I trust your faithfulness more than my need to be justified. Soften my heart in your compassion.

SAME STANDARD

The Lord hates double standards—
that's hypocrisy at its worst!

PROVERBS 20:23

Hypocrisy is not representative of the nature of our steadfast King. He offers the same standard for all—no exclusions or exceptions. His overwhelmingly abundant mercy is poured over all in the same measure. He does not offer a little love to some while offering his whole heart to others. The blood of Christ is sufficient for every person, no matter who they are, where they come from, or what they have done.

Do we truly believe this? If we do, we will apply it to our own lives, relationships, and interactions. If we somehow think that some are worthier of love than others, we have some inner work to do. We must reject the trap of pride and tribal thinking that elevates one group, language, or ethnicity above all others. God is God over all, and he does not discriminate. We need to be sure that we use the same measure for those outside our circles as we use for our families, our communities, and ourselves. There is no prejudice in the kingdom of heaven.

King of Justice, only you are perfect. May I question every bias within me that suggests that differences are dangerous. Shine your light of truth on my heart, mind, and life, and may I walk in integrity.

EMBRACE THE MYSTERY

It is the Lord who directs your life, for each step you take
is ordained by God to bring you closer to your destiny.
So much of your life, then, remains a mystery!

PROVERBS 20:24

There is only so much we can know in the here and now.
Think back to your younger years when you dreamed
of the future. How does your reality match what you
expected? Even if some of the major markers are there,
the details probably look different. No one can anticipate
what challenges they will face. Perhaps you have a job that
you dreamed of, but you live in a place where you never
imagined being. Maybe challenges delayed or changed
your plans altogether.

Knowing what we know now and recognizing
that there are details we will never be able to manifest by
wishful thinking, let's embrace the mystery. The one who
guides us is faithful and good, and his plans are better for
us than any we could make for ourselves. He sees what we
cannot, so we can trust him with our lives and delight in
the mysterious joys that unfold.

**Lord, I have learned to be content in my life, and I
want to grow in the awe and wonder of witnessing your
miracles of mercy continue to play out around and
within me. Open my eyes as I trust you.**

TRUSTWORTHY LEADERSHIP

Good leadership is built on love and truth,
for kindness and integrity are what keep leaders
in their position of trust.

PROVERBS 20:28

Charisma may win some favor in the short term, but without tried-and-true character, charisma alone will not provide good leadership. Instead of judging leaders on how charming they are, we should look to the legacy of their lives. Have they built loving and trusting relationships in their families and communities? Consider whether they are known for their kindness and integrity.

Without trust, there is room for all sorts of trouble. First, we must look at ourselves and consider where we can build upon the foundation of Christ's kingdom values in our own lives. Jesus said that we will be judged with the same measure we use against others. Instead of overly focusing on the flaws of others, let's shift our focus to examine our own hearts first. Do we lead as well as we want others to?

Jesus Christ, your leadership is so full of love and truth. You call people up and out of their shame and their complacency. Search me, know me, and refine me in the light of your mercy so that I will stand the tests of this world with your love as my core motivation.

PAIN, A GREAT TEACHER

When you are punished severely,
you learn your lesson well—
for painful experiences do wonders to change your life.

PROVERBS 20:30

Not every painful circumstance in this life is a direct result of our own actions; not every challenge is a punishment. Most of us know that the fruit of discipline can lead to our transformation. Instead of framing every painful period as a punishment, let's look at how the pain can teach us to become more like the Lord—more loving, more open, and more kind.

If you have experienced any sort of great loss in your life—the death of a loved one, for instance—you probably know the feeling of instant kinship with those who have also grieved deeply. It is like being initiated into a club that no one wants to join. No one likes to be in pain, but we can empathize with others in a deeper way when we know the experience ourselves. Instead of trying to avoid the pain that is so clearly with us, let's turn to it and ask what it has to teach us. What wisdom there is in this!

Savior, I want to know the wonders of expanding in your love as much as I have known the pain of expanding in grief. Transform me in the process. Thank you.

STEERED BY THE KING

It's as easy for God to steer a king's heart for his purposes
as it is for him to direct the course of a stream.

PROVERBS 21:1

As God's children, we have become priests and royalty in
his kingdom. First Peter 2:9 says, "You are God's chosen
treasure—priests who are kings, a spiritual 'nation'
set apart as God's devoted ones. He called you out of
darkness to experience his marvelous light, and now he
claims you as his very own." He claims us as his very own.
It is as easy for him to steer our hearts for his purposes
as it is for him to direct a stream. What a wonderfully
beautiful reality!

We can confidently live out the love of Christ
without the need to second-guess ourselves all the time.
When we trust that God will have his way no matter
what, we can live boldly and bravely. God is as much
Redeemer as he is Creator, so let's not let discouragement
darken our hope. He can do far more with us than we
could ever imagine.

**Redeemer, thank you for calling me your own. I openly
submit my heart to you again and again. You are my King,
and I am your willing servant. Use me for your glory.**

THE FRUIT OF FORESIGHT

Brilliant ideas pay off and bring you prosperity,
but making hasty, impatient decisions
will only lead to financial loss.

PROVERBS 21:5

Brilliant ideas are not get-rich-quick schemes. The fruit of God's kingdom and his ways last much longer than the wealth of any person, industry, or nation. Instead of rushing into decisions without proper due diligence or wise counsel, we must resist the hasty pull of impatience and instead weigh our decisions with wisdom and grounded advice.

There is tremendous benefit in strategic foresight. If we only look to the immediate benefits we could obtain, we may miss out on the lasting effects that put our long-term resources at risk. We can give space to consider any decision worth making. Haste leads to more risk than may be wise to take on. We should be purposeful and grounded in our decision-making. Brilliant ideas won't fade overnight; they will stand the test of time.

Jesus Christ, thank you for your wise counsel and for the reminder that hasty decisions are probably not worth the risk. Give me discernment in my decisions and time to consider the outcome of the opportunities presented to me today.

LESSONS LEARNED

Senseless people learn their lessons the hard way,
but the wise are teachable.

PROVERBS 21:11

Life is full of many lessons that we all must learn. Some learn the hard way, while others allow the wisdom of the instruction and experience of others to inform their practices. We see this in history, family systems, and the people around us. We must not be so full of pride that we won't allow the lived experience of others to teach us what not to do.

This is not to say that any of us can avoid failure. It is a part of life. But we can learn from the wisdom of those who have gone before us. We do not have to make the same mistakes they did, and we can start from a place of humble understanding. We can see this play out in the sciences. We have a basis of working knowledge, theories, and discoveries. We build upon what has already been discovered so we can go further. Let's do this with our spiritual lives as well.

Wise God, thank you for the wisdom that is all around me in the lived experiences and teachings of those who have gone before me. May my heart remain humble, trusting, and shrewd, building upon the blocks that have already been laid.

RIGHTEOUS INSTRUCTION

A godly, righteous person has the ability to bring the light
of instruction to the wicked even though he despises what
the wicked do.

PROVERBS 21:12

There are many examples of godly wisdom being given
to those who didn't choose righteousness for themselves
but benefited from the instruction of the wise. Daniel
and Joseph both had favorable positions with the rulers
of their day (in Babylon and Egypt, respectively). God
moved through them, even in the face of great danger,
and gave them favor to speak the truth to these leaders.

We don't have to agree with our leaders to offer
wisdom to them. It is more important that we stand in
truth and don't compromise our integrity to win the
favor of others. We must remain strong in the truth, and
we must not change in order to appease others. We can
present the truth with wisdom and care, but we should
not change our minds only to stoke a leader's ego. We can
trust God to do what he will, in the same way both Daniel
and Joseph did.

**Righteous One, help me to be truthful and wise in how I
interact with others—from leaders to acquaintances. May
I walk in the light of your kingdom's truth in every way.**

GENEROSITY THAT SOOTHES

Try giving a secret gift to the one who is angry with you and watch his anger disappear. A kind, generous gift goes a long way to soothe the anger of one who is livid.

PROVERBS 21:14

Kindness can break down the hardest of walls between us, and an intentional act of generosity can soothe the anger of another. Consider how you can actively use kindness and generosity to build a bridge where there has been offense, hurt, or anger. What can you do today to soften someone's heart toward you?

Although it is not our job to pacify everyone around us, it is wise to apply gracious generosity to the people in our lives. Perhaps we have strained relationships we want to save. Maybe we know people we need to interact with who harbor ill feelings against us. Let's apply the instruction of this proverb today. Even as we give, may we do it with hearts of generosity that don't expect anything in return. We should give out of kindness, not trying to manipulate a certain response. Only the person on the receiving end can choose how they will react, but as far as we're concerned, we can choose the generous way of Christ.

Generous Jesus, you give so much grace—grace upon grace! May I be like you in doing the same.

DEEPLY ROOTED SATISFACTION

To love pleasure for pleasure's sake
will introduce you to poverty. Indulging
in a life of luxury will never make you wealthy.

PROVERBS 21:17

When we find our satisfaction in things, we will never be truly gratified. The more we consume, the more we will want. We can see this very clearly in our consumerist society. If we are constantly yearning for the newest, latest, greatest of anything, we may just spend ourselves into debt and find that we are still not satisfied.

There is wisdom in restraint, and there is benefit to intentionality. We are constantly fed messages of what we need to finally complete our lives or to make us better, but in reality, that contentment does not come from anything we could buy. We need to be wary of how much time we spend consuming ads and messages that infiltrate our mindset. They are marketed to make us want more. Instead, let's spend more time unplugged, more time with the Lord, and more time meditating on his Word and kingdom values. We find our satisfaction in him and what he created us to do.

Wonderful One, you are the only one who can truly satisfy my soul. Thank you for the reminder that there are messages all around telling me otherwise. Help me to practice discretion and intentional rejection of the norms in favor of your ways.

PURPOSEFUL PLANS

The wicked bring on themselves the very suffering they
planned for others, for their treachery comes back
to haunt them.

PROVERBS 21:18

What we sow, we will reap. If we sow seeds of bitterness,
then we will have weeds of resentment in our lives. If we
plan to cause others suffering, we can expect to suffer
ourselves. We gain nothing in hurting others. Even
when we watch our enemies suffer, it will not bring us
satisfaction or joy. Perhaps you can forgive someone
today. Maybe you have a vendetta that you can let go of.
Ask the Lord to highlight a situation, if there is one, and
respond accordingly.

When we plan to do good, bless others, and offer
mercy-kindness and forgiveness, we will receive the fruit
of those seeds in our lives. When our plans are rooted
in the righteousness of Christ and his kingdom, we can
abandon the need for revenge. All plans are purposeful,
so we must be wise about what we meditate on.

Wise One, I don't want to wish suffering on others.
Help me forgive those I need to release. I need your
guidance to let go of my idea of what justice looks like.
Help me trust you and focus on how to be an agent of
mercy and goodness in this life.

TREASURES OF RIGHTEOUSNESS

The lovers of God who chase after righteousness will find all their dreams come true: an abundant life drenched with favor and a fountain that overflows with satisfaction.

PROVERBS 21:21

There is no one-size-fits-all approach to life. We should be more focused on the values that guide our footsteps than on the possible physical outcomes of our choices. We can leave comparison for those who resist the peace of God. The confidence of Christ is to be our foundation. When we chase after righteousness, we are not guaranteed lives free of pain, suffering, or trials, but we are promised abundant life with the satisfaction of the Spirit.

It is important to move our focus from the outward to the inner worlds of our hearts, souls, and lives. We can live in simplicity and still have the overflowing joy of Christ as our reward. As we become grateful stewards of what is ours, God expands our understanding in the wonderful scope of his perspective. Satisfaction is not in things bought or achieved but in the open and liberating love of God, which is available to us all without measure.

Righteous Lord, I choose to chase after you and your kingdom. I don't need fancy things to be satisfied. I just need you. Reveal where you are and what you are doing in and through me today.

WISE WARRIORS

A warrior filled with wisdom ascends into the high place and releases breakthrough, bringing down the strongholds of the mighty.

PROVERBS 21:22

Ephesians 6:11 advises, "Put on God's complete set of armor provided for us, so that you will be protected as you fight against the evil strategies of the accuser!" Our fight, the chapter of Ephesians goes on to say, is not with humans but with the oppressive principalities and authorities in rebellion against God's kingdom. As we wear the full armor that God has provided, we rise victorious with Christ in his triumph over evil.

We can use the wisdom of God to release the strategies of God's kingdom over regions, cities, and situations through our prayers. Let's ascend in the Spirit to the high place, where Christ is seated, and partner with him in our powerful prayers. Instead of fighting those around us, we can spend our energies fighting the influences behind them and releasing the kingdom of Christ over all of our struggles.

Victorious One, it is in your authority that I stand and partner with your purposes on the earth. When I am distracted by the injustices around me, remind me that wisdom is in seeking resolutions even beyond specific people. I choose to put on the full armor you offer.

SAGE SECRETS

Taking the easy way out is the habit of a lazy man, and it will be his downfall. All day long he thinks about all the things that he craves, for he hasn't learned the secret that the generous man has learned: extravagant giving never leads to poverty.

PROVERBS 21:25–26

The last line of this verse in Proverbs in the Septuagint reads, "The righteous lavish on others mercy and compassion." Whatever we generously give from a heart of compassion is never wasted. The kingdom principle of generosity always leads to us receiving more, for God's resources never diminish and are always overflowing. When we give grace, there is more grace for us. When we offer kindness, we make room to receive more kindness from our good Father.

We are never working from a deficit in Christ's kingdom. When we run dry, he is the river that rushes to fill us again. When we are hungry, he offers us nourishment to satisfy our souls. When we are thirsty, he is the living water that quenches our longing. Let's act in the same generosity of heart that our Father does. Extravagant giving never leads to poverty.

Generous Lord, you always offer more than I could ever conceive. Fill me so that I can pour out your mercy on others in even greater measure.

ULTIMATE VICTORY

You can do your best to prepare for the battle,
but ultimate victory comes from the Lord God.

PROVERBS 21:31

It is well and good that we prepare for what lies ahead.
We are not taken by surprise when we see what is clearly
coming. We must be sure to not mistake this verse as an
excuse to put off preparing for the future. At the same
time, no matter how much we prepare, the victory is not
in our efforts but in the hand of the Lord.

We do not act on behalf of God; we partner *with*
his purposes. Do we truly trust that the battle ultimately
belongs to the Lord? There are numerous examples in the
Bible that show the odds stacked against God's people, but
as they listen to his instruction and do as he asked, God
fights for them, even as they do their own part. We have
the privilege of partnering with God's purposes in our
lives, asking him for direction and vision and doing what
he says. Even as we walk it out, God fights with and for us.

**Great Redeemer, yours is the victory in life and in this
world. I trust you more than I trust my own senses.
Lead, guide, and transform me in your wisdom.**

RIGHTEOUS REPUTATION

A beautiful reputation is more to be desired than great riches, and to be esteemed by others is more honorable than to own immense investments.

PROVERBS 22:1

There are powerful, awful people in this world. There are also unassuming, wise, and merciful ones among us. It is much better to be known as a kindhearted and generous person than to have great wealth. Think through the guiding values of your life. Are you a person of your word, following through on your promises? Consider whether you are kind to all or only to those whom you can gain something from.

We should be representatives of righteousness in every area of our lives—not being compassionate with some and demeaning to others. God sees us in every interaction and circumstance. He does not excuse our lack of love, no matter how easily we can make excuses for ourselves. May we be people who esteem the favor of God more than the fickle favor of the powerful. As we live with integrity and honor, we should offer respect to everyone we meet. This is how a righteous reputation is born.

Jesus, I trust that caring more about your opinion than I care about the opinions of others will guide me into the beauty of integrity. I choose to live in the light of your kingdom and to follow your ways, no matter the cost.

PROBLEM SOLVERS

A prudent person with insight foresees danger coming and prepares himself for it. But the senseless rush blindly forward and suffer the consequences.

PROVERBS 21:3

We should heed the caution of wisdom as we move through this life. We don't have to reject sensibleness in order to embrace faith. In fact, it is good to consider the reasonable and practical aspects of life, including the foresight of possible challenges. Prudence leads to preparedness, and being prepared can bolster our faith.

Consider the people in your life who are natural problem solvers. Do they anticipate what could happen and prepare themselves for it? Perhaps you have not appreciated their anticipatory nature, but there is value in taking others' concerns seriously. Learning from them, we can look for how to be problem solvers, not brushing off the importance of foresight. It is the senseless who do not consider what is coming and who suffer for it.

Wise One, I know that you see everything—what has come before, what is happening now, and what is on the horizon. Help me to be more prudent and to take more seriously those who are good examples of natural prudence. I want to be prepared.

TENDER SURRENDER

Laying your life down in tender surrender before the Lord
will bring life, prosperity, and honor as your reward.

PROVERBS 22:4

There is no greater posture in life than to live in tender
surrender before the Lord. He is our Maker, and he is our
Sustainer. He knows our quirks, plans, and hopes. He has
our best at heart, wanting always what is life-giving for
us. He does not control or abuse his children. He loves us
with a love that is immeasurable, and it never, ever gives
up on us. He is an astoundingly patient and caring Father.

When we offer our surrender, not because we feel
we must, but because we love and trust the Lord, we
experience the liberation of his love in our lives. We have
the endless resources of his kingdom at our disposal. He
refreshes us when we are discouraged. He shines his light
of revelation on our confusion when we look to him. He
is worthy of all our trust, and he is worth yielding to no
matter the circumstance or sacrifice.

**Loving Jesus, I surrender to you out of love and honor.
I trust that you always have my best in mind, and you
work in practical acts of mercy in the lives of those who
trust you. Have your way in me.**

DEDICATED DIRECTIONS

Dedicate your children to God and point them in the way that they should go, and the values they've learned from you will be with them for life.

PROVERBS 22:6

Think through the values you want to instill in your children. Consider which standards you hope the next generation will uphold in their own lives. As you do, you can adjust your own approach to prepare them. Dedicate the young ones in your life to the Lord and to his mercy, and teach them how to rely on God in all things. Teach them how to trust in his timing and instruct them in the power of their actions as well as in what they say.

The lessons that truly mold us stay with us for life. Why, then, would we leave our directives to chance or to the whim of the moment? If we are purposeful with our own values, then we will also teach the younger generations the value of integrity. Wisdom never goes to waste. You can allow the fruit of the Spirit to be your guide as you parent and as you mentor young ones.

Great God, just as I have dedicated my own life, I also dedicate to your kingdom the lives of those I influence. May they learn the value of mercy, kindness, justice, and truth. May they walk in your ways and go even further than I have. Advance your kingdom in the next generation.

SEPTEMBER

PEACEFUL SOLUTIONS

Say goodbye to a troublemaker and you'll say goodbye
to quarrels, strife, tension, and arguments, for a
troublemaker traffics in shame.

PROVERBS 22:10

When tension strains our relationships, it can cause a
lot of strife within us. We cannot avoid arguments with
others; misunderstandings happen with everyone. It is
not the normal quarrels in relationships that the writer
of this proverb is addressing. Some people stir up trouble
wherever they go. Troublemakers who pick fights, cause
problems, and shame others regularly are not people to
whom we need to give full access to our lives.

In order to have healthy relationships, we need
to build better boundaries around our lives. There will
be times when the troublemakers that cause quarrels
are family, and we cannot say goodbye forever. We can,
however, be much more intentional with the time we give
them, the opportunities we offer to them, and the weight
we give their words. We can love others well when we
offer supports of loving care for our own souls.

**Lord, you are a peacemaker, not a shame trafficker.
Help me to have the wisdom, discernment, and
practical measures to promote peace in my home and
in my relationships. Thank you.**

RESERVOIRS OF REVELATION

God passionately watches over his deep reservoir of revelation-knowledge, but he subverts the lies of those who pervert the truth.

PROVERBS 22:12

The revelation-knowledge of God always reflects his heart. He will not condemn those he has promised to set free. He will not stop operating in generous grace and magnanimous mercy. We must be sure to weigh the word of the Lord as it comes through others against the nature of God. He will never go against himself, and he won't ever change.

We can find deep wells of wisdom in the presence of the Lord. Let's press into him today, looking to his wisdom over the world's. It is important to give ourselves time to receive from his overflowing fountain of mercy. He supplies fresh grace for us, and there is more revelation to expand our perspectives in him. When we seek the Lord, we find him. He reveals himself to those who look for him. With that in mind, may we put aside the temporary trappings of temptation and turn our energies toward the one who gives abundant life to the hungry.

Jesus, you refresh my soul in the waves of your mercy. Wash over me again today and renew my hope in you. Show me more of yourself, expanding my understanding of your great love.

READY IN SEASON

You'll become winsome and wise when you treasure the
beauty of my words. And always be prepared to share
them at the appropriate time.

PROVERBS 22:18

When we treasure something, we hold it close to our
hearts. We are sure to guard it, knowing how valuable it
is. We don't lose it easily or misplace it mindlessly. As we
treasure the Word of God, we meditate on it, letting its
transformative power go beyond our thoughts into our
hearts where it plants seeds that will grow. We are ready
to share his Word at the appropriate time if we give it
proper attention and nurture it with care.

We prepare our hearts and minds in Christ by
leaning on the support of the Holy Spirit and by giving
God our devoted attention on a regular basis. We cannot
be prepared to share wise words if we neglect wisdom's
instruction in our lives. As we live out wisdom, we should
also allow time to meditate on how we are being changed
by the wisdom that guides us.

**Wise Leader, I want to treasure the beauty of your
words and the beauty of who you are more and more as
I grow. Thank you.**

SUPPORT THE POOR

Never oppress the poor or pass laws with the motive of crushing the weak. For the Lord will rise to plead their case and humiliate the one who humiliates the poor.

PROVERBS 22:22–23

When we use our power, privilege, or resources for the Lord, we help lift the weak instead of crushing them further into poverty. God is never in support of oppression, and we shouldn't be either. We need to look at the systems we support, how we give and to whom we give our money. This surely affects and reflects on what we claim to believe.

Jesus personified this approach in his life and ministry. He didn't turn away anyone who wanted to follow him. He challenged the religious who used the law to oppress the poor. He spent much of his time with those to whom others wouldn't give the time of day. We are not called to be appeasers of the powerful but to be powerhouses of mercy to all.

Liberator, you set the captives free, and you heal the sick. You don't turn away from the weak or ostracized; you go to them. May I be just like you.

GENERATIONAL UNDERSTANDING

The previous generation has set boundaries in place.
Don't you dare move them just to benefit yourself.

PROVERBS 22:28

We are foolish if we neglect the wisdom and purposes
with which previous generations built boundaries.
This refers to moving property lines in order to benefit
ourselves over our neighbors, and it could also refer to
moving landmarks or memorials placed by ancestors.
The wisdom of Christ always moves in mercy, and this
includes physically, emotionally, and spiritually.

We need to be sure not to neglect the moral
boundaries that previous generations modeled either.
Where they sought to uphold the law of Christ's love,
let's give it due honor. We can learn many lessons from
previous generations—both what to repeat and what
not to repeat. In the clarity of hindsight, we should not
forget to look for what they did right, not only where
they missed the mark. We do well when we look to why
previous generations did what they did before we defend
or oppose carrying it on. Where there is mercy, there is
justice. We can stand on the truth of Christ and ascend
the steps that others have laid before us.

**Majestic Father, you are the same yesterday, today, and
forever. Though we often get you wrong, you never
forsake your faithfulness. Thank you.**

SHARPEN YOUR SKILLS

If you are uniquely gifted in your work,
you will rise and be promoted.
You won't be held back—you'll stand before kings!

PROVERBS 22:29

Whatever talents or skills you have, take the time to improve them even more through continued learning and hard work. As you sharpen these skills, you will find your efforts being rewarded. Don't worry about others around you; focus on what you are good at, spending time in both practice and refinement. Learn from those who are in that field already. Read about what others have done to improve. And keep doing it.

If you want to succeed in life, hard work is necessary. Don't resist the natural talents you have; as you embrace them and utilize them within your field, you will have a clearer understanding of where to put your time and energy. Follow the passion that God has put within you, use your gifts, and live according to his values. Put your head down and do the work, and at the right time, you will rise and be promoted.

Creator, thank you for making me uniquely in your image. I don't want to resist my nature—what you put in me—in order to fit someone else's mold. Give me clarity and vision as I put my hands to work.

CAREFUL CONSIDERATION

Don't compare yourself to the rich. Surrender your selfish
ambition and evaluate them properly. For no sooner do
you start counting your wealth than it sprouts wings
and flies away like an eagle in the sky—here today,
gone tomorrow!

PROVERBS 23:4–5

There is no need to spend our time and energy comparing
ourselves to the rich when Christ has liberated us to live
in the fullness of his love within our current reality. We
should be careful to know the motivations behind our
ambition. We need not blindly follow our ambition but
surrender it to the Lord. Jesus said in Luke 12:34, "Where
you deposit your treasure, that is where you fix your
thoughts—and your heart will long to be there also."

We have no further to look than our thoughts to
better understand the motivations of our hearts. With
careful consideration under the light of the Spirit's rays
of wisdom, we can surrender what is rooted in selfish
ambition and refocus our vision on the life-giving ways of
Christ. There is no gain in winning all the wealth in the
world at the cost of our own souls.

**Jesus, I want to walk in the light of your ways in every
area of my life, including in my finances. May I be
quick in generosity and slow in self-serving hoarding.
I surrender to you.**

PRUDENT PERCEPTIONS

Be sensible when you dine with a stingy man
and don't eat more than you should.

PROVERBS 23:6

If we find ourselves at the home of a stingy person, we
should be aware of how much we receive from them.
Though they may offer it willingly with their lip service,
in their hearts they are resentful. Pay attention to the little
comments they make offhandedly. This often will reveal
their true feelings. While we cannot read minds, if we
know a person's track record, we can act accordingly.

We must not ignore the areas of our own lives in
which we act grudgingly. Perhaps we do not have good
boundaries around what we give our yeses to, and we
often find ourselves in situations we wish we could get
out of. No one else is responsible for our agreements. We
need to be wise with what we agree to so that we may give
our enthusiastic participation rather than our waning
attention. When we are intentional with our generosity,
we can thrive in our practices and in our personal lives.

Generous Father, I'm so grateful that you are not stingy
with your love or with your resources. Help me to
have better discernment with others and with my own
offerings. Thank you.

PARTNER WITH THE FATHER

Never move a long-standing boundary line or attempt to take land that belongs to the fatherless. For they have a mighty protector, a loving redeemer, who watches over them, and he will stand up for their cause.

PROVERBS 23:10–11

The Father does not side with those who try to cheat others out of their inheritance. He never condones self-promotion at another's expense. He always leads with justice and mercy. Do we trust him to steadfastly follow through on his promises? If we do, there's no reason to try to trick others out of what is theirs in order to bolster what we have.

When we partner with the Father, we stand on the side of protecting the innocent, restoring moved boundaries, and offering mercy-kindness in all that we do. When we oppose the poor, we oppose the Lord. When we are overly focused on our own gain, we miss out on what the Lord wants to do through our service. There is much more to life than wealth and comfort, so let's be sure to focus our attention on what the Father is doing, what he is concerned with, and partner with him.

Faithful Father, I know that there is never an excuse for cheating others out of what is rightfully theirs. You are a mighty protector, a loving Redeemer, and I stand with you.

ANOINTED WORDS

My beloved child, when your heart is full of wisdom,
my heart is full of gladness. And when you speak
anointed words, we are speaking mouth to mouth!

PROVERBS 23:15–16

The wisdom of the Lord is given to us through his Spirit. It is offered to us through fellowship with himself. First John 2:27 says, "His anointing teaches you all that you need to know, for it will lead you into truth, not a counterfeit. So just as the anointing has taught you, remain in him." When we remain in the Lord, we have access to all that we need to know. With his Word living within us, he speaks directly to and through our yielded lives.

Consider how long it has been since you last spent devoted, distraction-free time with the Lord. Perhaps you can carve out even a few minutes of solitude to connect with the Spirit who is so very near. His loving wisdom offers what you need. Whatever you are deficient in, he is overflowing with. Look to him and find refreshment for your soul. Fill up on him, and you will have all you need to offer others in the anointing of his presence.

Anointed One, you are the wisdom that I crave. Fill me up with the riches of your Word, and let hope rise within me as you speak your life-giving and gracious words.

PASSIONATE WORSHIP

Don't allow the actions of evil men to cause you to burn with anger. Instead, burn with unrelenting passion as you worship God in holy awe.

PROVERBS 23:17

We cannot avoid the actions of others. Some people plot to do evil and cause harm to others, and they follow through on it. Though we are angry at the injustice of it, let's not allow rage to consume our beings. We can instead turn our passion to the Lord, who is good, just, and true. We can take our passion and use it to worship God in spirit and truth, asking for his wisdom and insight to settle us and refine our focus in practical ways that serve others.

Psalm 37:8 instructs us to "stay away from anger and revenge." In Psalm 86:15, we are reminded of God's powerful nature: "But Lord, your nurturing love is tender and gentle. You are slow to get angry yet so swift to show your faithful love. You are full of abounding grace and truth." God is so merciful. May we worship him in awe, "with clean hearts, free from frustration or strife" (1 Timothy 2:8), as we consider how good he is.

YAHWEH, I know that you are righteous and just, and you will not let the oppressed wither under the abuse of the wicked. I partner with you, and I will stand for justice and mercy at all times.

LIVING HOPE

Your future is bright and filled with a living hope that will never fade away.

PROVERBS 23:18

No matter what this season has looked like for you, no matter what you have gone through or left behind in your past, take heart in the wonderfully liberating mercies of Christ. Your future is bright. It is filled with a living hope that will never fade away because it is filled with the presence of Christ with you. Even the hardest days are full of the glory of the Lord.

It may be hard to recognize what is growing under the surface, but when it sprouts up, you will see that the seeds of mercy have been maturing, and not one day were you without the presence of the Lord. Even when you cannot see just yet all that God has been working in you, rest assured that you will. Take courage, for the living hope of Christ is your strength. Let his life within you revive your own. There is so much more to come and so much life ahead for you.

Redeemer, I yield my heart to you again. Revive my hope in you as you reveal where you have already been moving in the details of my life. You are my vision, Jesus. I look to you.

WELLS OF WISDOM

As you listen to me, my beloved child, you will grow in
wisdom and your heart will be drawn into understanding,
which will empower you to make right decisions.

PROVERBS 23:19

What we fill up on will either nourish or deplete us. No
matter what, it will affect our energy, our vision, and
our health. We should be sure to take our soul health as
seriously as we take our physical health. If we watch what
we eat, feeding ourselves nutrient-dense foods, but don't
take care of what we are filling our minds with, then we
neglect a vital part of our health.

We should strive to listen to the wise words of Jesus
and to those who have gone before us—both written
within Scripture and the annals of history. Those who
led with wisdom have much to offer us, and those who
promoted pursuing peace, grace, truth, and justice are
worth our attention. There is so much wisdom to grow
in. We have the Spirit who constantly fills us up with the
revelation-knowledge of the Lord. If we want to be drawn
to understanding, we must listen to the wisdom of God.

**Wise God, I take time to listen to you today. My heart
is an open door to you. As I go about my day, whisper
your words of life, leading me and instructing me in
your incomparable wisdom.**

DEVOTED CARE

Give respect to your father and mother,
for without them you wouldn't even be here.
And don't neglect them when they grow old.

PROVERBS 23:22

Our caregivers raised us, fed us, and gave us what we
needed when we were helpless. We were their dependents,
relying on their love and attention to protect and nourish
us. As they grow old, we have the opportunity to return
the favor. Many of us have known loved ones who,
whether because of age or sickness, became dependent on
us for care.

What an honor it is to offer loving care to those
who have raised us. Though no family system is perfect,
we should not neglect the opportunity to honor our
loved ones and to help them when they need it. When
we are able, may we offer our time, our resources, and
our attention to nourish, love, and protect those who are
vulnerable. There is blessing in it.

Jehovah, thank you for the reminder to honor older
generations. In a society that does not prioritize this,
I choose your kingdom ways. Even where there are
complicated feelings, I will not neglect the care that
I can provide. Move in mighty ways within my heart,
refining me in your love as I help those who raised me.

REPUTED CHARACTER

Don't be drunk with wine but be known as one who
enjoys the company of the lovers of God.

PROVERBS 23:31

Our character is built as much in the privacy of our own
homes as it is within the halls of community. When we
allow any substance more control over our lives than we
give the love of God, we are subject to its cravings. We
must recognize if there are any areas out of balance in our
private lives. Perhaps there are things that we turn to for
numbing, coping, or escaping more often than we turn to
the Lord.

Romans 6 is a great refresher for walking in the
freedom that Christ has offered us. "So tell me, what
benefit ensued from doing those things that you're now
ashamed of? It left you with nothing but a legacy of
shame and death. But now, as God's loving servants, you
live in joyous freedom from the power of sin" (vv. 21–22).
We are brought deeper into the holiness of God, found in
our union with Jesus Christ. We can live as those who are
truly free, then, from all our shame.

**Jesus Christ, I long for you more than I crave the things
of this world. I don't want to just know you with my
mind; I want to know you with my whole being.**

KINGDOM BUILDERS

Wise people are builders—they build families, businesses, communities. And through intelligence and insight their enterprises are established and endure.

PROVERBS 24:3

While the foolish don't think about what they can build that will stand the test of time, the wise are architects and builders who leave a lasting mark. Wisdom offers strategies to build legacies within families, businesses, and communities. The wisdom of God bolsters relationships and economies. It offers all that we need to grow and flourish.

Think about what you are building with your life. What are you investing in with your time, energy, and attention? Perhaps you have neglected areas that need some focus and care to come back into alignment with Christ. If so, today is a great day to do it. Grace overflows in the presence of Jesus, and there is so much mercy to redeem and restore even the most far-gone situation. Don't be afraid of admitting your weaknesses, for God's generous grace meets you in them. He rushes in to help you, giving you insight, strength, and support. Lean on him, and he will teach you how to rebuild.

Christ, I want to be a builder for your kingdom. I long to reflect the lavish love that liberates me in every area of my life. Be glorified as I partner with your purposes.

SPIRITUAL RICHES

Because of their skilled leadership, the hearts of people
are filled with the treasures of wisdom and the pleasures
of spiritual wealth.

PROVERBS 24:4

Wise builders are capable leaders. They can be trusted to
stand upon the foundation of mercy, truth, and justice
and use them as pillars upon which to build. When a wise
person shares his or her wealth of wisdom, others benefit
from the treasure by incorporating it into their own
hearts and lives.

Consider the spiritual riches that you have
garnered from the leadership of others. Which can you
share with others today? The King of kings and Lord of
lords is the one who rules and reigns over every leader.
Instead of being discouraged by the failures we see in
poor leadership, we can look to the example of those who
are doing it right and put that wisdom into practice.

**King of Kings, mold me into a vessel of love, integrity,
and justice. May my life be a reflection of your powerful
mercy, no matter who I am around or what I am doing.
I seek to honor you with all of my life—every part of it.
Fill me with the treasures of your wisdom, and I will
share them freely with those around me.**

WINNING WISDOM

Wisdom can make anyone into a mighty warrior,
and revelation-knowledge increases strength.

PROVERBS 24:5

Physical strength and endurance help us in many
situations in life, but spiritual strength is of much more
value. We should not neglect the training of our hearts,
minds, and spirits in the discipline of God's kingdom.
Romans 12:2 instructs us to "be inwardly transformed by
the Holy Spirit through a total reformation of how you
think. This," Paul goes on to say, "will empower you to
discern God's will as you live a beautiful life."

This is also echoed in 1 Timothy 4:8, which says,
"Athletic training only benefits you for a short season,
but righteousness brings lasting benefit in everything."
When we are transformed by the indwelling wisdom of
the Holy Spirit, his grace-strength becomes our own, and
his insights broaden our perspectives and understanding.
Wisdom can make anyone into a mighty warrior. Why
not you?

**Holy Spirit, thank you for your presence that dwells
within me. I surrender to your wisdom, and I ask for
your revelation-insight to light up my understanding
and liberate me in the areas where I've felt stuck. Give
me courage as I look to you.**

PURPOSE TO DO GOOD

If you plan to do evil, it's as wrong as doing it.
And everyone detests a troublemaker.

PROVERBS 24:9

If we do not grow weary of doing good, we reap our reward in due season (Galatians 6:9). If we trust in the Lord and do good, we experience the peace of God in our midst. We have nothing to hide when our hearts are focused on how we can serve others in love and extend the kingdom of Christ in our lives.

We already know that God looks at the heart and discerns our thoughts and intentions. It is as wrong for us to make evil plans in our hearts as it is to follow through on them. When we surrender our hearts to the Holy Spirit, we make room for the transformation of our inner worlds in his marvelous mercy. Romans 10:10 reminds us that "the heart that believes in him receives the gift of the righteousness of God—and then the mouth confesses, resulting in salvation." We will not be disappointed as we trust in him, and we are at our best when we look for ways to do good in the name of the Lord.

Liberating Lord, search my heart and know me. Reveal anything within me that goes against your mercy-kindness. Transform me as I follow you.

FAITHFULNESS UNDER PRESSURE

If you faint when under pressure,
you have need of courage.

PROVERBS 24:10

It is a reflection of our humanity when we waver in fear.
The courage we need to endure under pressure can be
bolstered by a great many things—an encouraging word
from a friend, a reminder of who we are, a commitment
to justice, etc. These are all reflections of how the Spirit
can use outside influences to strengthen our resolve.

If you find yourself running low on resources with
nothing left to give, don't try to suffer through on your
own any longer. There's no need to give up what you have
fought so hard to overcome. Reach out for support from
trusted sources. Make room to rest up in little ways if
that is all you have time for. Pray and ask the Lord for the
power of his grace to embolden your heart. He is so very
faithful to you, no matter the pressures you are under.
He will never abandon you, and he always has help at the
ready. Ask him for it today.

**Faithful One, thank you for your persistent presence in
my life. I rely on your grace to strengthen me, especially
when I am weak, worn, and weary. Bolster my courage,
Father. I need you.**

Move into Action

Go and rescue the perishing! Be their savior! Why would you stand back and watch them stagger to their death?

PROVERBS 24:11

When we have the power to affect change, to reach out to the hurting and bind their wounds, it is imperative that we not stand back and watch them suffer. We cannot help everyone, but we can certainly help some. There is no excuse for our inaction and indifference to the suffering that happens around us. It is courage that emboldens our hearts into action. It is compassion that propels us to reach out in practical acts of mercy.

Take this as your invitation to move from simply having good intentions to putting them into action today. When we see someone struggling, let's reach out to help. When we see the vulnerable being taken advantage of, we can step in. Jesus' love was not a comfortable bubble around him that kept him safe or sanitary. It moved him into action, self-sacrifice, and into the mess of others. He lifted others up, rebuked their abusers, and healed their wounds. Let's be like Jesus and live out the love we have stored up in our hearts.

Jesus, I want to be more like you. May I be unashamed of your love, reaching out to those who need help and advocating for the defenseless. May I never turn a blind eye when I can lend a helping hand.

SWEET AS HONEY

Revelation-knowledge is a delicacy,
sweet like flowing honey that melts in your mouth.
Eat as much of it as you can, my friend!

PROVERBS 24:13

When you fill up on the sweetness of revelation-knowledge, "then you will perceive what is true wisdom, your future will be bright, and this hope living within you will never disappoint you" (v. 14). The revelations of God bring satisfying sweetness to your soul, filling you up with the light of his life. There is an abundance of wisdom in his presence. You need never go without it.

True wisdom is found in Christ. When we look to his life, ministry, example, and testimony, we cannot help but be awed by his incomparable mercy. No one else loved so fully and selflessly. Who but Jesus can save our souls? He came to set the sinners free and to liberate the oppressed from their bondage. There is nothing that the power of Christ's love has not already conquered, so let's give ourselves to knowing him more and more.

Christ, your love has transformed me, and I pray that the power of your mercy will continue to liberate me from the limitations of my small thinking. Your revelations are like honey to my soul and like water to quench my thirst. You are always better than I expect at every turn.

CONTINUE TO RISE

The lovers of God may suffer adversity and stumble seven
times, but they will continue to rise over and over again.

PROVERBS 24:16

Even though you may suffer hardship in this life
and stumble many times, each time you rise again
to overcome. Why? Because the light of Christ is
your strength. Jesus was clear when he said, "In this
unbelieving world you will experience trouble and
sorrows, but you must be courageous, for I have
conquered the world!" (John 16:33). He has overcome
what we could never conquer on our own, and it is in his
victory that we stand (and rise over and over again).

    Don't allow the struggles of yesterday to cloud
your choices today. Don't let it discourage your hope for
tomorrow. You can only begin where you are—whether
that looks like rising from your stumbling or forging
ahead in determination. With Christ as your shield,
strength, and covering, you have all that you need to rise
up once more. Keep going and don't give up.

**Powerful One, you are my strength and my song. You
are my hope and my strong tower. I trust you more than
I do my own feelings. Bolster my hope in your presence
and refresh me in your love once again.**

CAREFUL NOW!

Never gloat when your enemy meets disaster, and don't be quick to rejoice if he falls. For the Lord, who sees your heart, will be displeased with you and will pity your foe.

PROVERBS 24:17–18

When we are under pressure from others who make our lives more difficult, it can be hard to resist the pull to rejoice when they experience a setback. However, we know that Christ does not gloat, and he does not lord his goodness over our imperfections. He extends mercy to all in the same measure. We must leave room for compassion, even with those who have hurt us.

This does not mean that a feeling of relief when our foes stop tormenting us is not valid, for it is. But we need to make sure we do not desire anyone's misfortune. We can let our relief lead us to worship the Lord rather than using it to revel in our enemies' failures. Love keeps our hearts humble and soft, even to those we would never choose to be around. The mercy of God is more powerful than our pettiness, so let's make sure we are yielding to his mercy at every turn.

Merciful Jesus, I humble myself before you and ask for your love to guard my heart and responses. May I walk in the light of your love in all that I do, including in how I handle someone else's misfortune.

UNMOVED BY STATUS

Those enlightened with wisdom have spoken these
proverbs: Judgment must be impartial, for it is always
wrong to be swayed by a person's status.

PROVERBS 24:23

It is tempting to fall under the influence of someone's
status—whether that's wealth, fame, or power. Under this
influence, we can be blinded to a person's humanity and
faults. Judgment must be impartial, not taking a person's
class, wealth, or race into account. It is important to
recognize first that we all have biases. Once we are aware
of them, we can actively counteract them with the mercy
of Christ as our standard.

In your dealings with others today, don't let a
person's status be a reason to compromise your values.
In the parable of the good Samaritan (Luke 10:25–37),
Jesus highlighted the importance of active mercy and the
meaninglessness of status or ethnicity when it becomes an
excuse to ignore the needs of another. As we are moved
with compassion in Christ, we will show kindness and
mercy to all, no matter who they are or what they look like.

**Compassionate Christ, your wisdom always instructs
in active love, and I have no excuse to show favor to
some and withhold it from others. Fill me with your
compassionate mercy, Lord, that it would become my
motivation.**

HONEST FEEDBACK

Speaking honestly is a sign of true friendship.

PROVERBS 24:26

Honesty can be trusted, and it builds the bonds of friendship rather than breaking them down the way that lies do. Ephesians 4:25 says, "Discard every form of dishonesty and lying so that you will be known as one who always speaks the truth." Speaking the truth is a sign of integrity. When you are honest, you have nothing to hide.

We cannot manage others' reactions so much that we refuse to show up genuinely in our relationships. If we do, we are the only ones who can take the blame for the misrepresentation of ourselves or our opinions. Especially in trusted relationships, we need to refuse to be anything but honest. It requires vulnerability and the willingness to clearly communicate, but it is worth it in the end.

Lord, you are true in all that you are and all that you do. I ask for your help to be genuine and honest in my communication and in my relationships. May I not shrink back from the risk of being vulnerable with my friends, for I know that it is a bond builder, even if it feels scary. Give me wisdom, and I will act on it.

DIVIDENDS OF HARD WORK

Professional work habits prevent poverty from becoming your permanent business partner. And: If you put off until tomorrow the work you could do today, tomorrow never seems to come.

PROVERBS 24:33–34

If we keep putting off until tomorrow what could be done today, we will build the habit of putting things off indefinitely. Instead of letting our inner resistance keep us from moving ahead in things that are achievable, we can take small steps of consistency and do what needs to be done now—or at least start the process.

Consistency is much more important than motivation. Often motivation follows our movement. What steps can you take today to get something done that you have been putting off? It could be as simple as doing a load of laundry or going to the gym or as complex as looking into graduate programs that interest you. Whatever it is, make consistent efforts, and you will reap the rewards.

Father, I don't want to stay stuck in patterns of procrastination. Help me to build consistent, small steps that will lead me to where I want to go. I know it doesn't have to be all or nothing. Thank you.

HIDDEN IN GLORY

God conceals the revelation of his word in the hiding
place of his glory. But the honor of kings is revealed by
how they thoroughly search out the deeper meaning of all
that God says.

PROVERBS 25:2

Do we simply accept the wisdom of God through the
vessel of others' views and understandings, or do we
search for the deeper meaning behind his Word in
partnership with his Spirit? The Spirit gives us a deep
understanding of God's Word, revealing with the help of
his presence what we did not previously grasp. If you have
ever felt a light bulb go off in your mind, you know this
feeling. When a question is answered subtly within you
and that answer expands your understanding, you have
experienced the revelation of God.

The glory of God is radiant. It surrounds him.
Whenever we feel the expansively deep presence of God,
wisdom is near. May we hide ourselves in the glory of
God, searching for the deep wells of his wisdom. We need
not only be satisfied by surface knowledge. There is so
much more to discover as we delve into his depths.

**Glorious God, I come to you with a hungry heart and
an open mind today. As I spend time in your presence,
reveal a deeper truth of your character that I have not
yet grasped. I'm waiting on you.**

PURIFYING FIRE

If you burn away the impurities from silver,
a sterling vessel will emerge from the fire.

PROVERBS 25:4

We each have the opportunity to be refined by the fires of God's purifying presence. As we do, the core of who we are will shine brighter. Though silver will never be gold and gold will never be platinum, their true natures shine brightest when the impurities are burned away. No matter who we are or what we are made of, we can trust the refining process of our Creator. Even when the fires of life burn hot, he can use them to purify us.

Think through your life. Are there any areas that have been tried by fire? Perhaps you have experienced financial or relational upheaval. Maybe a sickness has rendered you weaker than you knew was possible. Trust the Lord, for he holds you even in the fire. As you go through the pain, know that the unimportant things in life melt away in the process. Your faith is being strengthened as you trust him, and he will not let you go.

Refiner, I trust you to hold me together even when I feel as if everything is falling apart. Refine my character in the trials of life so that I may come out clearer, stronger, and more myself than ever before.

HUMBLE PLACES OF HONOR

Don't boast in the presence of a king or promote yourself by taking a seat at the head table and pretending that you're someone important.

PROVERBS 25:6

It is much better for us to allow the leaders around us to promote us rather than to distinguish ourselves in places of importance. This is a matter of respect, not of confidence. In all things, we should remain humble. If we take ourselves too seriously, we may find ourselves humbled by others.

God is our King, and he promotes us at the right time. We can trust him to open doors of opportunity as we faithfully serve him. We don't have to concern ourselves with who sees us. As we work hard and lead with integrity, God will cause others to see our faithfulness. Even if we live small lives, God's favor can shine brightly over our hearts as we yield to his leadership in all we do. There's nothing wrong with being out of the spotlight. That is where many of the most amazing people dwell.

Jesus, I honor your leadership and love in my life. Though I want to be validated for what I do, may I never crave it so much that I reach for it. I want, more than anything, to be favored by you.

OCTOBER

PRACTICAL PATIENCE

Don't be hasty to file a lawsuit.
By starting something you wish you hadn't,
you could be humiliated when you lose your case.

PROVERBS 25:8

When we impulsively react in offense, we leave the grounding wisdom of the Lord. Wisdom is deliberate, and it takes its time. It does not react to unforeseen challenges with hasty frustration. There is always room to step back, slow down, and consider the effects of the actions we intend to take, especially if it is a drawn-out process that we might regret initiating.

The Spirit is our help in all things. "The Holy Spirit takes hold of us in our human frailty to empower us in our weakness" (Romans 8:26). If you don't yet notice the difference between reacting in haste or in grounded wisdom, ask the Spirit to help you discover the signs within yourself. A good place to start is to always take a step back when you feel your nervous system heightening before you make a rash decision. Patience is not just a virtue of the Spirit but is also a practice of walking in wisdom.

Great God, help me to slow down and reach out to the Spirit when I feel overwhelmed and in my weakness so that I don't rush headlong into decisions I will regret.

TRUSTWORTHY FRIENDS

Don't reveal another person's secret just to prove a point in an argument, or you could be accused of being a gossip and gain a reputation for being one who betrays the confidence of a friend.

PROVERBS 25:9–10

Discretion is an important element to learn in our conversations and interactions. If we expose someone with information given in confidence, we break the trust not only of their friendship but also of the people we are revealing it to. Gossips are not simply those who like to talk; they are people who cannot be trusted with private information. This is not a reputation anyone desires.

If we value our friends, we will learn to keep our mouths shut, even when others provoke us. It is not our place to share secrets that were offered to us in confidence in order to prove a point. It is an entirely different matter to seek counsel and help when a friend offers us information that reveals they are in danger. Let's look to the example of Christ and the wisdom of the Spirit to direct us. In short, our motivations will reveal how we should proceed.

Jesus, you are the most trustworthy friend available. Thank you for knowing me, loving me, and caring for me through all my weaknesses, failures, and struggles. May I be a trustworthy friend.

TREASURED WORDS

Winsome words spoken at just the right time are as appealing as apples gilded in gold surrounded with silver.

PROVERBS 25:11

An aptly spoken word can be as beautiful a gift as any you could imagine. Have you ever been extremely discouraged but were bolstered by the encouragement of a friend? Perhaps you could not figure out what decision to make, and wise counsel from someone helped to clarify your direction. Think through the times when the wisdom of Christ challenged you and gave you courage.

May you speak with intention today, being careful about what you say to others. Instead of mindlessly complaining, choose what you will give airtime. Let it start first in your thoughts, taking each captive. Second Corinthians 10:5 says, "We capture, like prisoners of war, every thought and insist that it bow in obedience to the Anointed One." When we do this in our minds, it will allow us to speak the words of Christ and his kingdom— words that bring life, hope, peace, and joy. These are words to be treasured.

Lord, I submit my thoughts to you, and I offer my heart to you again. Fill me with the wisdom of your Word and transform my mind in your perfect peace. I want to speak words that give hope and courage and are filled with love.

CROWNED WITH BEAUTY

When you humbly receive wise correction, it adorns your
life with beauty and makes you a better person.

PROVERBS 25:12

It is an honorable trait when we listen with open hearts.
Those who already think they know what they need to
know will resist the wise correction of Christ. Even wise
kings and sages, scholars and thought leaders recognize
the supreme importance of a curious and open mind. We
may know more today than we ever have, but there are
still mysteries to uncover, understanding to garner, and
experience to appreciate.

We become better people when we are open to
admitting where we get it wrong. From there, we can
move forward in expanded knowledge. Let's consider how
willing we are to listen to others. When we humble our
hearts, we learn from interactions with those who have
more experience than we do. We benefit when we readily
accept the correction of wisdom in our lives. As we allow
truth to pierce our hearts, we are transformed by its
correction. Let's not resist the changes that come with the
journey of life.

**Beautiful One, only you know all, see all, and understand
all. I look to you and to your character to weigh the
wisdom I receive from those around me. I choose to lead
with love and follow your ways with a humble heart.**

INVIGORATING CONFIDENCE

A reliable, trustworthy messenger refreshes the heart
of his master, like a gentle snowfall at harvest time.

PROVERBS 25:13

What an amazing relief it is to know the ones we can rely
upon in life. Whether it is in our workplaces, our families,
or our communities—we find a certain confidence and
freedom in knowing the ones we can reach out to and trust
to follow through on what they say they will do. May we be
reliable and trustworthy workers, friends, and neighbors—
and may we know this type of person in our lives.

If you have someone who comes to mind as you
think through this today, reach out to them and thank
them for being someone you can trust. Express the
benefit that they bring to your life and offer the genuine
gratitude you feel. Then consider how you, too, can grow
in dependability. If there are areas of improvement you
have been putting off for no good reason, today is the day
to move ahead. Determine today to be as reliable as those
you admire and follow through on a delayed promise.

**Trustworthy One, more than anyone else, I know that
you are reliable in love and justice. You are faithful
to your promises. May I be a dependable reflection of
your loyal love.**

REFRESHING TRUTHS

Clouds that carry no water and a wind that brings no
refreshing rain—that's what you're like when you boast
of a gift that you don't have.

PROVERBS 25:14

It is important to recognize what our lives are filled with.
Are we heavy with the wisdom of God? If we are full of
the presence of the Spirit, we will operate in the gifts he
has given us. Instead of bragging about who we think we
are, we can live out the truth of who we are in him and
humbly walk in the power of his love. When we do, we
are like glory clouds raining down God's goodness in the
lives of those we meet.

The wind of the Spirit brings new life. There is
redemption-rain on its way. As we let the Spirit's breeze
move us, we can bring refreshing truths to the people of
God. Whatever we are full of will overflow. May we spend
time in the presence of God, receiving his instruction,
wisdom, and overflowing mercy. As we fill up on the
goodness of his presence, he moves us where he wants us
to go, bringing the refreshing relief of his kindness into
every place we step.

**Glorious Spirit, you are the wind, and I am a cloud
waiting to be moved by you. Fill me with more of your
mercy, revealing the heart of the Father in deeper ways.**

A GENTLE APPROACH

Use patience and kindness when you want to persuade
leaders and watch them change their minds right
in front of you. For your gentle wisdom will quell the
strongest resistance.

PROVERBS 25:15

Soft words of truth can melt the strongest defenses. When
you want to persuade someone of a view that they have
been resistant to, the way to go about it isn't through
mockery or force. It is with patience and kindness that
hard hearts can soften to hear other perspectives. Be
intentional in your approach, and you will watch the
power of gentle wisdom transform even the skeptic right
in front of you.

A willingness to hear different viewpoints is
important. We should take constructive criticism and
consider opinions that go against our own, especially
when we are in leadership roles. As we do, we can
demonstrate how to be affable to those who present their
opposing views with patience and kindness. When we
practice humble listening, we may just find that there is
wisdom in what others have to say and not just in our
own opinions.

**Lord, thank you for the gentleness and strength of your
love. You are unwavering in mercy, and yet you never
force it on anyone. May I follow your kind lead in my
own relationships and interactions.**

JUST ENOUGH

When you discover something sweet, don't overindulge
and eat more than you need, for excess in anything can
make you sick of even a good thing.

PROVERBS 25:16

There is room for most pleasures in life. We should not
reject the goodness that God so freely offers for us to
experience. But wisdom reminds us that we can ingest too
much of even a good thing. We should not lose sight of
moderation in our lives. We can savor the sweet things, to
be sure. We can also stop ourselves from overindulging. We
will only dull our senses and make ourselves sick if we don't.

Galatians 5:16 says, "As you yield to the dynamic
life and power of the Holy Spirit, you will abandon the
cravings of your self-life." The cravings of the self-life are
the things that serve only us, not the greater good. If we
spend our lives seeking to satisfy our own cravings, how
short-sighted we are. Let's instead look for ways to expand
our reach, serve others in love, and share the good things
we have with those who have less than we do. What
blessing there is when we share the sweet things of this
life with others.

**Father, help me to practice moderation and generosity,
sharing the goodness in my life with others.**

HEALING WORDS

Lying about and slandering people are as bad as hitting them with a club, or wounding them with an arrow, or stabbing them with a sword.

PROVERBS 25:18

If you've ever been affected by the hurtful words of someone else, then you know the power that they hold. Words can build, and words can destroy. They can offer hope, and they can cause discouragement. They can wound, and they can heal. Words are tools, and the types of tools we use matter. They matter to our own soul-health, our relationships, and the world around us.

Think of ways you can build others up with your words today. Perhaps you can repair trust that has been broken. We must be aware not only of our own speech but also of our responses to others when they wield wounding words. It's important to be honest about how others' words affect us. No change can take place when there is no awareness or accountability. Be brave enough to set a standard and to allow others to know when they have hurt you.

Healer, thank you that I don't have to walk around helpless against the tide of others. May I be an encourager, a healer, and a builder with my words. May I also be a defender and a truth-teller. You make me brave enough to be honest.

TIMING MATTERS

When you sing a song of joy to someone suffering in the deepest grief and heartache, it can be compared to disrobing in the middle of a blizzard or rubbing salt in a wound.

PROVERBS 25:20

Context is so very important. Compassion does not ignore what others are going through even when we are in moments of rejoicing. Seasons come and go, so we should be wise about how we interact with those who are suffering. We do not act the same at a wedding as we do a funeral, after all.

Our God is full of compassion. When we are suffering, he comforts us. May we look for ways to comfort those suffering around us. Second Corinthians 1:4 talks about how the Father "always comes alongside us to comfort us in every suffering so that we can come alongside those who are in any painful trial. We can bring them this same comfort that God has poured out upon us." The more comfort we have received in our own suffering, the more we have to offer others. As we draw near to those who are grieving, whether we can relate or not, we can offer them our presence and comfort without needing to fix them.

Comforter, help me to be sensitive to those I am around so that I may offer comfort, not more heartache.

REFRESHINGLY GOOD NEWS

Like a drink of cool water refreshes a weary, thirsty soul,
so hearing good news revives the spirit.

PROVERBS 25:25

Think about the last piece of good news you received.
How did it make you feel? A good report can bring relief,
joy, celebration, tears, and renewed hope. It can feel as
welcome as the sun breaking through a cloudy day. It can
be poignant and life changing.

Consider the angel who encountered the shepherds
outside of Bethlehem after Jesus' birth. The shepherds
were terrified by the radiant splendor before them. The
angel's response was this: "Don't be afraid, for I have
come to bring you good news, the most joyous news the
world has ever heard! And it is for everyone everywhere!"
(Luke 2:10). This exceedingly good news was that Jesus,
the Messiah—a rescuer for us all—was born. We know
through the accounts of the Gospels that he came to
be our Savior, rescuing us from the perils of sin and
death and liberating us in his merciful sacrifice. What
wonderful news this is to rejoice in today.

**Savior, thank you for your life, death, and resurrection.
Thank you for liberating me completely in your
limitless love. I adore you, and I worship you.**

NO NEED TO STRIVE

It's good to eat sweet things, but you can take too much.
It's good to be honored, but to seek words of praise is not
honor at all.

PROVERBS 25:27

It is better to be honored by another than to search
for ways to elevate ourselves. If we crave the praise of
others, we will never be satisfied. We will constantly look
for more affirmation. We must be sure that our worth
and identity are rooted and grounded in the love of
Christ. When they are, we don't have to go searching for
validation elsewhere.

There is a difference between wanting to be
honored and fishing for honors. When we live as devoted
lovers of God, our focus is on what is ours to do—how we
can serve others and live out our love well. When we are
driven and distracted by what we can gain from others, it
may drive us to say and do things that are not honoring to
them or to us. As we humble our hearts and stand upon
the foundation of who we are in Christ, we can allow him
to honor us when others don't.

**Worthy One, help me to not go seeking after the praise
of others when I can find myself surefooted and secure
in your love.**

In Season

It is totally out of place to promote and honor a fool, just like it's out of place to have snow in the summer and rain at harvest time.

PROVERBS 26:1

In the proper season, both snow and rain are beneficial. They are needed to help plants grow. In the wrong season, however, they can be harmful. It is also harmful to affirm and honor a fool who has not had time and experience to mature. It is out of place, and those who witness it will not take it well. A fool also leaves many enemies in their wake, so this must be taken into account.

Our character is shown through how we build our lives and how we treat people. It is important to know what those who are close to us say about our character. We must not be deceived by hollow charm but truly look at the fruit of a person's life and nature before we honor him or her with promotions and praise.

Holy God, refine my character in your mercy and build me up in your gracious truth. I want to be about your business—not the business of making myself great. May I partner with you in honoring others who faithfully show up in service.

Inescapable Returns

An undeserved curse will be powerless to harm you.
It may flutter over you like a bird,
but it will find no place to land.

PROVERBS 26:2

When we walk in the light of the Lord, submitting to
his kingdom ways, we have nothing to fear. When we
move in his love, we do not look for ways to harm others.
Undeserved curses thrown at us will have no place to
land. God knows our hearts, and we can rest assured that
he will protect us when others falsely accuse us.

We should be careful, then, how we live. If we live
without reproach, all of the accusations will fall away
as others investigate our lives. When they look under
the surface, what will they find? For those with baseless
accusations, slandering us without reason, the returns will
go right back to them. Let's be careful, then, too, about
those against whom we make accusations. All will be made
clear, and God does not overlook even a single detail.

**Just Judge, you see everything as clear as day. You know
me, and you know the ones I struggle to love. Help me
to remain humble and steadfast in your mercy, living
righteously and without shame.**

CLEVER RESPONSES

If you're asked a silly question, answer it with words
of wisdom so the fool doesn't think he's so clever.

PROVERBS 26:5

Though foolish people may run off their mouths,
thinking they know more than others, let wisdom guide
your response. Remember the traits of godly wisdom,
as revealed in James 3:17; it is "always pure, filled with
peace, considerate and teachable. It is filled with love and
never displays prejudice or hypocrisy in any form." When
your response is filled with the wisdom of heaven, it will
display the nature of Christ.

So, if today someone asks you a silly question,
don't scoff or take the bait. Answer it with grounded
wisdom. How many times did Jesus do this with the
religious leaders who tried to ensnare him? In fact, Jesus
often answered people's questions with a question of his
own. Wisdom doesn't shut people down; it gives them
the opportunity to think differently. What a wonderful
example to follow!

**Wise Jesus, I am in awe of the wisdom that you showed
in your responses to people's questions. I'm so glad you
aren't afraid of curiosity too. Help me to be wise and
trust your ways more than the pride of self-certainty.**

RELIABLE PRESENCE

You can never trust the words of a fool,
just like a crippled man can't trust his legs to support him.

PROVERBS 26:7

It is good to know whose word you can trust and whose you cannot take at face value. It is a difficult reality that not all people in our lives can be trusted with knowledge or access to the vulnerable parts of us—but it is true. The trustworthy, though not perfect, are able to tell the truth, honor others, and follow through on their promises.

There is so much information out there and sometimes not enough personal context to know who is telling the truth and who is not. We cannot be expected to be able to know it all. We can, however, be wise in how we ingest information. The fruit of a person's character can do a lot to reveal the trustworthiness of their words. Especially for those we live and interact with on a regular basis, we can decipher who is worthy of our trust.

Worthy God, you are loyal in love and faithful to your promises. I trust you to guide me in wisdom to know whom I can depend on and to be a trustworthy friend myself.

HONORABLE HEART POSTURE

There's only one thing worse than a fool,
and that's the smug, conceited man
always in love with his own opinions.

PROVERBS 26:12

God created us to live in the freedom of his love, and Christ came to point us back to that intended reality. He broke down every barrier that stood in the way of our ability to live free from shame, the shackles of sin, and the limitations of death. Do we live in the liberty that Christ has offered us? How incredibly the Father both loves us and pursues us with the passion of his heart!

May we turn to the Lord today, who is incredibly rich in mercy. "Even when we were dead and doomed in our many sins," Ephesians 2:5 says, "he united us into the very life of Christ and saved us by his wonderful grace!" When we are focused on the wonderfully life-giving love of Christ, our attention is turned from how we can serve ourselves to how we can live out his marvelous mercy in every area of our lives.

Wonderful Savior, thank you for your liberating love that sets me free from having to go back to the error of my ways over and over again. I love your wisdom more than my own opinion, and I worship you in awe and wonder today.

WASTED ENERGY

It's better to grab a stray dog by its ears
than to meddle in a quarrel that's none of your business.

PROVERBS 26:17

Arguments require emotional energy. Why then would
we spend our precious energy on disagreements that
are none of our business? We need not meddle in the
affairs of others. It is wise for us to stay out of contentious
quarrels that have nothing to do with us. Prudence keeps
us from jumping into every fight to negotiate peace;
instead, we get to wisely choose our peace-making efforts.

If you feel emotionally depleted in some areas,
consider if you can step out of those activities or
relationships. Perhaps there are fights you can disengage
from. If we do not protect our own peace, no one else
will do it for us. Consider all the things you can get roped
into on social media. How many are actually worth your
engagement, and which are a waste of your energy?
Consider how you can implement this wisdom in your
life so that you can focus on the things that truly matter.

**God of Wisdom, thank you for your wisdom and
your peace. Give me discernment as I recognize what
requires my engagement and what doesn't. Thank you
for your help.**

QUELLING QUARRELS

It takes fuel to have a fire—a fire dies down when you run out of fuel. So quarrels disappear when the gossip ends.

PROVERBS 26:20

Fires are stoked when we add logs to them. Quarrels are prolonged when we keep adding fuel to their cause. If we recycle the same information over and over, we may keep ourselves in cycles of chaos. Let's not refuse to let go of the past, ruminating and reminding ourselves and others of mistakes that have already been forgiven.

Verse 22 says, "Gossip is so delicious, and how we love to swallow it! For slander is easily absorbed into our innermost being." When we leave compassion out of our conversations, we don't consider what is behind the actions of another. Though we cannot know for sure anyone else's intentions, we do know that God does. We can trust God to do what we are ill-equipped to do and choose to love and honor others with our speech, thoughts, and actions. These lend to peaceful solutions.

Peace Bringer, I don't want to be argumentative and always looking to prove others wrong. I know that only comes at my own expense in the end. Help me to remain humble and compassionate in all of my interactions and conversations.

DECEPTIVE CHARM

Smooth talk can hide a corrupt heart
just like a pretty glaze covers a cheap clay pot.

PROVERBS 26:23

Though charm can be deceiving, what a person is truly made of will be made clear. We must not allow flattery and smooth-talking to distract us from problematic and chaotic situations around the person in question. We need to have the discernment to look past the veneer, which we are equipped to do by weighing the fruit of a person's actions and what they say.

Wise people are genuine, real, and honest. Their actions match their words, and they seek restoration and forgiveness when they fail (not only when they are called out). Though charm can woo a person's favor in the short term, it is not a solid foundation for a lasting relationship. Proverbs 31:30 says, "Charm can be misleading...but this virtuous woman lives in the wonder, awe, and fear of the Lord. She will be praised throughout eternity." Look for the virtues of a person's life, and you will find their motivations.

Steadfast One, your wonderful nature is so much better than the fleeting charm of anyone in this world. Thank you for your loyal love. May I reflect it with integrity and honor all the days of my life.

TEST THE FRUIT

Don't be drawn in by the hypocrite, for his gracious
speech is a charade, nothing but a masquerade covering
his hatred and evil on parade.

PROVERBS 26:25

Directly before this verse lies the warning: "Kind words
can be a cover to conceal hatred of others, for hypocrisy
loves to hide behind flattery" (v. 24). Flattering words are
not necessarily the indication of a kind person. Though
their words may seek to soothe the ego, the hearts of
hypocrites do not act out of mercy.

Jesus rebuked the religious scholars who
questioned why his disciples didn't follow the traditions
that the scholars thought proved a person's holiness. In
Mark 7, Jesus said, "You are hypocrites!…'These people
honor me with their words while their hearts run far away
from me!…For they continue to insist that their man-
made traditions are equal to the instructions of God'"
(vv. 6–7). We can test our own hearts and the judgments
we make, offering ourselves as clay to be molded by the
mercy of Christ, our King.

Jesus, may the fruit of my yielded heart produce a crop
of righteousness for your kingdom. Where pride keeps
me from hearing you, I ask you to correct me. I want to
be a person of integrity who repents whenever necessary
and surrenders to your ways above the ways of culture.

MANIFEST MOTIVATIONS

Don't worry—he can't keep the mask on for long.
One day his hypocrisy will be exposed before all the world.

PROVERBS 26:26

We can trust God to make all things clear. In Luke 12:2, Jesus said, "Everything hidden and covered up will soon be exposed. For the façade is falling down, and nothing will be kept secret for long." Even secrets spoken behind closed doors will be revealed. We don't have to worry whether wickedness will be exposed or not. It will be. We can trust God to do it.

We should evaluate our own motivations in light of this. Are we living to serve merely our own interests, or are we abiding by wisdom's statutes? Wisdom is peace loving. It does not foster division. Wisdom is merciful, demonstrating kindness, compassion, and forgiveness to others. It is considerate and willingly places the needs of others above ourselves whenever possible. Wisdom does not show partiality to others based on our own benefit and preferences. It is a reflection of the limitlessness of God's love—with grace, justice, and mercy on display.

Lord, search me and know me. Reveal if there is any self-serving hypocrisy in my heart and root it out in your love. I want to live by your values.

SECURE LOVE

Hatred is the root of slander
and insecurity the root of flattery.

PROVERBS 26:28

When we know our worth, rooted in the identity that Christ has given us, we rest in the security of who we are. We don't need to prove ourselves to anyone, for the Lord sees us, knows us, loves us, and accepts us as we are. We have no need to tear others down in order to lift ourselves up. The feasting table of our God and King has room for all, and we don't need to compete for our place.

How convinced are you that no one can take your place in the kingdom of heaven? God's affection for you is not threatened by the love he has for anyone else. You are unique and specially loved. You don't have to fight for his attention. Whenever you call to him, he hears you. Whenever you look to him, his gaze is upon you already. He is not distracted by the needs of others, for there is room in his marvelous mercy for all who hunger and thirst. Let the incomparable affection of your Father boost your confidence today.

Father, I am grateful that I don't need to compete in your kingdom. I am free to love you, to be me, and to support others in their triumphs as I wait for my own.

OPENHANDED SURRENDER

Never brag about the plans you have for tomorrow, for you don't have a clue what tomorrow may bring to you.

PROVERBS 27:1

This verse isn't suggesting that we shouldn't make plans and follow through on them. Rather, it speaks of the larger attitude with which we should approach life. If we brag about things that we will accomplish, we leave out the necessary and inevitable truth that unforeseen challenges will arise as well. Instead of conceitedly finding our satisfaction in what we accomplish and lording it over others, we should humbly keep our perspective open to the mysteries that the future will unfold.

James 4:14 says, "You don't have a clue what tomorrow may bring. For your fleeting life is but a warm breath of air that is visible in the cold only for a moment and then vanishes!" Though we make plans for our lives, only the Lord knows how they will play out. He sees the end from the beginning and everything in between. There is not a detail that he misses. We can trust him with openhearted surrender to lead us through this life.

Faithful One, I'm so grateful that you know all things and that I don't have to. I trust you to guide me through the hills and the valleys of this life with steadfast love. I humble my heart before you.

LET IT HAPPEN

Let someone else honor you for your accomplishments,
for self-praise is never appropriate.

PROVERBS 27:2

Have you ever spent time around people who were full of themselves? Self-importance is not an appealing trait to most, and it certainly does not reflect the kingdom of heaven. Even Jesus, the Son of God, did not praise himself. He showed the Father's likeness through his lived-out love, letting the integrity of his teaching and lifestyle cohesively reveal who he was. He always deserved the honor, and still does, but he did not force people to recognize him.

Can you identify any areas where you have been striving for validation? Perhaps you have been concerned with being overlooked, so you insecurely insert yourself to make sure others notice you. Take the advice of this proverb and let someone else honor you for your accomplishments. Share passionately with your friends about what you are doing, but don't brag about your accomplishments to people you don't even know. Let it happen naturally. God will never overlook you, and he will honor you for what you do, even if no one else does.

Worthy Jesus, help me to focus on what my work is today. I do it unto you, for your glory. Be honored in my life and in my hard work.

LOVE'S CHALLENGE

It's better to be corrected openly if it stems from hidden love. You can trust a friend who wounds you with his honesty, but your enemy's pretended flattery comes from insincerity.

PROVERBS 27:5–6

An honest word that challenges you out of love is better than insincere flattery from someone who does not care about you. Even if the honest truth hurts, it is better to know it than to be blinded by superficial praise. Don't let offense cloud your heart. Consider the source. If a trusted friend offers you an honest viewpoint, then take it into consideration. Humbly evaluate what he or she has to say and ask further questions if needed.

Those who love us want the best for us. We may not agree on all things, but we can hear each other out, nonetheless. The vulnerability of authentic concern is worth the risk for those we love. We should not hold back honesty when staying quiet does more harm than good. Love is not passive, and it is not indifferent. We should offer honest challenges when need be and love our friends well.

Jesus, I don't want to shy away from the wise input of friends, colleagues, family, and mentors in my life. Help me discern and remain humble when confronted with correction.

LEAVE ROOM

When your soul is full, you turn down even the sweetest honey. But when your soul is starving, every bitter thing becomes sweet.

PROVERBS 27:7

When we have eaten until we are overly full, not even our favorite treats appeal to us. It is the same with our souls. When we are filled with too much information, entertainment, or distraction, our souls will not crave the sweet Word of God. The Word of God is like revelation-honey—sweet to the soul's taste and satisfying our hearts in expanded awareness of who God is.

We must be aware of what we are filling our souls with. Are they things that can never satisfy, or are we being nourished first with the Word of God? Jesus Christ is the Word. He who was, is, and is to come offers us the fellowship of his Spirit. Take time today and every day to fill up on the wonders he offers. Jesus quoted in Matthew 4:4, "Bread alone will not satisfy, but true life is found in every word that constantly goes forth from God's mouth." Let's feast on the true life offered to us.

Father of All, thank you for your wonderful Word that I can feast upon each day. Speak to me and reveal divine revelations that will awaken my understanding in new, life-giving ways today.

BEAUTIFULLY SWEET FRIENDSHIPS

Sweet friendships refresh the soul and awaken our hearts with joy, for good friends are like the anointing oil that yields the fragrant incense of God's presence.

PROVERBS 27:9

There is nothing in life that more sacredly reveals the heart of God than the intimacy of souls in friendship. Heart to heart, God longs for close relationship with us. He wants us to know him and to trust him, just as we do our faithful friends. Friendship with God is an incredible gift, and each good friend we have is a reflection of God's wonderful love.

Think through the refreshing relationships in your life. Which friendships challenge, rejuvenate, and encourage you? Identify those with whom you feel utterly seen, known, and accepted. Good friends are those that bring you joy and also those whom you can both celebrate and mourn with. Sweet friendships awaken our hearts in the way that God wants to awaken us with his sincere friendship. We must not forget the importance of time spent with our wonderful God, for we were made to know him and to be known by him. We were created to walk hand in hand in gardens of glory with the King of kings.

Creator, thank you for the beautiful friendships I have in my life. Most of all, thank you for the friendship I have with you.

BUILD STRONG CONNECTIONS

Never give up on a friend or abandon a friend of your father—for in the day of your brokenness you won't have to run to a relative for help. A friend nearby is better than a relative far away.

PROVERBS 27:10

Wherever you find yourself, don't give up on the friends around you. Build strong connections within your community, and you will have help when you need it. The relationships you have are important—both within and outside of the church body. Show up for your friends in their time of need, and good friends will do the same for you.

It is so very important to build and maintain healthy relationships. If you find yourself isolated, look at the point of connections you already have in your life and build from there. You are not as alone as you feel. Reach out to someone whom you have lost touch with for no other reason than time or space. Tend to the friendships in your life, and you will always have someone to turn to in a time of need.

Friend of the Fatherless, thank you for your help in my time of trouble. May I treat my friends the way you do, and may I experience the strength of support that I long for.

THE JOY OF OBEDIENCE

My son, when you walk in wisdom, my heart is filled with gladness, for the way you live is proof that I've not taught you in vain.

PROVERBS 27:11

As we grow and mature, putting the wisdom we've learned into practice, those who taught us and faithfully walked with us until this point have reason to rejoice. What parents are not proud when their child willingly lives by the values that they tried so diligently to instill in him? In the same way, our Father in heaven is filled with gladness when we walk in his ways.

Consider the godly wisdom you have integrated into your life. You can rejoice just as much as the Father does, for he delights in your obedience. Everything that God advises us to do is with our best interest in mind and at heart, so we can freely give ourselves to following the wisdom of his kingdom in every area of our lives.

Wise Father, I choose to walk in your ways, for I know that they are best. Your law of love is worth laying aside my biases and opinions. Your love is better than life.

Be Prepared

A wise, shrewd person discerns the danger ahead and
prepares himself, but the naïve simpleton never looks
ahead and suffers the consequences.

PROVERBS 27:12

It is with discernment that we can look ahead and
recognize the dangers that we need to prepare for.
Innocence can keep a person from discerning what is
ahead, but if we have lived long enough and still refuse to
take wise precautions, we will suffer the consequences of
our lack of foresight.

We can absolutely have full faith in God and still
prepare ourselves. One does not preclude the other.
Let's get rid of the notion that having faith in God must
mean that we don't take our futures seriously. We cannot
control what happens, but we can prepare ourselves with
discernment as the days change and signs of the times
arise. What have you been putting off that you can take
care of? Is it drafting a will for your descendants or putting
some savings away? Whatever it is, seize the opportunity
that today affords you and trust God with the rest.

**God, thank you for the gift of discernment that does
not make me tremble in fear but motivates me into
action and preparation. Give me wisdom as to what I
need to do.**

November

ATMOSPHERES OF PEACE

An endless drip, drip, drip, from a leaky faucet and the
words of a cranky, nagging wife have the same effect.

PROVERBS 27:15

Perpetual sounds of a problem that needs to be fixed can
wear not only on our minds but also on our souls. We
should be aware of the kind of atmospheres we promote
within our homes. Do we stir up chaos or seek to meet (or
have others meet) endless demands, or do we encourage
peace? Our speech and actions are reflections of our
hearts. When we address and soothe the heart issues, the
quality of our relationships will improve.

If we have done what we can to address issues
within our relationships and they are still not improving,
there is wisdom in realizing that we are not responsible
for how others behave. We each have a part to play, and
if we are actively doing our own part and seeking to
understand the other person, we can rest assured. Though
we cannot control the reaction of others, including our
loved ones, we can sow peace, nonetheless, through hearts
of love.

**Prince of Peace, thank you for the peace I have found in
you. Increase it even more as I soak in the presence of
your mercy. Do what only you can do and bring peace
to the chaos I cannot control.**

Iron Sharpens Iron

It takes a grinding wheel to sharpen a blade,
and so one person sharpens the character of another.

PROVERBS 27:17

The book of Proverbs warns us many times to abstain from senseless arguments and refrain from being a quarrelsome person. There is a difference, however, between being someone who looks to start arguments and those who are willing to have a friendly debate. The former is ego-driven and stirs up chaos. The latter offers alternative perspectives in a conversation meant to broaden and challenge our viewpoints. One tears down while the other seeks to build and refine.

Friendly discussions are beneficial for all parties willing to participate. Do you shrink back from sharing your viewpoint because you hate conflict, or do you offer it, knowing that someone who knows you well will not define you by one opinion? The more we know each other, the deeper we can prod about our biases and our outlooks. As iron sharpens iron, so a friendly debate sharpens each person involved.

Refiner, with a heart of love and curiosity, I know that an argument can help refine my views and expand my understanding. May I never resist a loving challenge to see things differently.

TENDING AND YIELDING

Tend an orchard and you'll have fruit to eat. Serve the Master's interests and you'll receive honor that's sweet.

PROVERBS 27:18

The things we tend to will grow, and what we care for will flourish. We must be aware, then, where we are putting our time, attention, and love. What do we allow to fill our minds and pull our hearts? Serving the Lord is not an obligation but a display of love. Jesus said, in Matthew 6:33, "Above all, constantly seek God's kingdom and his righteousness, then all these less important things will be given to you abundantly."

It is better to serve the interests of God than to chase down our own. Our interests may change with the shift of the winds, but the values of God's kingdom are secure. When we put God first, it does not mean we opt out of living our lives. It means that we invite his fullness to lead, guide, and redirect us when necessary. We choose to live from his extensive mercy rather than self-protective fear. Let's be sure to incorporate the ways of Christ within our choices as we follow hard after him.

Holy God, I want to serve you more than I want to serve myself because I know there is true and lasting satisfaction in your ways.

WONDERFULLY UNIQUE INTERESTS

Just as no two faces are exactly alike,
so every heart is different.

PROVERBS 27:19

Do you recognize that your unique thought patterns, perceptions, skills, and talents are a gift from a creative Maker? It is not a bad thing to resist the pull of uniformity within systems. Unity is reflected in the position of our hearts, not in the ways we express ourselves. A shared belief system in the kingdom of God does not mean that we all need to have the same lifestyles, clothing choices, or interests. Our businesses and hobbies are diverse. This is the way it is meant to be.

God knows our hearts, and he does not judge us based on our appearance. May we resist the pull to judge people based on where they live, what they do for work, or how they dress. We get to dive into the passions of our hearts, for God put them there for a reason. Let's pursue our gifts, hone our skills, and broaden our horizons. The kingdom of God is anywhere his mercy dwells, and it dwells with each of us.

Father, thank you for creating me in your image. I want to live in the fullness of your love and in the best capacity of who you have created me to be.

CHARACTER TESTING

Fire is the way to test the purity of silver and gold,
but the character of a man is tested by giving him
a measure of fame.

PROVERBS 27:21

Fame brings with it certain privileges that are only afforded to the powerful. When people achieve fame, they often face opportunities for temptation in ways that they couldn't have anticipated. If we are not rooted in the values of God's kingdom, and we don't know the power of our choices or the importance of our identity as children of God, then we may find ourselves compromising for the sake of ease or passing pleasure.

Even when we fail and fall, God's mercy is near to restore us. When we surrender to his love, we allow the powerful redemption of Christ's resurrection life to free us from false senses of security. This is so much better than boosting our egos with pride and distracting ourselves with fleeting gratification. As we yield to Christ, our character will stand the tests of life. As we turn to the Lord again and again, we offer ourselves as living sacrifices for his glory.

Glorious One, your love is even better than life. There are endless pleasures in your wisdom—things that won't rust or lose their luster. I choose your ways, Father. I choose you. Have your way in me.

CAREFUL ATTENTION

A shepherd should pay close attention to the faces of his flock and hold close to his heart the condition of those he cares for.

PROVERBS 27:23

We should not lose sight of the important people in our life as our vision broadens and expands in the compassion of Christ. We need to first care for those closest to us, and then we can tend to the needs of others. When we are preoccupied beyond our own little spheres of influence, the people closest to us may suffer.

First Timothy 5:4 is a reminder that we should provide for our families. "If [widows] have children or grandchildren at home, then it is only proper to let them provide for the ones who raised them when they were children, for kindness begins at home and it pleases God." It's important we do not neglect our close relationships; instead, let's do as the proverb says and hold close to our hearts the condition of those we care for. Let's provide for, support, and be there for our loved ones.

Tender Father, thank you for your close watch and care of your children. May I not neglect the needs of my own family, friends, and community, for if I remain unengaged in support at home, I have lost sight of what truly matters.

HONORING WHAT WILL LAST

A man's strength, power, and riches
will one day fade away;
not even nations endure forever.

PROVERBS 27:24

Nothing outside the kingdom of heaven (aside from God himself) will last forever. We must make sure that we are living for the things that will endure. Power, strength, and wealth will one day fade away. Though we may gain a little in this life, we should make sure our attention and affections are placed in the kingdom of Christ.

If you knew this was your last year on earth, how would you change the way you live? Looking back over your life up until this point, what are the things you wish you would have gone after and the things you would have walked away from? Only you can choose how you will live from this point onward. Store up the treasures of heaven, build upon your relationships, and live with mercy-kindness, courage, passion, and hope.

Everlasting Father, in you there is no beginning and no end. You are the source of all life, and to you all will return. I want to live my life with purpose, in a way that matters in eternity. Help me to refocus and refine my life in your ways.

FEARLESS COURAGE

Guilty criminals experience paranoia even though no one threatens them. But the innocent lovers of God, because of righteousness, will have the boldness of a young, ferocious lion!

PROVERBS 28:1

When we hide in the shadows, we fear what may be exposed in the light. When our consciences are heavy with guilt, we live in cages of our own making. Instead we should be like the innocent lovers of God this proverb speaks of and have the boldness of young, ferocious lions. Our true confidence is in the righteousness of Christ that has covered us, liberated us, and restored us in peace.

No matter what our past, we can choose the liberation of God's love at any moment. Even if we still must face the natural consequences of our choices, our consciences can be clean. First John 1:7 says, "If we keep living in the pure light that surrounds him…the blood of Jesus, his Son, continually cleanses us from all sin." When we are purified, we can walk in the confidence of Christ— what he has done, who he is, and what he offers us.

Christ, I will be courageous as I walk in the light of your righteousness. I submit my life to you. May it glorify your name and be full of your love, peace, and powerful redemption.

RESTORERS OF PEACE

A rebellious nation is thrown into chaos, but leaders anointed with wisdom will restore law and order.

PROVERBS 28:2

When we are anointed with wisdom, we uphold the values of God's kingdom in justice, equality, and mercy. Corrupt leaders cause chaos, while wise leaders promote peace. Let's think through what it would look like for our values to align with the kingdom of Christ. Are there things that need to change? In many ways, what the kingdom of God values goes against what the world values.

May we be humble of heart, never thinking ourselves too good to serve others. The best leaders are the servant leaders—the ones who don't just delegate and sit back but who get in the trenches with those they lead. It is important to recognize what sort of example we are setting for those we work with. Are we leading by example, or do we believe that our status elevates us from doing the little things? We can promote peace with our actions as well as our words. Let's be people who live openheartedly and authentically, doing the best we can with what we have. God is in the details.

Lord, when I look at your example of leadership, I can't help but be stunned. You do not ask anything of us that you would not do yourself. May I reflect your purehearted goodness in my own role.

TRUTH LOVERS

Those who turn their backs on what they know is right
will no longer be able to tell right from wrong. But those
who love the truth strengthen their souls.

PROVERBS 28:4

It is not enough to have been taught right from wrong; we
must put it into practice in order to actually live out our
faith. What we believe, we will act upon. Our lives reveal
the attitudes of our hearts. When we value the principles of
God's Word, implementing his instructions into our choices
and lifestyles, our souls are strengthened in his truth.

When we start down a road that leads us away
from the truth of God's kingdom, his nature, and his
promises, we may become confused as to what in life
truly matters. We may struggle to know what is right or
wrong—not only for us but also for the world around us.
The foundation of God's unchanging truth is a firm place
to stand. He never changes. Opinions come and go—
nations rise and fall—but the Lord is faithfully the same
through it all.

**Glorious God, you are the forever and unchanging
standard of truth. I don't put my hope in doctrines or
ideas. I put my hope in you. I build my life upon you.
I choose to walk in your ways because you are worthy.**

LIGHT OF JUSTICE

Justice never makes sense to men devoted to darkness, but those tenderly devoted to the Lord can understand justice perfectly.

PROVERBS 28:5

Justice does not make sense to those devoted to darkness because it stands against everything they do. In Isaiah 1:17, seeking justice is described as follows: "Rescue the oppressed. Uphold the rights of the fatherless and defend the widow's cause." If we live by the just ways of the Lord, we cannot support systems of oppression or abuse.

In the kingdom of God, in fact in the very heart of God, every life matters. Every person is valuable. He created each in his image. The poor are loved the same as the rich. The sick are as precious as the healthy. What we find annoying in others is not just tolerated by God, but he sees through to the very heart of a person and loves them. May we never use our faith as an excuse to be indifferent to injustice or turn aside when we see powerful people abusing the vulnerable. The light of justice shines on us all, and we will have to account for everything we do both in the open and in secret.

Just King, I am devoted to you, and I commit to pursuing your justice with my life as much as I pursue your mercy.

REWARDS OF RESISTANCE

Those who tempt the lovers of God with an evil scheme
will fall into their own traps. But the innocent who resist
temptation will experience reward.

PROVERBS 28:10

None of us can escape the inevitable temptations that life
throws our way. Even Jesus was tempted. In the forty days
Jesus spent in the wilderness, he was tempted in multiple
ways. He used Scripture and faith to resist the enemy. We
can do the same.

As we resist temptations that lead us away from
the values of Christ and his kingdom, our faith and
resolve are strengthened. When we are weak, we have the
strength of the Spirit to empower us to endure. When
we have nothing left to support ourselves, we have the
support of the Holy Spirit to help and rescue us. We
must not forget that we have the power of his presence to
overcome any and every temptation that comes our way.

**Victorious One, I stand in your triumph over death
and rise in the strength of your Spirit with me. When I
am weak, may I be strengthened by you. Help me stand
strong in you.**

RICH IN WISDOM

The wealthy in their conceit presume to be wise, but a poor
person with discernment can see right through them.

PROVERBS 28:11

Having many resources does not mean that a person
is wise. Some people are born into privilege, and they
have not had many lessons to test the strength of their
character. Others may have powerful wealth but weak
integrity. We should not assume that just because some are
successful in the eyes of the world that they are people of
wisdom. With discernment, we can see how they interact
with others, the reputations that they have, and the fruit of
their lives. Are they generous? Are they humble?

As for us, we can nourish our souls with the
wealth of wisdom found in the Scriptures. We get to give
ourselves to knowing God better through meditating on
his Word, talking with others about him, fellowshiping
with the Spirit, and worshiping him. Even the poorest
and simplest among us can share in the wealth of Christ's
kingdom, even now.

**Jesus Christ, I want to be wealthier in your wisdom
than in any other thing. I trust your heart and your
ways. Teach me and give me discernment to recognize
true wisdom in others.**

KISSED BY MERCY

If you cover up your sin you'll never do well.
But if you confess your sins and forsake them,
you will be kissed by mercy.

PROVERBS 28:13

Whatever we seek to cover up will be revealed someday.
Let's give up trying to conceal our failures and
wrongdoings and instead confess them to the Lord and
turn away from them. As we turn to the Lord, we can
embrace the mercy he offers us abundantly whenever we
look to him. His love is strong, and it is powerful enough
to overcome our sins. What a wonderful hope we have!

When was the last time you were kissed by mercy?
If there is something that you've been resisting offering to
the Lord, may you find the motivation you need to give it
to him. Allow his light to shine on the dark places of your
heart, and he will bring restoration, redemption, and new
life. His mercy does not shame; it resurrects.

**Merciful Lord, there is no one like you. You are so
generous, so loving, and so true. I trust your heart,
and I offer what I have been holding back. I don't want
anything but your powerful love to have a hold over me.**

TENDER JOY

Overjoyed is the one who with tender heart trembles before God, but the stubborn, unyielding heart will experience even greater evil.

PROVERBS 28:14

When we catch a glimpse of God's greatness, we cannot help but tremble with humble awe. He is so much more powerful, so much wiser, so much more than we could ever think or imagine. What joy we experience when we revel in his glory, for in that place we realize that nothing compares to him.

As Psalm 100:4–5 says,

You can pass through his open gates with the password of praise…
For YAHWEH is always good and ready to receive you.
He's so loving that it will amaze you—
so kind that it will astound you!

There is nothing you need to hold back as you come to the Lord today. Even if you approach him with fear and trembling, you will come away filled with joy.

King Jesus, I come with praise and gratitude, longing to encounter an even greater glimpse of your glorious nature. Reveal yourself to me as I worship you with an open, overjoyed heart.

DRENCHED IN BLESSING

Life's blessings drench the honest and faithful person, but
punishment rains down upon the greedy and dishonest.

PROVERBS 28:20

What beautiful blessings exist in the wonderful fellowship
of God! He who created joy and gladness offers it to his
people. We experience kindness in connection to others
and deep love in committed communities. What joyful
delight there is in the gift of relationships, work to keep us
busy, and the pleasures of life.

Think about what you are thankful for in your
life. Which blessings make you recognize the Father's
goodness? Pour out your heart in gratitude today and
consider how you can be a blessing to others. Be creative
in how you show generosity. Maybe you can give a gift
that might bolster a friend's hope. What wonderful hope
there is in the generous fellowship of Christ within you—
more than enough to infuse and creatively inspire you in
goodness.

**Generous Father, thank you for all that you have given
me. I don't want to lose sight of the wonders of your
blessings in my life. May I be a conduit of your love
to others, as well, as I live to be a reflection of your
generosity.**

FOCUSED VALUES

A greedy man is in a race to get rich,
but he forgets that he could lose
what's most important and end up with nothing.

PROVERBS 28:22

"What use is it," Jesus asked, "to gain all the wealth and power of this world, with everything it could offer you, at the cost of your own life?" (Mark 8:36). All the wealth of this world will not satisfy, and we could waste our lives trying to achieve what does not matter in eternity.

It is much better to live with grounded values, loving those around us and feeding our souls with the nourishment of God, than it is to live striving for empty goals that will pass away as soon as we do. As we embrace the Lord, we can live for his purposes. Let's surrender to his ways, for they are better than the ways of this world. We can focus our vision on the one who never fails and live for his favor. He always knows best, teaching us with the wisdom of his eternal truth. We experience true life when we let go of our lives for the sake of the gospel.

Jesus, I want to live fully focused on you—your ways, your goodness, and your faithfulness. As I do, may my life be marked and transformed by your living mercy.

WELCOMING CRITIQUE

If you correct someone with constructive criticism,
in the end he will appreciate it more than flattery.

PROVERBS 28:23

A person who wants to grow in wisdom welcomes constructive criticism. In the same way, we should be sure that when we offer critiques, they are helpful and not just shaming. Others may not welcome the input of our opinion without our desire to help them. On the other hand, when we offer critiques about things we know nothing about, we show a lack of wisdom altogether.

Proverbs 15:32 warns, "Refusing constructive criticism shows you have no interest in improving your life, for revelation-insight only comes as you accept correction and the wisdom that it brings." We must be humble and realistic enough to recognize that perfection is unattainable. Allowing the process of failure and correction can expand our knowledge and teach us to persevere. We cannot act on what we do not know, but as we learn, we can adjust our approach.

Wise Father, thank you for the freedom to try and fail and try again. I don't rely on my own limited understanding, but I lean into the constructive help of others. May I always be humble enough to learn from others and to never give up listening to sage advice.

CAREFUL TRUST

To make rash, hasty decisions shows that you are not
trusting the Lord. But when you rely totally on God,
you will still act carefully and prudently.

PROVERBS 28:25

How we make decisions can reflect where our trust lies. If
we make our choices hastily, rushing in without caution,
we may be propelled by the fear of missing out or the
mindset of scarcity. The wisdom of God is grounded and
clear. There is no need to be rash! Haste is an anxious
response. You can make a quick and wise decision,
weighing different components well. You can also let
anxiety and tunnel vision move you in a direction that
does not benefit you.

Trust totally in God, and you don't have to worry
about details. Make the most careful decision you can
with what information you have and trust God to help
you handle the things that you cannot foresee. Isaiah
26:3 says, "Perfect, absolute peace surrounds those whose
imaginations are consumed with [God]; they confidently
trust in [him]." Let's fill our minds with who the Lord is
and put our confidence in his faithfulness.

**Good God, I trust that you are faithful, true, and
merciful. Help me to stay grounded in your wisdom
in the decisions I make, refusing to let fear rush me to
make a premature decision.**

LIBERATING REVELATIONS

Self-confident know-it-alls will prove to be fools.
But when you lean on the wisdom from above, you will
have a way to escape the troubles of your own making.

PROVERBS 28:26

God is grander than we can imagine. He does not just
save us from the troubles that come our way, outside of
our own control, but he also helps us escape the troubles
we create for ourselves. Whose love does that? The source
and author of love, whose being exudes mercy-kindness.
His love breaks chains and creates dry paths in the middle
of rushing rivers to provide his people a way out of their
captivity.

As Paul declared, so may we: "Now I live with the
confidence that there is nothing in the universe with the
power to separate us from God's love. I'm convinced that
his love will triumph over death, life's troubles, fallen
angels, or dark rulers in the heavens. There is nothing in
our present or future circumstances that can weaken his
love" (Romans 8:38). What gloriously good news that is!
Nothing can weaken his love, and this love is our glorious
victory in life and in death.

**Glorious Jesus, what a waste of time it would be to
pretend that I know better than you do. I lean on your
wisdom, and I welcome your loving leadership over my
life—in every single area.**

RIGHTFUL PLACES OF HONOR

When wicked leaders rise to power, good people go into hiding. But when they fall from power, the godly take their place.

PROVERBS 28:28

Wicked leaders, focused on their own agendas and hungry for power, cause chaos not only for their own nations but also for the nations around them. Good people go into hiding because corrupt leaders look for ways to get rid of them. We saw this with Saul and David in the Bible. We see it still happening in nations around the world today.

In time, when the wicked fall from power, the wise and godly ones will take their place. We must not give in to corruption or give up living good, honorable lives, serving others in love and justice. We need not compromise our own values when the powerful try to assert control over us. Christ's kingdom is unshakable, and it will not fall to any leader on this earth. As we live for the glory and the recognition of God, we must refuse to take part in systems of abuse and oppression. With clean consciences, we will stand before the Lord, and he will honor us. What greater goal could there be?

Worthy One, refine my heart in the values of your kingdom that I may stand on its steadfast and unmoving tenets. I will follow you no matter what.

REASON TO REJOICE

Everyone rejoices when the lovers of God flourish,
but the people groan when the wicked rise to power.

PROVERBS 29:2

The qualities of godly leadership are clear in the fruit of a person's life. Humble, teachable attitudes lend to people who are willing to listen to wise counsel. Honesty and openness build trust. Godly leaders don't seek to control others, but they offer rules that help people thrive. They are merciful and compassionate, offering chances for restoration and redemption. They sow seeds of peace and do not start fights with others. They stand in truth, on the side of the vulnerable, and liberate the oppressed. They uphold justice and do not show favor to powerful people.

So much more can be said of godly leaders. Perhaps you see some of these traits in yourself. Which qualities do you want to grow in? Even if you do not aspire to leadership, living a life of quiet honor will bring peace, joy, and benefit to those around you. How you live matters. It is to your honor when others rejoice because of your part in their lives. May you recognize the people who bring you joy and celebrate them today.

Joyful Jesus, I want to live in the integrity of your kingdom and your ways. Transform me in your love as I continually submit my heart to your Spirit.

STRENGTH IN JUSTICE

A godly leader who values justice is a great strength and example to the people. But the one who sells his influence for money tears down what is right.

PROVERBS 29:4

When leaders don't value or administer justice, the people revolt. Justice is not only the upholding of law and order. Justice also protects the vulnerable and administers appropriate sentences to those who act as if they are above or outside of the law. May we be people who value justice not merely as an ideal but also as a practice in our own lives.

In Isaiah 1:17, the Lord speaks on this: "Learn what it means to do what is good by seeking righteousness and justice! Rescue the oppressed. Uphold the rights of the fatherless and defend the widow's cause." When we walk in God's justice, God is pleased. Psalm 37:28 says, "The Lord loves it when he sees us walking in his justice." As we persevere in love, justice, and mercy, God will move at just the right time. He honors every movement of mercy in our lives, and he doesn't forget a single moment of surrendered trust.

Christ, may your justice rule and your mercy shine bright for all to see. May your godly leaders rise to take their places, and may the wicked go the way of the decaying earth.

GROUNDED AND GENUINE

Flattery can often be used as a trap to hide ulterior
motives and take advantage of you.

PROVERBS 29:5

Though flattery can evoke within us a feeling of
fulfillment for a moment, we should not only take people
at their word but also look to their actions to back up
what they say. When we are grounded in wisdom, we
will not be distracted by disingenuous compliments. We
should be genuine in the compliments we give, too, not
using them as tools of manipulation.

Some people use attention, admiration, and
affection in order to make others feel safe and dependent
upon them. However, this does not last. When one's
hidden motive is to take advantage of someone, the flattery
turns to control. Grounded love, sincere compliments, and
true affection have no need to take advantage of others.
The love of Christ does not seek to control us. It sets us
free. May our love do the same for others.

**Loving Jesus, may I be genuine in mercy and kindness.
I don't want to manipulate others—not for my own
benefit or for any other reason. May I be grounded in
your love that fuels my identity, giving up the need to
find it in anyone else. Thank you.**

SYSTEMS OF INFLUENCE

God's righteous people will pour themselves out for the poor, but the ungodly make no attempt to understand or help the needy.

PROVERBS 29:7

God's Word makes no qualms about the importance of helping the poor. Jesus surprised the religious elite of his day by spending time with those whom they considered the fringes of society. He dined with tax collectors. He touched the sick, healing their diseases. He went to the poor and encouraged them. His love knew no bounds—not based on culture, class, or gender. May we remove the boundaries that keep us from serving the less fortunate with generosity of resources, heart, and attention.

According to today's verse, we can tell who the righteous and unrighteous are depending on how they interact with or seek to understand the poor. Considering this, let's be honest with ourselves about where we land. As the children of God, we are called to use our influence to help those who are poor not simply by putting bandages on their problems but also by changing the systems that keep them stuck in cycles of poverty.

Righteous One, I don't want to neglect your heart for the poor. I recognize that I am no better than anyone else even if I am better off economically. May your love move me into action as I look for ways to serve the poor.

HOLY HONESTY

Violent men hate those with integrity,
but the lovers of God esteem those who are holy.

PROVERBS 29:10

People with integrity refuse to be tempted by power or money. Their values are impenetrable, for they stand on the truth and integrity of God's wisdom. Even when others threaten their livelihoods, they cannot be convinced to compromise their values. May we walk in the light of honesty, no matter what. May we live as pure reflections of Christ's mercy, no matter who is watching or who isn't.

What we do in private is as important to our character as what we do for others to see. It is important that we be genuine in love, open in humility, and strong in truth. Integrity does not mean that we never falter. It does not mean that we are perfect. It does, however, mean that we seek to correct our wrongs, to be authentic in every circumstance, and to be uncorrupted by power or greed. We cultivate integrity as we openly surrender our lives to God and to his kingdom ways.

Holy God, I want to stand in the truth of who you are, who I am in you, and the love that you've called me to. May my heart be uncorrupted by the pull of power. May the power of your mercy always have precedence.

UNIFYING VISION

When there is no clear prophetic vision, people quickly
wander astray. But when you follow the revelation of the
Word, heaven's bliss fills your soul.

PROVERBS 29:18

When there is no collective purpose, we each go our
own ways. While some are naturally motivated to make
a difference for the better in the lives of those around
them, others can easily be swept away by the pull of self-
serving power. If we follow the Word, we will be people of
purpose, vision, and unity. We will have an inner strength
of truth guiding us as we allow the wisdom of God to
refine our values and our approaches to others.

The mercy of God is a tremendous motivator,
and being united to serve others in a beneficial way can
greatly unify people from different backgrounds. Let's not
lose hope; we can look for ways to serve others, support
those who are already doing the work, and be a beacon
of light to those in need of encouragement. As we look
outward and we move on behalf of others, we will find
our own souls moved.

**Merciful Lord, thank you for your mercy that moves
in perpetual motion toward people. I don't want to be
stagnant in self-service. Show me where connecting
with others in united vision can propel me further into
your purposes.**

A PEACEFUL HEART

The source of strife is found in an angry heart,
for sin surrounds the life of a furious man.

PROVERBS 29:22

Unchecked anger does not lead to righteousness but to a life of chaos. James 1:19–20 advises to "be slow to become angry, for human anger is never a legitimate tool to promote God's righteous purpose." Paul also advised against letting anger take root in our hearts in Ephesians 4:26–27: "Don't let anger control you or be fuel for revenge, not for even a day. Don't give the slanderous accuser, the Devil, an opportunity to manipulate you!"

We are called to be agents of peace, to pursue mercy in all of our interactions, and to create atmospheres of safety for those around us. An angry heart is like a ticking time bomb. It will go off and cause destruction. Let's yield our hearts to the Prince of Peace and ask his Spirit to transform our inner worlds in the perfect harmony of his presence.

Prince of Peace, I don't want to be ruled by anger, and I don't want to be manipulated by fear or chaos. Create in me a pure, peaceful heart that finds its rest and confidence in you. May I bring calm to others and be a place of refuge in a chaotic world.

FEARLESS CONFIDENCE

Fear and intimidation is a trap that holds you back.
But when you place your confidence in the Lord,
you will be seated in the high place.

PROVERBS 29:25

Who of us has not experienced the confining feelings of fear? When our nervous systems react in fear, we can feel rushed to act or shutdown and frozen. Our bodies were created to protect us from danger, and our responses are often immediate when we sense danger is near. It is one thing to have an initial reaction to fear and another to choose to stay stuck in cycles of it.

With our confidence in God, his peace fills us and becomes our regulator. As we put our total trust in his faithfulness, we don't have to brace for the worst in helplessness. Even as we prepare for hard times, we can do it with a fearless confidence that God is sovereign and he is with us. We are motivated to partner with him in mercy and to courageously rise up in adversity when we allow his values to permeate our hearts. He partners with his people to do immeasurably more than we could ever imagine.

Good Father, I surrender my heart in hope to your limitless love. Fill me with boldness as I follow you and break me free from cycles of fear and intimidation.

INJUSTICE IS ALWAYS WRONG

The wicked hate those who live a godly life,
but the righteous hate injustice wherever it's found.

PROVERBS 29:27

In the kingdom of God, there is never an excuse for injustice. There is no place for bitterness or hatred. There is no excuse for discrimination or prejudice. Does this sound impossible? Nothing is impossible with Christ, and we must look to his standards as the example and not the standards of the world around us—not the confines of history or our present struggles.

Nothing can keep us from the powerful love of Christ, and this is a truth that transcends time, space, and human divisions. We must not let the disheartening biases and systems of oppression so prevalent in our world keep us from doing better. We must not let the realities of our world keep us from living for the values of Christ's kingdom, where there is "a vast multitude of people…made up of victorious ones from every nation, tribe, people group, and language" (Revelation 7:9). Let us be arbiters of justice and unity, of inclusion and marvelous mercy.

Creator, I know no class or racial discrimination exists in your kingdom. May I live with your values as my foundation no matter what.

December

EVEN MORE TO LEARN

I've yet to learn the wisdom that comes from the full
and intimate knowledge of you, the Holy One.

PROVERBS 30:3

None of us has reached the pinnacle of knowledge in this
world. In fact, even the most brilliant thought leaders of
our day in their niche fields of expertise have more to
discover. Why would we, then, think that we could have a
handle on God's majestic wisdom? There is so much more
to discover than a million lifetimes could afford. As we
remain teachable, we get to pursue the expansion of our
understanding in the wonderfully mysterious journey of
following the Lord.

When we recognize how little we actually know
in the grand scope and scheme of things, we position
our hearts to learn without the resistant barriers of pride
getting in the way. When we are quick to admit what
we do not know, we make room to learn. We must not
give up on this lifelong journey of knowing the Lord. He
constantly reveals himself to those who seek him, so let's
not remain in the comfort of stagnancy.

**Wonderful One, I want to know you more every
single day I live, move, and have my being. Reveal the
wonders of your mysterious love as I encounter you in
my life. I love you.**

CHRIST, OUR REIGNING MASTER

Who is it that travels back and forth from the heavenly realm to the earth? Who controls the wind as it blows and holds it in his fists?…What is his name? And what is the name of his Son? Who can tell me?

PROVERBS 30:4

In John 3:13, Jesus revealed, "No one has risen into the heavenly realm except the Son of Man who also exists in heaven." He is the one who travels back and forth between earth and heaven. He controls the winds of his Spirit. Jesus Christ is the master of heavenly knowledge and wisdom. It is in him and through him that we find the fullness of God.

"The same one who descended is also the one who ascended above the heights of heaven, in order to begin the restoration and fulfillment of all things" (Ephesians 4:10), and that One is Jesus. We are fulfilled in the glorious goodness of Christ. He has the wisdom to guide us into the everlasting goodness of his kingdom. Why would we look for better solutions elsewhere then? Let's look to Christ, today and every day, for the wisdom to reign in life and to endure in suffering.

Holy One, you are the King who rules over all. You have my heart and my allegiance. Have your way in my life.

PURE PROMISES

Every promise from the faithful God is pure and proves to be true. He is a wraparound shield of protection for all his lovers who run to hide in him.

PROVERBS 30:5

As Numbers 23:19 points out, "God is not a man, that he should lie" (KJV). He doesn't change his mind like we humans do so often. What he speaks, he follows through on. What he promises, he carries through. There is not a promise that goes unfulfilled. He is the way, the truth, and the life. There is nothing in this world, or outside of it, that is impossible for him to accomplish.

Do we truly trust the faithfulness of God? Peace is available for those who believe that he does what he sets out to do. Let's run into the shelter of his embrace, allowing his presence to wrap around our souls as our shield and strength. Whatever adversity we face, God is with us in the powerful peace and liberating love of his presence. He will strengthen us in his grace, empower us with his loyal love, and guide us with his wisdom. More than any other, he can be trusted, for he will never fail.

Faithful Father, bolster my courage in your powerful presence and infuse hope within my heart. I rely on you, Perfect One.

EARNEST PRAYER OF SURRENDER

Empty out of my heart everything that is false—every lie, and every crooked thing. And give me neither undue poverty nor undue wealth—but rather, feed my soul with the measure of prosperity that pleases you.

PROVERBS 30:8

What would it look like if we trusted not only that the Lord can meet our needs but also that his purposes for us are larger than we could dream for ourselves? We don't have to reach a certain measure of wealth to be favored by God. He favors the poor as much as he does any other. We don't measure our success based on the size of our bank accounts but on the level of satisfaction we find in the Lord.

May we willingly pray this prayer of surrender, as the writer of this proverb did. It is important to submit our hearts to God's refining wisdom. When God empties our hearts of lies, crooked passions, and pursuits, it can be a painful process. Let's not give up. Instead, we can lean into the divine love of the Refiner, celebrating every movement in mercy that triumphs over the cycles of fear and defeat that we have been stuck in.

God, I truly want to walk in your wisdom. I want to live according to your ways even when it goes against my previous understanding.

ULTIMATE CONTENTMENT

May my satisfaction be found in you. Don't let me be so
rich that I don't need you or so poor that I have to resort
to dishonesty just to make ends meet. Then my life will
never detract from bringing glory to your name.

PROVERBS 30:9

True and lasting satisfaction will never be found in the
resources of this world. Though a life of wealth may make
things easier for us, it does not guarantee the contentment
of our souls nor the wisdom of our hearts. It is important
that we value God's kingdom more than we do our own.
May we be satisfied with the perfect provision of his hand—
that we would not be too poor to meet our needs and that
we would not be so rich that we feel we don't need him.

There is beauty in a life of simplicity, with our
needs met and our souls satisfied in the values of Christ's
powerful and everlasting kingdom. May our eyes see and
our ears hear what God is doing and saying. We must
hunger and thirst for his righteousness more than we
hunger and thirst to fill our bellies and our homes. As
we seek first the kingdom of heaven, our priorities will
become straight. Then we will experience true satisfaction.

**Jesus, my prayer is simple: be what satisfies and fulfills
my soul.**

RISING JUSTICE

There is a generation rising that uses their words like swords to cut and slash those who are different. They would devour the poor, the needy, and the afflicted from off the face of the earth!

PROVERBS 30:14

As voices of injustice rise, may the voices of the righteous rise even louder! Let us live with justice as our motto and with mercy as our motivation. Our actions should speak louder than our words. May we be a generation, from old to young, that no longer lets the oppression of powerfully abusive voices dictate our values or our hope.

Now is when the people of God should rise up as healers of the broken, defenders of the vulnerable, and protectors of the weak. We can bind up the brokenhearted, living out the Messiah's mission from Isaiah 61. We get to partner with Christ in our response to evil. We get to affect change through the power of his love lived out. We must not let the voices of those who threaten to drown out goodness be our barometer of hope. As we look to the Unchanging One, we can transform the world with servant-hearted mercy.

Messiah, I partner with your purposes and choose to be an agent of justice, mercy, and freedom. I will not bow or cower to the injustices around me. I will live out your love.

MARVELOUS MYSTERIES

There are four marvelous mysteries that are too amazing to unravel—who could fully explain them? The way an eagle flies in the sky, the way a snake glides on a boulder, the path of a ship as it passes through the sea, and the way a bridegroom falls in love with his bride.

PROVERBS 30:18–19

The four examples used in these verses have to do with movement and mystery. Is this not indicative of the Spirit? The way an eagle soars on winds indicates how we can soar above our problems and limitations. It is a picture of the overcoming life. The way a snake glides on a boulder is a picture of our sin that was placed on the Rock, Jesus Christ.

Our lives, like ships passing through the sea, sail on the high seas of mystery until we reach our destiny. There are many details of our journeys that we cannot anticipate, but God guides us through the waters. We can see the beautiful picture of a wedding as a metaphor for the mystery of love our heavenly Bridegroom pours out on us, his church, as he romances us and sweeps us off our feet. What a mystery love is!

Father, increase my understanding of the mysteries of your goodness. I am in awe of you.

NO LESSON TOO SMALL

The earth has four creatures
that are very small but very wise.

PROVERBS 30:24

No lessons are too small, no creatures so insignificant
that we cannot learn from them. God reveals himself not
only through glimpses of himself in humanity but also in
the created world around us. There are lessons in acorns,
seedlings, and sparrows. Revelations of God are hidden in
the soil, in the cells that we cannot see with the naked eye.
Snowflakes and grains of sand contain beautiful glimpses
of glory.

May we have the eyes of children, finding wonder
in the simplest things around us. Perhaps the awe of
childlike wonder can awaken the children within us still.
We can find so much beauty in the natural world. There
is so much pleasure in its fruits, its rivers, and its valleys.
Let's allow our hearts to awaken in the wonder of small
lessons of wisdom that open the crevices of our curiosity.

**Marvelous God, I want to be awakened in awe, like
children are when they encounter something new and
wonderful. Just as roly-polies can fascinate a child for
hours, may I be entranced by the wisdom I find in the
simple things around me. Open my eyes to see more of
you as I am living my simple life.**

BOLSTERED BY DILIGENCE

The feeble ant has little strength, yet look how it diligently gathers its food in the summer to last throughout the winter.

PROVERBS 30:25

Though ants are small and seemingly insignificant, they diligently collect the food they need to get through the barrenness of winter. There is an innate drive to gather what they need and to work through the summer's warm days.

In the same way, preparing for the future is a mark of true wisdom. When we anticipate the needs of the next season, we can spend our resources, time, and attention sensibly. Foresight is a tremendous gift, though not often praised until barren seasons come. May we recognize the value of preparation before a time of emergency comes. We can be grounded in peace in the present moment and still work diligently for the future. We must resist the pull of anxiety and the lull of ignorance and instead practice the grounded balance of wisdom in our lives.

Father, give me vision and discernment to know what is worth my time and investment and what is unnecessary. May I live with wisdom as my guide, in times of sufficiency and in times of need. Help me to have foresight that is rooted in your gracious peace.

NESTLED IN SAFETY

The delicate rock-badger isn't all that strong, yet look how it makes a secure home, nestled in the rocks.

PROVERBS 30:26

Just as the rock-badger finds its home in the high place, we can also find our security in the cleft of the Rock of Ages. Though we are weak, the grace of God is our strength. As David prayed in Psalm 61, "When I'm feeble and overwhelmed by life, guide me into your glory, where I am safe and sheltered" (v. 2). When we are hidden in the glorious presence of Christ, fear loses its power over us.

Even in our weakness, we can crawl into the cleft of God's presence. What a beautiful picture this is of safety, security, and peace. "Lord, you are a paradise of protection to me. You lift me high above the fray. None of my foes can touch me when I'm held firmly in your wraparound presence" (Psalm 61:3). Lifted high above our troubles, we can rest in the hiddenness of God's protective arms. May we know the peace of God that passes all understanding, no matter the circumstances we face.

Protector, I climb into the hidden place of your glory today. As I turn to you, wrap around me with the tangible peace of your presence. Settle my heart and keep me safe.

AWAKENED IN PURPOSE

The locusts have no king to lead them,
yet they cooperate as they move forward by bands.

PROVERBS 30:27

In the book of Joel, there is a prophetic declaration from the prophet on behalf of the Lord. The locust army points us to the awakening army, mentioned in Joel, that is coming to devour the works of the enemy. The King of Glory guides this army from on high, even though he cannot be seen, and leads them as one.

May we be found, motivated, and deployed as one, with the vision of Christ and his kingdom as our deliverer and our master. We cannot ignore the rising use of power to abuse, manipulate, destroy, and hinder love's liberation in our world. We can choose to side with the kingdom of heaven, using not violence but service and mercy to wage war on injustice. May our hearts be awakened in the purpose to which we were called: "To walk holy, in a way that is suitable to your high rank, given to you in your divine calling" (Ephesians 4:1).

Jesus, you are my leader, and I will not bow my knee to any other power. Your ways are better than the ways of the rulers of this world, and I want to be aligned with you in all I do and stand for. Be glorified.

POSITIONED BY GOD

The small lizard is easy to catch as it clings to the walls with its hands, yet it can be found inside a king's palace.

PROVERBS 30:28

No matter who you are, how insignificant you feel (like the small lizard), God can put you in meaningful places where you can be used for his glory. Have you ever found yourself in a situation that, when you took a step back, surprised you? God is really good at sneaking up on us and putting us in places we never dreamed we would be. He gives us opportunities that can astound us.

Let's be faithful with what we have and where we are, and let God promote us in his timing. We don't have to fight for a place at the table. He can put us in significant places where he can use us for his glory. Remember Jesus' words in Luke 16:10: "The one who faithfully manages the little he has been given will be promoted and trusted with greater responsibilities."

Powerful One, I will not neglect the importance of faithfulness in the seemingly small things in my life. I trust that in your timing, you will open doors I can't anticipate as I serve you.

An Answer to Prayer

Listen, my dear son, son of my womb.
You are the answer to my prayers, my son.

Proverbs 31:2

Who in your life is an answer to prayer? Think of your family, friends, colleagues, and community. Perhaps you can remember a time when you prayed for what you now have. Take some time to offer gratitude to the Faithful One—the one who not only hears you but also answers you. May the answered prayers of your life breathe fresh hope into the ones you are still waiting on.

It is good for us to recognize and verbalize our deep love for others. We can get so caught up in the nitty-gritty of day-to-day life that we forget to share what we love about others with them. If there is something that you are grateful for in a relationship, share it with that person today. If you remember an answered prayer in the form of certain people in your life, let them know what they mean to you. Gratitude shared is a bridge-builder and love-extender to those around us.

Lord, thank you for the answered prayers and for the wonderful goodness of your tangible love in my life. My heart overflows with thanksgiving as I consider all that you have done.

No Regrets

Keep yourself sexually pure from the promiscuous,
wayward woman. Don't waste the strength of your
anointing on those who ruin kings—
you'll live to regret it!

PROVERBS 31:3

Let's have the foresight, discernment, and wisdom
that keeps us from wasting our strength on things that
will only deplete and dishonor us as well as diminish
our legacies. When we give in to temptation, letting
something or someone else have power over us, we
will live to regret it. This is not to say that there is no
redemption. We know, of course, in Christ there is. We
can live in the liberating love of Christ and still be wise
about what we do or don't do.

Hebrews 7:26 says that Christ "is the High Priest
who perfectly fits our need—holy, without a trace of evil,
without the ability to deceive, incapable of sin, and exalted
beyond the heavens!" We come to him, offering the
sacrifice of our hearts to him. He is perfect and holy, and
he purifies us in his presence. Let's look to him whenever
we are tempted, for he will provide a way out for us that
leads us away from regret (see 1 Corinthians 10:13).

**God, I don't want to live foolishly, ignoring wisdom's
directions in my life. May I be an overcomer,
empowered by your grace. You are my strength.**

STAYING SOBER-MINDED

When they drink they forget justice
and ignore the rights of those in need,
those who depend on them for leadership.

PROVERBS 31:5

We should be wary about anything that compromises
our ability to judge soundly and that has us act in ways
that dishonor the values that we claim to live by. If any
activity causes us to lose our ability to watch our mouths
or advocate for the defenseless, we should steer clear of it.
When we abandon the ways of justice and mercy, we can
no longer be the people God calls us to be.

Especially when we lead others, we need to be
diligent about not putting ourselves in compromising
positions. If we become drunk with power, overlooking
and ignoring the rights of those in need, we do not
deserve the position of leadership. If any sort of addiction
has a hold over our hearts, then we are compromised in
integrity. We will forsake justice before we give up the
thing that has a hold on us. So, then, we need to jealously
guard our affections, our peace, and our liberty in Christ.

**Lord Jesus, I want to be sober-minded and in line with
your justice, mercy, and truth. Liberate me in your
love and set me free from anything that keeps me from
living out the light of your truth in my life.**

Called for a Purpose

You are to be a king who speaks up on behalf of the
disenfranchised and pleads for the legal rights of the
defenseless and those who are dying.

PROVERBS 31:8

As agents of God's kingdom—as children of the Most
High—we are to lead with justice, mercy, and truth. We are
to uphold the values of Christ over our own preferences.
We are to advocate for the vulnerable and marginalized.
We are to be defenders of the weak and the dying.

We should evaluate if this is true of the causes that
we get behind. Are we truly looking to make a difference
in the wise ways that reveal the heart of the Father to
the world? If so, we will be willing to sacrifice our own
comfort and the need to please people who don't align
with God's ways. We can become like Paul, who, in
Galatians 1:10, said, "My supreme passion is to please
God. For if all I attempt to do is please people, I would fail
to be a true servant of Christ."

Messiah, I choose your ways, your will, and your
purposes over pleasing others. I want to be someone who
advocates for the marginalized, no matter what powerful
voices try to dissuade me. Your love is meant for all.

RULING IN RIGHTEOUSNESS

Be a righteous king, judging on behalf of the poor
and interceding for those most in need.

PROVERBS 31:9

Our ministry, as sons and daughters of the Righteous
One, is to be reflections of our Father in the way we live.
"True spirituality that is pure in the eyes of our Father
God," James 1:27 says, "is to make a difference in the
lives of the orphans, and widows in their troubles, and to
refuse to be corrupted by the world's values."

Do we make a difference in the lives of those in
need, refusing to be corrupted by the world? If not, then
our religion is as shallow and empty as the promise of a
liar. Isaiah 58:7 encourages, "Share your food with the
hungry! Provide for the homeless and bring them into
your home! Clothe the naked! Don't turn your back on
your own flesh and blood!" When we follow the Word
of the Lord, he drenches us in the light of his favor. The
glory of YAHWEH goes before us, shining bright for all to
see. As we live out his righteousness in practical ways, we
cannot overlook the enormously important element of
putting our faith into practice.

**Righteous One, forgive me for how I have overlooked
the importance of advocating for the poor, weak, and
vulnerable. I partner with you.**

WONDERFUL WORTH

Who could ever find a wife like this one—
she is a woman of strength and mighty valor!
She's full of wealth and wisdom.
The price paid for her was greater than many jewels.

PROVERBS 31:10

This verse is the beginning of a Hebrew acrostic poem describing the virtue of the perfect bride. This woman is both a picture of what a virtuous wife looks like and a beautiful allegory of the victorious end-time bride of Jesus Christ, full of virtue and grace. The price he paid for her was greater than the wealth of the world's storehouses. The sacred blood of the Lamb of God is invaluable.

Through Christ, we have access to the wealth and wisdom of the Father's kingdom. He calls us his own, giving us his very name. It is our identity in him that provides the power we need to be overcomers in this life. God saw us in our most natural state, defenses down, and decided that we were worth winning in glorious redemption. What a God! What wonderful worth he has proclaimed over us. What a reason to rejoice!

Glorious Jesus, thank you for the lengths to which you went to reveal the Father's heart to us. Thank you for seeing me, knowing me, and making me your own. I am yours, Lord.

WORTHY OF CONFIDENCE

> Her husband has entrusted his heart to her,
> for she brings him the rich spoils of victory.
> All throughout her life she brings him
> what is good and not evil.
>
> PROVERBS 31:11–12

Jesus will not be ashamed to display his virtuous bride to the world. She will not bring disgrace to his name. As the church, we are the bride of Christ. He trusts his heart to his honorable bride. Are we worthy of this kind of confidence? Let's consider how we reflect the values of our bridegroom in what we choose and how we live.

We should strive to each be found worthy of the trust that Jesus gives us. As we draw closer to him, he becomes our covering and strength, and he transforms us by the glorious new life of his Spirit. May we not shrink from him out of fear or shame but draw even nearer in our weakness, letting him love us to life over and over again. He is worthy of our confident trust, no matter what.

Loving Christ, you are my confidence and strength. May I be found worthy of the confidence of your love as I generously share it with others. You are so incredibly good to me.

EAGER TO WORK

She searches out continually to possess that which is pure
and righteous. She delights in the work of her hands.

PROVERBS 31:13

As honorable people of God, as we work with our own
hands, we can effect change through loving acts of
practical mercy in our lives. What gifts do we have to
work with? What skills do we have to use for God's glory?
As we seek the kingdom of God and his righteousness,
we can use our natural gifts to further the kingdom of
heaven. We must not undervalue the power that our work
submitted to the values of Christ can have.

Just as we have five fingers on each hand, so
the church has five ministries to work with: apostles,
prophets, evangelists, pastors, and teachers. The present
work of Christ on the earth is represented through these
ministries of the church. The delight of the virtuous bride
is to equip others and to help those in need.

**Father, as I offer you the work of my hands, move
through my life in wondrous acts of mercy. As you
move through the ministries of your church, may you
be glorified.**

DIVINE SUPPLIES

She gives out revelation-truth to feed others. She is like a
trading ship bringing divine supplies from the merchant.

PROVERBS 31:14

There is plenty of divine revelation to pass along as we
carry the truth of God to the world around us. We are
carriers of God's glory. We are vessels that, when yielded
to God, are full of his wisdom. We must not forget the
importance of filling our ships before we try to help
others in need. We need to spend time in the harbor of
God's presence, where he fills us with all that we need to
bring to others.

Consider the divine supplies you see that the world
needs. Don't forget to account for what you are running
low on as well. As you anchor in the Spirit's presence, he
will take inventory of what you need. Open up the rooms
of your heart and let him roam around. There is glorious
provision for you when you do.

**Lord, instead of relying on my own strength, abilities,
and resources, I first come to you today. I don't want
to run on empty. Fill me with all that I need in your
presence. Share your revelation-truth with me today
and empower me with your grace. You are my limitless
source.**

ARISE WITH ANOINTING

Even in the night season she arises and sets food on the table for hungry ones in her house and for others.

PROVERBS 31:15

Isaiah 60:1 reads, "Rise up in splendor and be radiant, for your light has dawned, and YAHWEH's glory now streams from you!" It is with this type of glory that we arise with purpose and strength to feed the hungry ones around us. Even in the dark seasons of life, as we persevere in Christ's love and intercede for those in need, we labor in the night season to help others.

It is time to arise with anointing and go forth in the marvelous mercy of God's presence. We never need to go out on our own strength. God is faithful to guide us in confidence and in peace as we follow him. Let's put all our trust in him, for he is faithful in all that he does. He never loses sight of his purposes, and as we partner with him, he will direct us in his ways.

Great God, thank you for the grace of your presence that empowers me to partner with you in hard times as well as in times of plenty. You are my source, my strength, and my vision.

USHERING IN NEW LIFE

She sets her heart upon a field and takes it as her own.
She labors there to plant the living vines.

PROVERBS 31:16

As we partner with the purposes of Christ, we are branches producing the fruit of his kingdom. In John 15:1–2, Jesus said, "I am a true sprouting vine, and the farmer who tends the vine is my Father. He cares for the branches connected to me by…pruning every fruitful branch to yield a greater harvest." Just as a branch that is severed from the vine will not bear fruit, so if our lives are not intimately joined to Christ, they will be fruitless.

A fruitful life is the result of living in union with Christ as our source. We must not neglect the supreme importance of cultivating deep fellowship with the Spirit who leads us into all truth. What a tremendous gift we have in relationship with God! Nothing separates us from his love, and we are transformed by his living mercy at work within our hearts.

Lord, as you transform my life, may your mercy reach others through me. I am yours, feeding off the nourishment of your Word, presence, and wisdom.

ANOINTED WITH POWER

She wraps herself in strength, might,
and power in all her works.

PROVERBS 31:17

Wrapped in strength, we are ready for whatever faces us.
This verse speaks to the anointing power of Christ in us to
do the greater things Jesus spoke of. "I tell you this timeless
truth: The person who follows me in faith, believing in me,
will do the same mighty miracles that I do—even greater
miracles than these because I go to be with my Father!"
(John 14:12). When we follow Christ in fullhearted
devotion, taking him at his word and implementing his
wisdom in our lives, we are anointed with the same power
that resurrected Christ from the dead.

May we take Jesus seriously and follow him in
faith. We can walk out the wonders of his mercy as we
ask him to do greater things through us. Jesus said, "Ask
me anything in my name, and I will do it for you!" (John
14:14). Let's ask for miracles, signs, and wonders as we
walk in the power of his presence.

**Almighty God, it is your power that raises the dead to
life, heals the sick, and redeems the lost souls. Your love
is greater than the grave, and I want to ask for, seek,
and walk in the power of your mercy.**

LAMPS OF
EVERLASTING OIL

She tastes and experiences a better substance,
and her shining light will not be extinguished,
no matter how dark the night.

PROVERBS 31:18

Jesus was born into a dark world, where darkness had taken hold. He was born in secret, and his life was hidden from the powerful King Herod, who sought to slaughter the baby boys in Bethlehem. But Jesus was a shining light that could not be extinguished. In the same way, Jesus said, "Your lives light up the world. For how can you hide a city that stands on a hilltop?…Don't hide your light! Let it shine brightly before others" (Matthew 5:14, 16).

May our prayer lives burn the midnight oil as we partner with Christ's purposes on the earth. Our lifestyles of consistent prayer help us overcome the darkness that surrounds us. As we unashamedly follow Christ on his path of laid-down love, we allow the light of his mercy to shine brightly through our actions. We become beacons of radiant hope as we prayerfully walk in the ways of God, for they are nourishment and life to us.

Light of the World, you are the One I look to. Thank you, Jesus, for coming into the darkness and shining your glorious light. You are radiant.

EXTRAVAGANT GENEROSITY

*She is known by her extravagant generosity to the poor,
for she always reaches out her hands to those in need.*

PROVERBS 31:20

A wise person does not only provide for the needs of her own household or family; she also reaches out in extravagant generosity to the poor. The parable of the good Samaritan reminds us that generosity fueled by compassion is more important than our status in society. God is extraordinarily generous with us. His mercy is without end, and he freely offers it to us. May we reflect the incredible kindness of his heart by being liberal with our own service and giving.

Generosity is a heart posture. No matter how little we have, we can practice it. Jesus highlighted a poor widow's offering to illustrate this: "I tell you the truth, this poor widow has given a larger offering…For the rich only gave out of their surplus, but she sacrificed out of her poverty and gave to God all that she had to live on, which was everything she had" (Mark 12:43–44). When we give to the poor, we make an offering to God. We should not evade the opportunity or responsibility to help those in need.

Merciful Jesus, thank you for your incredible generosity. I want to live a life of poured-out love through practical means. May I be a living reflection of you.

Unafraid of the Unexpected

She is not afraid of tribulation, for all her household is covered in the dual garments of righteousness and grace.

PROVERBS 31:21

Under the garments of grace, we are found righteous in the sight of the Father. Through Christ, we have found our perfect peace and freedom from fear. We can rest in the confidence of God's faithfulness to do all that he promised. Let's support one another in love, encouraging one another as the days grow cold. May we be harbors of safety, gathered together in homes of peace.

No matter what comes, God sees it all. He is prepared for all that is to come, and there is not a single situation where he is powerless or at a loss for what to do. We can lean on him, cling to him, in the summer months and through the long, cold winter. With his grace as our strength, we will face whatever comes with fearless confidence in his faithfulness.

Faithful One, because of your loyal love, I know that I have nothing to fear. Even when tensions rise around me, your peace is my portion. My confidence is in you.

BENEFIT TO ALL

Even her works of righteousness
she does for the benefit of her enemies.

PROVERBS 31:24

Our surrendered lives are not only a benefit to those we care for but also to our enemies. There are no dividing lines in the hearts of those who are yielded to the limitless love of the Lord. We must be sure to show generosity to all, not withholding from those we disagree with when they are in need. Our faithful work is not only to be offered to those we agree with but also to our communities at large.

The mercy of Christ is offered freely to all. We cannot live under the delusion that we must decide who is worthy of it and who is not. Grace is a gift freely offered to all without restriction. Whether one accepts it or not is his or her own choice, but we should never withhold it. Jesus said, "Love your enemy, bless the one who curses you, do something wonderful for the one who hates you, and respond to the very ones who persecute you by praying for them" (Matthew 5:44). Let's follow his loving lead, for there is no higher way.

Redeemer, I clothe myself in your compassion, and I ask for the power of your grace to rise up from within, motivating me in mercy.

JOYFUL ANTICIPATION

Bold power and glorious majesty are wrapped around her
as she laughs with joy over the latter days.

PROVERBS 31:25

As we set our hearts on the promised second coming of
our Lord Jesus, looking ahead to the glorious fulfillment
of his promises and the wonderful reign of his kingdom,
we can rest in joyful anticipation. No matter what we face
now, there are better days ahead—a time when the Lord
will wipe every tear from our eyes and death will be but a
distant memory.

As we live with the values of Christ's kingdom as
our own, we experience the victory of his resurrection
as our own. He is our triumphant King, and as we wait
in anticipation of the fulfillment of all things, we look
ahead with hope. No matter what difficulties you are
facing today, may you lift your eyes to Jesus, the "author
and finisher" of your faith (Hebrews 12:2 KJV). Set your
eyes on him and ask for a glimpse of the coming glory
you have to look forward to in the powerful peace of his
kingdom.

**Lord Jesus, I fix my eyes on you today. Encourage my
heart in hope as I do. You are my King and my God. My
heart fills with joy as you reveal yourself in new ways.**

FAITHFUL CARETAKERS

She watches over the ways of her household
and meets every need they have.

PROVERBS 31:27

We must not neglect the importance of caring for our households. Love seeks to meet the needs of those around us. It reaches out in practical ways. It is reliable and trustworthy. It is loyal and generous. When we treat others with care and respect, we reveal the heart of God to each of them. There is no excuse for ignoring the practical needs of our loved ones.

First Timothy 5:8 says, "If a believer fails to provide for their own relatives when they are in need, they have compromised their convictions of faith and need to be corrected, for they are living worse than the unbelievers." Conviction of faith flows to the practical aspects of our lives. May we be people of integrity, living as authentically in love within the walls of our own homes as we do outside of them. Our families should receive the best of us as we meet their emotional needs as well as their physical ones. Let's offer them our best.

Loving Lord, may those closest to me receive the best of me. May I be quick to apologize when I hurt them, and may there be a wealth of love, security, respect, and honesty present in my home.

EVERLASTING VIRTUES

Charm can be misleading, and beauty is vain and so quickly fades, but this virtuous woman lives in the wonder, awe, and fear of the Lord. She will be praised throughout eternity.

PROVERBS 31:30

When we live in the wonder, awe, and fear of the Lord, it spills out into every area of our lives. The mercy of God weaves the details of our days into the wonderful tapestry of his great redemption. There is restoration for the broken, healing for the sick, comfort for the grieving, and connection for the lonely in the generous presence of God.

May we live in awe of God's marvelous mercy—not only in our own lives but also in the interconnectedness of humanity. No situation is too far gone that he cannot restore. No power on the earth can overwhelm or disarm his love. He is faithful and true. As we fix our eyes on him, we will find our hope rising to meet the magnitude of his goodness. Let us live for what truly matters. With our attention on Christ and our lives as living reflections of his love, we surely will.

Everlasting God, it is to you I offer my heart, soul, and life. I choose to walk in the light of your ways, trusting your hand to guide me along the way.

About the Author

Brian Simmons is the lead translator of The Passion Translation®. The Passion Translation (TPT) is a heart-level translation that uses Hebrew, Greek, and Aramaic manuscripts to express God's fiery heart of love to this generation, merging the emotion and life-changing truth of God's Word. The hope for TPT is to trigger inside every reader an overwhelming response to the truth of the Bible and to reveal the deep mysteries of the Scriptures in the love language of God, the language of the heart. Brian is currently translating the Old Testament.

After a dramatic conversion to Christ in 1971, Brian and his wife, Candice, answered the call of God to leave everything behind and become missionaries to unreached peoples. Taking their three children to the tropical rain forest of Central America, they planted churches for many years with the Paya-Kuna people group. Brian established leadership for the churches that Jesus birthed and, having been trained in linguistics and Bible translation principles, assisted with the translation of the Paya-Kuna New Testament.

After their ministry overseas, Brian and Candice returned to North America, where Brian began to passionately work toward helping people encounter the risen Christ. He and his wife planted numerous ministries, including a dynamic church in New England (US). They also established Passion & Fire Ministries, under which they travel full time as Bible teachers in service of local churches throughout the world.

Brian is the author of numerous books, Bible studies, and devotionals that help readers encounter God's heart and experience a deeper revelation of God as our Bridegroom-King, including *Throne Room Prayer*, *The Sacred Journey*, *Prayers on Fire*, *The Divine Romance*, and *The Vision*.

Brian and Candice have been married since 1971 and have three children as well as precious grandchildren and great-grandchildren. Their passion is to live as loving examples of a spiritual father and mother to this generation.